CW00347275

Database Modeling & Design: The Fundamental Principles

Second Edition

The Morgan Kaufmann Series in Data Management Systems

Series Editor, Jim Gray

Database Modeling & Design: The Fundamental Principles, Second Edition
Toby J. Teorey

Database: Principles, Programming, and Performance
Patrick O'Neil

Readings in Database Systems, Second Edition
Edited by Michael Stonebraker

Atomic Transactions
Nancy Lynch, Michael Merritt, William Weihl, and Alan Fekete

Query Processing for Advanced Database Systems
Edited by Johann Christoph Freytag, David Maier, and Gottfried Vossen

Transaction Processing: Concepts and Techniques
Jim Gray and Andreas Reuter

Understanding the New SQL: A Complete Guide
Jim Melton and Alan Simon

Building an Object-Oriented Database System: The Story of O_2
Edited by François Bancilhon, Claude Delobel, and Paris Kanellakis

Database Transaction Models for Advanced Applications
Edited by Ahmed K. Elmagarmid

A Guide to Developing Client/Server SQL Applications
Setrag Khoshafian, Arvola Chan, Anna Wong, and Harry K.T. Wong

The Benchmark Handbook for Database and Transaction Processing Systems, Second Edition
Edited by Jim Gray

Camelot and Avalon: A Distributed Transaction Facility
Edited by Jeffrey L. Eppinger, Lily B. Mummert, and Alfred Z. Spector

Readings in Object-Oriented Database Systems
Edited by Stanley B. Zdonik and David Maier

Database Modeling & Design: The Fundamental Principles

Second Edition

TOBY J. TEOREY

Morgan Kaufmann Publishers, Inc.
San Francisco, California

Executive Editor: Bruce M. Spatz
Production Manager: Yonie Overton
Assistant Editor: Douglas Sery
Production Coordinator: Julie Pabst
Copyeditor: Gary Morris
Text Design & Composition: Rebecca Evans & Associates
Cover Design: Rebecca Evans & Associates
(based on first edition cover, designed by Gary Head)
Printer: Edwards Brothers, Inc.

Editorial Offices:

Morgan Kaufmann Publishers, Inc.
340 Pine Street, Sixth Floor
San Francisco, CA 94104

Published 1990. Second Edition 1994

Printed in the United States of America

98 97 96 5 4 3

Library of Congress Cataloging-in-Publication Data

Teorey, Toby J.
Database modeling & design : the fundamental principles / Toby J. Teorey. — 2nd ed.
p. cm.
Rev. ed. of: Database modeling and design. 1990.
Includes bibliographical references and index.
ISBN 1-55860-294-1 (pbk.)
1. Relational databases. 2. Database design. 3. Database management. I. Teorey, Toby J. Database modeling and design. II. Title.
QA76.9.D26T45 1996
005.75'6—dc20 96-12120
CIP

To Matt, Carol, and Marilyn

CONTENTS

PREFACE

Data modeling and database design have undergone significant evolution in recent years, since the domination of business applications by the relational data model and relational database systems. Before the relational era, however, the dominating data models were the hierarchical and network models, characterized by IMS and CODASYL-style database systems, respectively. Database design for these systems depended on knowledge of both the logical and physical characteristics of the data model. More recently, however, the relational model has allowed the database designer to focus on these characteristics separately. Object-oriented databases, the next generation, are also based on a separation of the logical and physical aspects, but go further by integrating the data manipulation and data definition mechanisms.

In this second edition we continue to concentrate on techniques for database design in relational database systems, starting with the entity-relationship approach for data requirements specification and conceptual modeling; but we also look ahead to the common properties in data modeling and operations between the relational and the object-oriented model. We cover the database life cycle from requirements analysis and logical design to physical design for local, distributed, and multidatabases. The discussion of basic principles is supplemented with an entirely new and clear common example, a company personnel and project database, based on real-life experiences and thoroughly classroom tested. This edition also provides an extended set of problems at the end of Chapters 2 through 6, 8 through 9, and Appendix A, with Solutions to Selected Exercises at the end of the book.

Organization

The database life cycle is described in Chapter 1. We also review the basic concepts of database modeling. Entity-relationship (ER) modeling is a popular method for the conceptualization of users' data requirements. Currently, there is no standard ER model, and published articles and textbooks have introduced an enormous variety of constructs and notation to represent fundamental modeling concepts. In Chapter 2 we present the most fundamental ER concepts and provide a simple set of notational constructs—that is, the Chen notation—to represent them. We then provide guidance to reading some of the most common alternative notations used in the literature. We look at ER models at two levels: the simple level that is currently used in most computer-aided software engineering (CASE) tools and which satisfies requirements for end-user readability, and a complex level that is useful to database designers who want to clearly define complex relationships.

Chapters 3 and 4 show how to use ER concepts in the database design process. Chapter 3 is devoted to direct application of ER modeling in logical database design. Chapter 4 explains the transformation of the ER model to the relational model and to SQL syntax specifically.

Chapter 5 is devoted to the fundamentals of database normalization through fifth normal form, showing the functional equivalence between the ER model and the relational model for the higher normal forms. Chapter 6 introduces the concepts of physical design, access methods, and join strategies, and illustrates how to modify a relational schema to be more efficient when usage for specific applications is well known. The case study in Chapter 7 summarizes the techniques presented in Chapters 1 through 6 with a new problem environment.

Chapters 8 and 9 present two approaches to data allocation strategies in distributed and multidatabases. Chapter 8 presents the fundamentals of fragmentation and data allocation in a distributed database system, and the case study in Chapter 9 illustrates the connection between logical design and distribution of data in relational database systems. Chapter 10 introduces the basic concepts in the estimation of dependability: availability, reliability, and mean transaction completion time in a repairable distributed or multidatabase system—that is, one that automatically generates transaction restarts.

An extensive review of the popular relational database query language SQL is presented in the appendix for those readers who lack familiarity with database query languages.

This book can be used by the database practitioner as a useful guide to database modeling and its application to database designs from the business and office environments to scientific and engineering databases. Whether you are a novice database user or an experienced professional, this book offers new insights into database modeling and the ease of transition from the ER model to the relational model, including the building of standard SQL data definitions. Thus, whether you are using DB2, SQL/DS, Oracle, Ingres, Sybase, NonStop SQL, or any other SQL-based system, the design rules set forth here will be applicable. The case studies used for the examples throughout the book are from real-life databases that were designed using the principles formulated here. This book can also be used by the advanced undergraduate or beginning graduate student to supplement a course textbook in introductory database management or for a stand-alone course in data modeling or database design.

Typographical Conventions

For easy reference, entity names (Employee, Department, and so on) are capitalized from Chapter 2 forward. Throughout the book, table names (**product**, **product_count**) are set in boldface for readability.

Acknowledgements

I wish to acknowledge my co-authors in several relevant papers that contributed to the continuity of this book: Deb Bolton, Jarir Chaar, Yang Dongqing, Jim Fry, Wei Guangping, John Koenig, Kunle Olukotun, Dick Spencer, and Amjad Umar. Joe Celko, Jim Gray, Bill Grosky, Dave Roberts, and Behrooz Seyed-Abbassi provided valuable technical criticism. The Star Trek problem was designed by Paul Helman and Marilyn Mantei, and several ER model problems and other suggestions were provided by Nauman Chaudhry, Carol Fan, Nayantara Kalro, Ji-Bih Lee, Dan O'Leary, John DeSue, and Dan Skrbina. I wish to thank the Department of Electrical Engineering and Computer Science (EECS), the Center for Information Technology Integration (CITI), and the University of Michigan for providing computer resources for writing and revising. The entire manuscript was written using Microsoft Word 5.0 and MacPaint 2.0. Pat Corey and Ann Gordon provided excellent detailed critiques of the original manuscript, and Rosemary Metz was always there for anything that needed fixing. Finally, thanks to Julie for offering Ludington, and not giving up.

Solutions Manual

A solutions manual to all exercises is available. Contact the publisher for further information.

CHAPTER 1

INTRODUCTION

Database technology began to replace file systems in the mid-1960s. Since that time database modeling and design has slowly evolved from an art to a science that has been partially implementable as a set of software design aids. Many of these design aids have appeared as the database component of computer-aided software engineering (CASE) tools, and many of them offer interactive modeling capability using a simplified data-modeling approach.

In this chapter we review the basic concepts of database management and introduce the role of data modeling and database design in the database life cycle.

1.1 Data and Database Management

The basic component of a file in a file system is a *data item*, which is the smallest named unit of data that has meaning in the real world—for example, last name, first name, street address, id-number, and political party. A group of related data items treated as a unit by an application is called a *record*. Examples of types of records are order, salesperson, customer, product, and department. A *file* is a collection of records of a single type. Database systems have built upon and expanded these definitions: In a relational database, a data item is called an *attribute*, a record is called a *row* or *tuple*, and a file is called a *table*.

A *database* is a more complex object; it is a collection of interrelated stored data that serves the needs of multiple users within one or more organizations, that is, interrelated collections of many different types of tables. The motivation for using databases rather than files has been greater availability to a diverse set of users, integration of data for easier access and update for complex transactions, and less redundancy of data.

A *database management system (DBMS)* is a generalized software system for manipulating databases. A DBMS supports a logical view (schema, subschema); physical view (access methods, data clustering); data definition language; data manipulation language; and important utilities such as transaction management and concurrency control, data integrity, crash recovery, and security.

Relational database systems, the dominant type of systems for well-formatted business databases, also provide a greater degree of data independence than the earlier hierarchical and network (CODASYL) database management systems. *Data independence* is the ability to make changes in either the logical or physical structure of the database without requiring reprogramming of application programs. It also makes database conversion and reorganization much easier. Relational (and object-oriented) DBMSs provide a much higher degree of data independence than previous systems; they are the focus of our discussion on data modeling.

1.2 Data Modeling and the Entity-Relationship Approach

Schema diagrams were formalized in the 1960s by Charles Bachman. He used rectangles to denote record types and directed arrows from one record type to another to denote a one-to-many relationship among instances of records of the two types. The entity-relationship (ER) approach for conceptual database modeling, the approach emphasized in this book, was first described in 1976 by Peter Chen. The Chen form of ER models uses rectangles to specify entities, which are somewhat analogous to records. It also uses diamond-shaped objects to represent the various types of relationships, which are differentiated by numbers or letters placed on the lines connecting the diamonds to the rectangles. Since the original definition of entities and relationships, the ER-modeling technique has undergone a variety of changes and extensions, including the implementation of experimental database management systems using the ER data model.

The overriding emphasis in ER modeling is on simplicity and readability. The goal of conceptual schema design, where the ER approach is most useful, is to capture real-world data requirements in a simple and meaningful way that is understandable by both the database designer and the end user. The end user is the person responsible for accessing the database and executing queries and updates through the use of DBMS software, therefore having a vested interest in the database design process.

The ER model has two levels of definition, one which is quite simple and another which is considerably more complex. The simple level is the one used by most current CASE tools. It is quite helpful to the database designer in communicating with end users about their data requirements. At this level, one simply describes, in diagram form, the entities, attributes, and relationships that occur in the system to be conceptualized and whose semantics are definable in a data dictionary. Specialized constructs, such as "weak" entities or mandatory/optional existence notation, are also usually included in the simple form. But very little else is included, in order to avoid cluttering up the

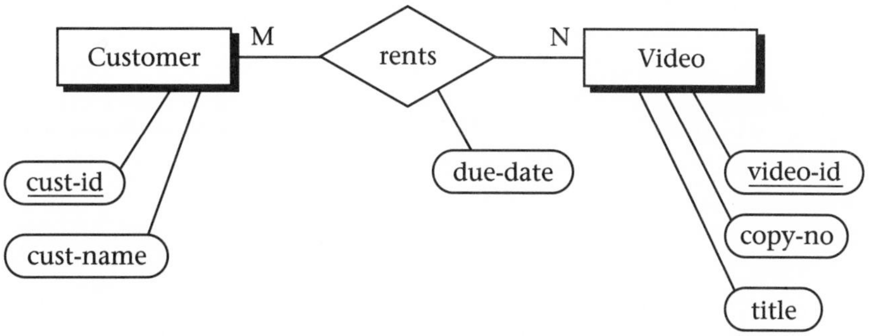

Figure 1.1 Example ER model

ER diagram while the designer's and end user's understanding of the model are being reconciled.

An example of a simple form of ER model is shown in Figure 1.1. We use the Chen notation for this example and throughout the rest of this book because it is the most common form in the literature today. In this example we want to keep track of videotapes and customers in a video store. Videos and customers are represented as entities Video and Customer, and the relationship rents shows a many-to-many association between them. Both Video and Customer entities have a few attributes that describe their characteristics, and the relationship rents has an attribute due date that represents the due date for a particular video rented by a specific customer.

From the database practitioner's standpoint, the simple form of the ER model is the preferred form for both database modeling and end-user verification. It is easy to learn and it is applicable to a wide variety of design problems one might encounter in industry and small businesses. We will also see that the simple form is easily translatable into SQL data definitions, and thus it has an immediate use as an aid for database implementation.

The complex level of ER model definition includes concepts that go far beyond the original model. It includes concepts from the semantic models of artificial intelligence and from competing conceptual data models such as the binary relationship model and NIAM methodology (see Chapter 2 for an overview of some NIAM concepts). ER modeling at this level helps the database designer capture more semantics without having to resort to narrative explanations. It is also useful to the database application programmer because certain integrity constraints defined in the ER model relate directly to code—code that checks range limits on data values and null values, for example. However, such detail in very large ER diagrams actually detracts from end-user understanding. Therefore, the simple level is recommended as a communication tool for database design verification.

1.3 The Database Life Cycle

The database life cycle incorporates the basic steps involved in designing a global schema of the logical database, allocating data across a computer network, and defining local DBMS-specific schemas. Once the design is completed, the life cycle continues with database implementation and maintenance. This chapter contains an overview of the database life cycle. In succeeding chapters we will focus on the database design process from the modeling of requirements through distributed data allocation (Steps I through IV below). We illustrate the result of each step of the life cycle with a series of diagrams in Figures 1.2 through 1.4. Each diagram shows a possible form of the output of each step so the reader can see the progression of the design process from an idea to actual database implementation. These forms are discussed in much more detail in succeeding chapters.

I. ***Requirements analysis.*** The database requirements are determined by interviewing both the producers and users of data and producing a formal requirements specification. That specification includes the data required for processing; the natural data relationships; and software platform for the database implementation. As an example, Figure 1.2 shows the concepts of products, customers, salespersons, and orders being formulated in the mind of the end user during the interview process.

II. ***Logical design.*** The *global schema,* which shows all the data and their relationships, is developed using conceptual data-modeling techniques such as ER. The data-model constructs must ultimately be transformed into normalized (global) relations, or tables. The global schema development methodology is the same for either a distributed or centralized database.

a. *ER modeling.* The data requirements are analyzed and modeled by using an ER diagram that includes, for example, semantics for optional relationships, ternary relationships, supertypes, and subtypes (categories). Processing requirements are typically specified using natural language expressions or SQL commands along with the frequency of occurrence. Figure 1.2b shows a possible ER model representation of the product/customer database in the mind of the end user in Figure 1.2.

b. *View integration.* Usually, when the design is large and more than one person is involved in requirements analysis, multiple views of data and relationships result. To eliminate redundancy and inconsistency from the model, these views must eventually be consolidated into a single global view. View integration requires the use of ER semantic tools such as identification of synonyms, aggregation, and generalization. In Figure 1.2 two possible views of the product/customer database are merged into a single global view based on common data for customer and order.

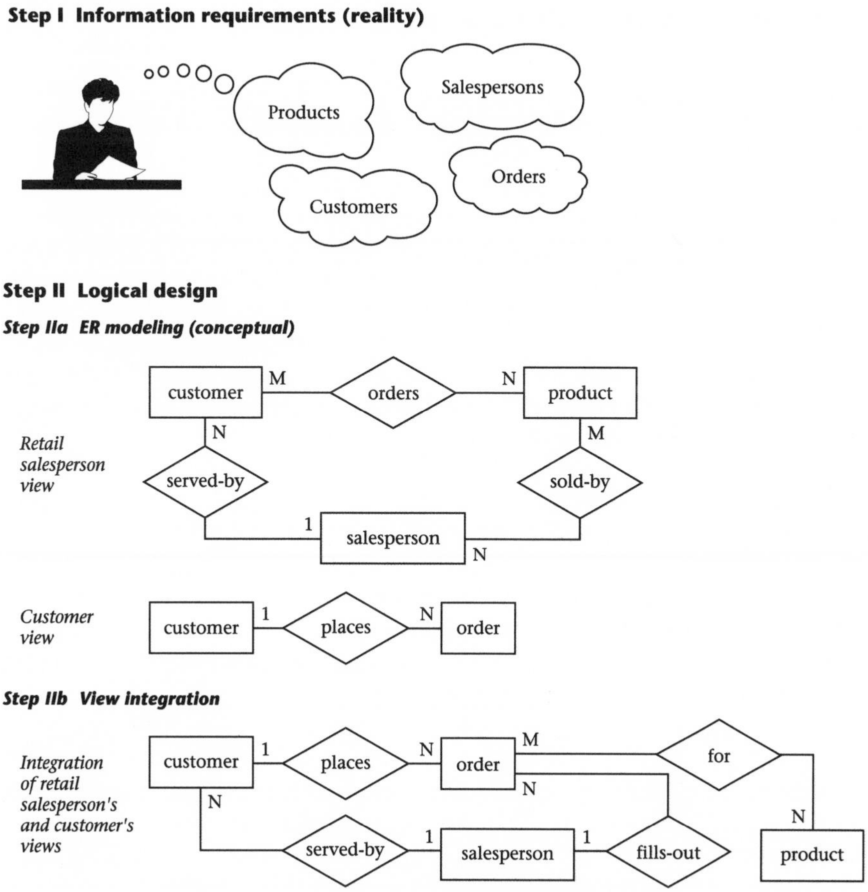

Figure 1.2 Database life cycle: requirements and logical design

c. *Transformation of the ER model to SQL tables.* Based on a categorization of ER constructs and a set of mapping rules, each relationship and its associated entities are transformed into a set of candidate relational tables. We will show these transformations in standard SQL in Chapter 4. Redundant tables are eliminated as part of this process. In our example, the tables in Figure 1.3 are the result of transformation of the integrated ER model in Figure 1.2.

d. *Normalization of tables.* Functional dependencies (FDs) are derived from the ER diagram. They represent the dependencies among data elements that are keys of entities. Additional FDs and multivalued dependencies (MVDs), which represent the dependencies among key and nonkey attributes within entities, can be derived from the requirements specification. Candidate relational

Step IIc Transformation of the ER diagram to SQL tables

Customer

cust-no	cust-name	....

Product

prod-no	prod-name	qty-in-stock

Order

order-no	sales-name	cust-no

Order-line

order-no	prod-no

Salesperson

sales-name	addr	dept	job-level	vacation-days

Step IId Normalization of SQL tables (3NF, BCNF, 4NF, 5NF)

Decomposition of tables and removal of update anomalies

Salesperson

sales-name	addr	dept	job-level

Sales-vacations

job-level	vacation-days

Step III Usage refinement

Customer

cust-no	cust-name

Order

order-no	sales-name	cust-no

Customer / refined

cust-no	cust-name	sales-name

Figure 1.3 Database life cycle: ER-to-SQL, normalization, and usage refinement

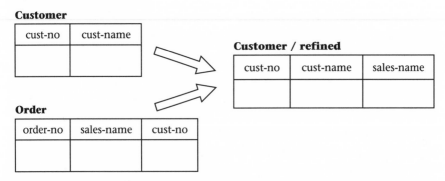

tables associated with all derived FDs and MVDs are normalized to the highest degree desired using standard normalization techniques. Finally, redundancies that occur in normalized candidate tables are analyzed further for possible elimination, with the constraint that data integrity must be preserved. An example of normalization of the tables defined here is shown in Figure 1.3.

III. ***Usage refinement.*** In this step the global schema is refined in limited ways to reflect processing requirements if there are obvious large gains in efficiency to be made. Usage refinement consists of selecting dominant processes on the basis of high frequency, high volume, or explicit priority; defining simple extensions to tables that will improve query performance; evaluating total cost for query, update, and storage; and considering the possible effects of denormalization. The justification for this approach is that, once local site physical design begins, the logical schema is considered to be fixed and is thus a constraint on efficiency. The database designer would like to remove this inflexibility if possible. Nevertheless, the usage refinement step makes assumptions about the physical design environment such that one may consider it to be actually an advanced stage of physical design. Usage refinement is illustrated in Figure 1.3 with the extension of the customer table to include sales-name to be more efficient for database queries such as, "Who is the salesperson for a customer named Pamela Wilson?"

IV. ***Data distribution.*** Data fragmentation and allocation are also forms of physical design because they must take into account the physical environment, that is, the network configuration. However, this step is separate from local schema and physical design, because design decisions for data distribution are still made independently of the local DBMS.

A *fragmentation schema* describes the one-to-many mapping used to partition each global table into fragments. Fragments are logical portions of global tables that are physically located at one or several sites of the network. A data *allocation schema* designates where each copy of each fragment is to be stored. A one-to-one mapping in the allocation schema results in nonredundancy; a one-to-many mapping defines a replicated distributed database. An example of the allocation of a fragmented and partially replicated database is shown in Figure 1.4, where various subsets of the whole database are allocated to different sites in a computer network.

Three important objectives of database design in distributed systems are:

- the separation of data fragmentation and allocation,
- control of redundancy, and
- independence from local database management systems.

Step IV Data distribution

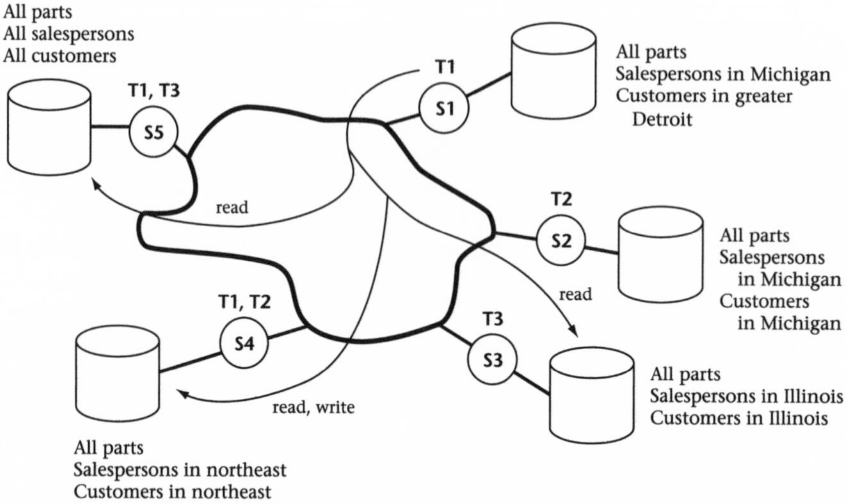

S1 = Ann Arbor, S2 = Detroit, S3 = Chicago, S4 = Boston, S5 = New York

Decisions: fragmentation, replication, allocation

Objectives: min response time, min communication cost, max availability

Step V Local DBMS schema and physical design

SQL (relational)

```
create table customer
   (cust_no integer,
   cust_name char(15),
   cust_addr char(30),
   sales_name char(15),
   prod_no integer,
   primary key (cust_no),
   foreign key (sales_name)
      references salesperson,
   foreign key (prod_no)
      references product);
```

CODASYL (network)

```
schema name is order-db

record name is customer
location mode is calc using cust-no
duplicates not allowed
02 cust-no pic x(10)
02 cust-name pic x(20)
02 cust-addr pic x(25)

set name is served-by
owner is salesperson
member is customer
```

Physical design parameters: Indexing, access methods, clustering

Figure 1.1 Database life cycle: data distribution and physical design

The distinction between designing the fragmentation and allocation schema is important: The first one is a logical, the second a physical mapping. In general, it is not possible to determine the optimal fragmentation and allocation by solving the two problems independently since they are interrelated.

However, near-optimal solutions can be obtained with separable design steps, and this is the only practical solution available today.

V. ***Local schema and physical design.*** The last step in the design phase is to produce a DBMS-specific physical structure for each of the site databases and to define the *external user schema*. In a heterogeneous system, local schema and physical design are site-dependent. The logical design methodology in Step II simplifies the approach to designing large relational databases by reducing the number of data dependencies that need to be analyzed. This is accomplished by inserting ER modeling and integration steps (Steps IIa and IIb) into the traditional relational design approach. The objective of these steps is an accurate representation of reality. Data integrity is preserved through normalization of the candidate tables created when the ER model is transformed into a relational model. Some examples of SQL data definition language table definitions are given in Figure 1.4.

VI. ***Database implementation, monitoring, and modification.*** Once the design is completed, the database can be created through implementation of the formal schema using the data definition language (DDL) of a DBMS. Then the data manipulation language (DML) can be used to query and update the database, as well as set up indexes and establish constraints such as referential integrity. The language SQL contains both DDL and DML constructs; for example, the "create table" command represents DDL, and the "select" command represents DML.

As the database begins operation, monitoring will indicate whether performance requirements are being met. If they are not being satisfied, modifications should be made to improve performance. Other modifications may be necessary when requirements change or end user expectations increase with good performance. Thus the life cycle continues with monitoring, redesign, and modifications.

Most CASE tools available today focus on Steps II, V, and VI of the database life cycle. Within Step II, the ER modeling, view integration, transformation to SQL, and normalization substeps are all commonly supported by many (but not all) tools. Within Step V, transaction modeling has become commonplace, and automatic application generation is provided by some tools. An excellent survey of both CASE tools that offer database design and purely database design tools can be found in [BCN92]. In the next chapter we look first at the basic data-modeling concepts, then—starting in Chapter 3—we apply these concepts to the database design process. The detailed steps in the database life cycle are illustrated using examples taken from real-life databases.

1.4 Summary

Knowledge of data-modeling and database design techniques is important for database practitioners. Among the variety of data-modeling approaches, the ER model is arguably the most popular in use today because of its simplicity and readability. A simple form of the ER model is used in most CASE tools and is easy to learn and apply to a variety of industrial and business applications. It is also a very useful tool for communicating with the end user about the conceptual model and verifying the assumptions made in the modeling process. A more complex form, a superset of the simple form, is useful for the more experienced designer who wants to capture greater semantic detail in diagram form and avoid having to write long and tedious narrative to explain certain requirements and constraints over and over again.

The database life cycle shows what steps are needed in a methodical approach to database design from logical design, which is independent of the system environment, to data distribution in a computer network and to local physical design, which is based on the details of the database management system chosen to implement the database.

Literature Summary

Much of the early data-modeling work was done by Bachman, Chen, Nijssen, Senko, and others [Bach69, Bach72, Chen76, NvS79, Senk73]. Database design textbooks that adhere to a significant portion of the database life cycle described in this chapter are [TeFr82, Howe83, Hawr84, Wied83, Yao85]. For general textbooks on database systems, consult [Spro76, Date86, Ever86, KoSi91, Ullm88, ElNa94, Maci89]. Some of the early research in CASE tools for the ER model was done by [TeHe77, CFT84, Rein85], and a comprehensive survey was written by David Reiner in [BCN92]. More on CASE tool information can be found in the *DBMS* annual review of database software [DBMS93].

[Bach69] Bachman, C.W. "Data Structure Diagrams," *Database* 1,2 (1969), pp. 4–10.

[Bach72] Bachman, C.W. "The Evolution of Storage Structures," *Comm. ACM* 15,7 (July 1972), pp. 628–634.

[BCN92] Batini, C., Ceri, S., and Navathe, S. *Conceptual Database Design: An Entity-Relationship Approach,* Benjamin/Cummings, Redwood City, CA, 1992.

[Chen76] Chen, P.P. "The Entity-Relationship Model—Toward a Unified View of Data," *ACM Trans. Database Systems*1,1 (March 1976), pp. 9–36.

[CFT84] Cobb, R.E., Fry, J.P., and Teorey, T.J. "The database designer's workbench," *Information Sciences* 32,1 (Feb. 1984), pp. 33–45.

[Codd90] Codd, E.F. *The Relational Model for Database Management*, Version 2, Addison-Wesley, Reading, MA, 1990.

[Date89] Date, C.J. *A Guide to the SQL Standard* (2nd Ed.), Addison-Wesley, Reading, MA, 1989.

[Date90] Date, C.J. *An Introduction to Database Systems*, Vol. 1 (5th Ed.), Addison-Wesley, Reading, MA, 1990.

[DBMS93] Special Issue: 1993 Database Buyer's Guide, *DBMS* 6,7 (Sept. 1993).

[ElNa94] Elmasri, R. and Navathe, S.B. *Fundamentals of Database Systems* (2nd Ed.), Addison-Wesley/Benjamin/Cummings, Redwood City, CA, 1994.

[Ever86] Everest, G.C. *Database Management: Objectives, System Functions, and Administration*, McGraw-Hill, New York, 1986.

[Hawr84] Hawryszkiewycz, I. *Database Analysis and Design*, SRA, Chicago, 1984.

[Howe83] Howe, D. *Data Analysis and Data Base Design*, Arnold Pub., London, 1983.

[KoSi91] Korth, H.F. and Silberschatz, A. *Database System Concepts* (2nd Ed.), McGraw-Hill, New York, 1991.

[Maci89] Maciaszek, L. *Database Design and Implementation*, Prentice-Hall International, New York, 1989.

[Rein85] Reiner, D., Brodie, M., Brown, G., Friedell, M., Kramlich, D., Lehman, J., and Rosenthal, A. "The Database Design and Evaluation Workbench (DDEW) Project at CCA," *Database Engineering* 7,4 (1985), pp. 10–15.

[Senk73] Senko et al. "Data Structures and Accessing in Data-base Systems," *IBM Syst. J.* 12,1 (1973), pp. 30–93.

[Spro76] Sprowls, R.C. *Management Data Bases*, Wiley/Hamilton, Santa Barbara, CA, 1976.

[TeHe77] Teichroew, D. and Hershey, E.A. "PSL/PSA: A Computer Aided Technique for Structured Documentation and Analysis of Information Processing Systems," *IEEE Trans. Software Engr.* SE-3,1 (1977), pp. 41–48.

[TeFr82] Teorey, T. and Fry, J. *Design of Database Structures*, Prentice-Hall, Englewood Cliffs, NJ, 1982.

[Ullm88] Ullman, J. *Principles of Database and Knowledge-Base Systems*, Vols. 1 & 2, Computer Science Press, Rockville, MD, 1988.

[Wied83] Wiederhold, G. *Database Design* (2nd Ed.), McGraw-Hill, New York, 1983.

[Yao85] Yao, S.B. (editor) *Principles of Database Design*, Prentice-Hall, Englewood Cliffs, NJ, 1985.

CHAPTER 2

THE ER MODEL: BASIC CONCEPTS

This chapter defines all the major entity relationship concepts that can be applied to the database life cycle. In Section 2.1, we will look at the simple level of ER modeling described in the original work by Chen and extended by others. In particular, we will use the Chen ER notation throughout the text. The simple form of the ER model is used as the basis for effective communication with the end user about the conceptual database. Section 2.2 presents the more advanced concepts that are less generally accepted but useful to describe certain semantics that cannot be constructed with the simple model.

2.1 Fundamental ER Constructs

2.1.1 Basic Objects: Entities, Relationships, Attributes

The basic ER model consists of three classes of objects: entities, relationships, and attributes.

Entities

Entities are the principal data objects about which information is to be collected; they usually denote a person, place, thing, or event of informational interest. (This book drops the older term "entity set" and uses entities to represent entity types.) A particular occurrence of an entity is called an *entity instance*, or sometimes an *entity occurrence*. In our example, employee, department, division, project, skill, and location are all examples of entities. For easy reference, entity names will henceforth be capitalized throughout this text: Employee, Department, and so forth. The entity construct is a rectangle as depicted in Figure 2.1. The entity name is written inside the rectangle.

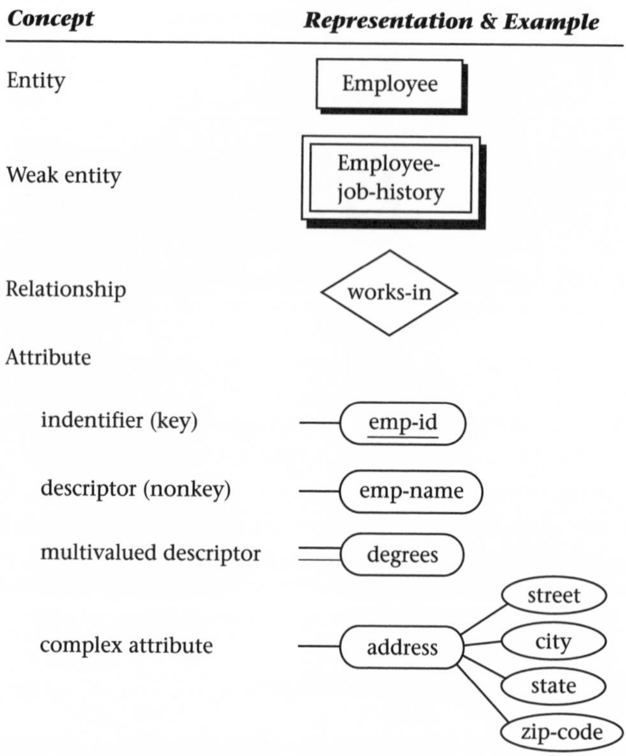

Figure 2.1 Fundamental ER constructs: basic objects

Relationships

Relationships represent real-world associations among one or more entities, and as such, have no physical or conceptual existence other than that which is inherited from their entity associations. A particular occurrence of a relationship is called a *relationship instance* or, sometimes, *relationship occurrence.* Relationships are described in terms of degree, connectivity, cardinality, and existence. These terms are defined in the sections that follow. The most common meaning associated with the term relationship is indicated by the connectivity between entity occurrences: one-to-one, one-to-many, and many-to-many. The relationship construct is a diamond which connects the associated entities, as shown in Figure 2.1. The relationship name is written inside the diamond.

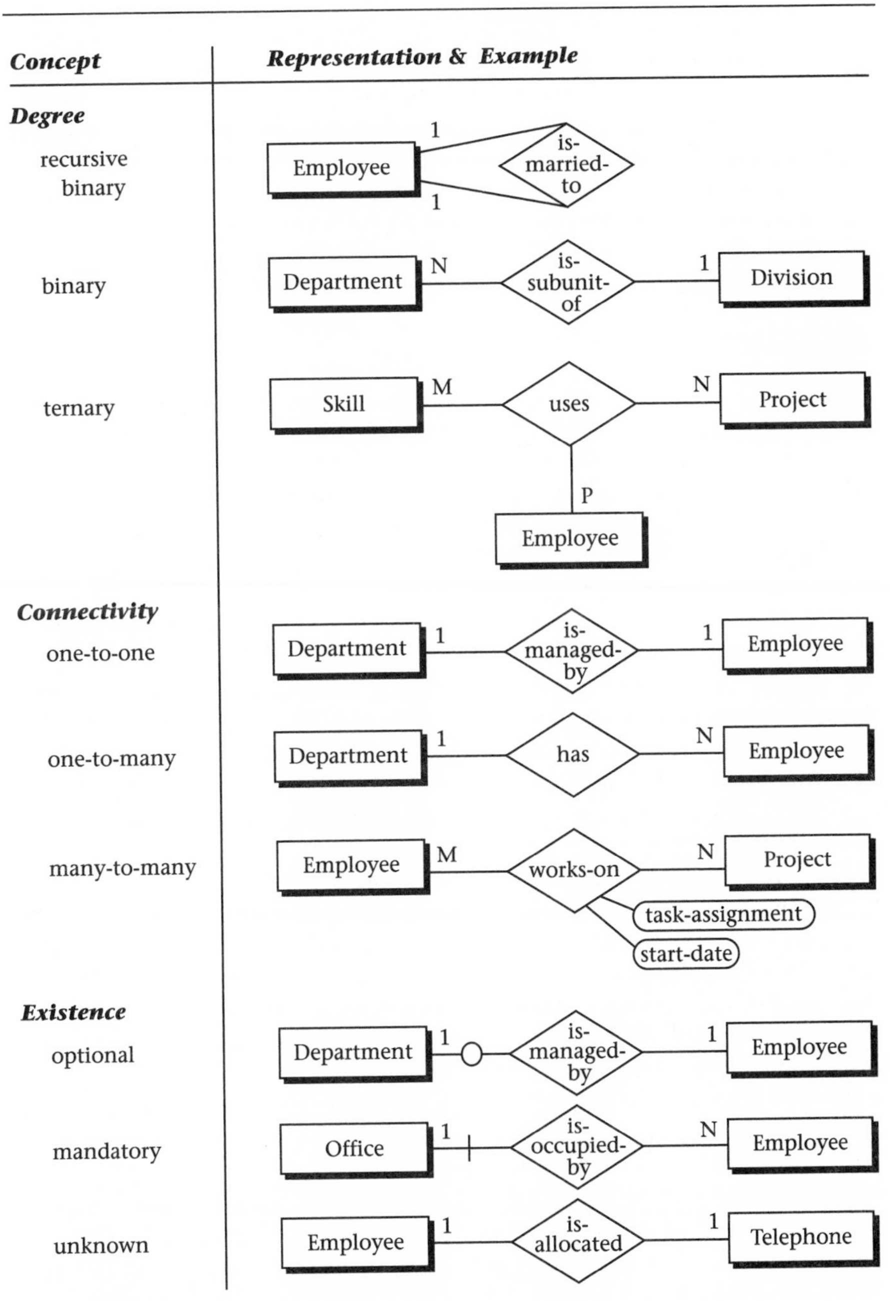

Figure 2.2 Fundamental ER constructs: relationship types

A *role* is defined as the function an entity plays in a relationship. For example, the role works-on defines the function of the entity Employee in the relationship between Employee and Project in Figure 2.2. The role name and relationship name are equivalent. Convention dictates that role names should act as verbs (if possible) between the nouns for entity names and, for readability, should be read from left to right or top to bottom in ER diagrams. In the example we read "(An) Employee works on (a) Project" as a way of describing the relationship. Unfortunately, we cannot always set up our role names so easily, but we try!

Attributes

Attributes are characteristics of entities that provide descriptive detail about them. A particular occurrence of an attribute within an entity or relationship is called an attribute value. Attributes of an entity such as Employee may include emp-id, emp-name, emp-address, phone-no, fax-no, job-title, and so on. The attribute construct is an ellipse with the attribute name inside (or oblong as shown in Figure 2.1). The attribute is connected to the entity it characterizes.

There are two types of attributes: identifiers and descriptors. An identifier (or key) is used to uniquely determine an instance of an entity; a descriptor (or nonkey attribute) is used to specify a nonunique characteristic of a particular entity instance. Both identifiers and descriptors may consist of either a single attribute or some composite of attributes. For example, an identifier or key of Employee is emp-id, and a descriptor of Employee is emp-name or job-title. Key attributes are underlined in the ER diagram, as shown in Figure 2.1.

Some attributes, such as specialty-area, may be multivalued. The notation for multivalued attributes is shown with a double attachment line, as shown in Figure 2.1. Other attributes may be complex, such as an address that further subdivides into street, city, state, and zip code. Complex attributes are constructed to have attributes of their own; sometimes, however, the individual parts of a complex attribute are specified as individual attributes in the first place. Either form is reasonable in ER notation.

Entities have internal identifiers that uniquely determine the existence of entity instances, but weak entities derive their identity from the identifying attributes of one or more "parent" entities. Weak entities are often depicted with a double-bordered rectangle (see Figure 2.1) which denotes that all occurrences of that entity are dependent for their existence in the database on an associated (strong) entity. For example, in Figure 2.1 the weak entity Employee-job-history is related to the entity Employee and dependent upon Employee for its own existence. Another typical form for a weak entity is a multivalued attribute associated with an entity or a many-to-many relationship between two entities, so that the identity dependence is more obvious. As an example, in Figure 2.2 the relationship works-on between Employee and Project could be redefined as a weak entity Works-on, having a one-to-many relationship with Employee and a one-to-many relationship to Project. Note that Works-on must be the "many" side of each of the two new relationships (see Section 2.1.3).

2.1.2 Degree of a Relationship

The degree of a relationship is the number of entities associated in the relationship. Binary and ternary relationships are special cases where the degree is 2 and 3, respectively. An n-ary relationship is the general form for any degree n. The notation for degree is illustrated in Figure 2.2.

The binary relationship, an association between two entities, is by far the most common type in the natural world. In fact, many modeling systems use only this type. In Figure 2.2 we see many examples of the association of two entities in different ways: Division and Department, Department and Employee, Employee and Project, and so on. A binary recursive relationship—for example, married-to in Figure 2.2—relates a particular Employee to another Employee by marriage. It is called recursive because the entity relates only to another instance of its own type. The binary recursive relationship construct is a diamond with both connections to the same entity.

A ternary relationship is an association among three entities. This type of relationship is required when binary relationships are not sufficient to accurately describe the semantics of the association. The ternary relationship construct is a single diamond connected to three entities as shown in Figure 2.2. Sometimes a relationship is mistakenly modeled as ternary, when it could be decomposed into two or three equivalent binary relationships. When this occurs, the ternary relationship should be eliminated to achieve both simplicity and semantic purity. Ternary relationships are discussed in greater detail in Sections 2.2.3 and 5.5.

An entity may be involved in any number of relationships, and each relationship may be of any degree. Furthermore, any two entities may have any number of binary relationships between them, and so on for any n entities (see n-ary relationships defined in Section 2.2.4).

2.1.3 Connectivity and Cardinality of a Relationship

The *connectivity* of a relationship describes the mapping of the associated entity occurrences in the relationship. Values for connectivity are either "one" or "many." For a relationship between entities Department and Employee, a connectivity of one for Department and many for Employee means that there is at most one entity occurrence of Department associated with many occurrences of Employee. The actual number associated with the connectivity is called the *cardinality* of the relationship connectivity. Cardinality describes the constraints on the number of entity instances that are related through a relationship, as we see illustrated below.

Figure 2.2 shows the basic constructs for connectivity for binary relationships: one-to-one, one-to-many, and many-to-many. On the "one" side, the number 1 is shown on the connection between the relationship and one of the entities, and on the "many" side, the letter N (and sometimes the letters M or P) is used on the connection between the relationship and the entity to designate the concept of many. In the one-to-one case, the entity Department is managed by exactly one Employee and each Employee manages exactly one Department. Therefore, the minimum and maximum cardinalities on the is-managed-by relationship are exactly one for both Department and Employee.

In the one-to-many case, the entity Department is associated with ("has") many Employees. The maximum cardinality is given on the Employee (many) side as the unknown value N, but the minimum cardinality is known as one. On the Department side the minimum and maximum cardinalities are both one, that is, each Employee works within exactly one Department.

In the many-to-many case, the entity Employee may work-on many Projects and each Project may have many Employees. We saw that the maximum cardinality for Employee and Project was M and N, respectively, and the minimum cardinalities were each defined as 1.

Some situations are such that the actual maximum cardinality is known. Let us assume, for example in Figure 2.2, that the entity Employee in the many-to-many relationship may be a member of a maximum of three Projects (N=3); thus, the maximum cardinality is 3 on the Project side of the works-on relationship. Reading from right to left in the same relationship, we may be told that the entity Project may contain a maximum of 15 Employees (M=15). Thus, 15 is the maximum cardinality of Employee in the works-on relationship. The minimum cardinalities in all relationships of any type are either zero or one, depending on whether the relationship is optional or mandatory, respectively (see Section 2.1.5). In this example the minimum cardinalities are one for both Employee and Project.

2.1.4 Attributes of a Relationship

Attributes can be assigned to relationships as well as to entities. An attribute of a many-to-many relationship such as the works-on relationship between the entities Employee and Project (Figure 2.2) could be task-assigned or start-date. In this case, a given task-assigned or start-date is common only to an instance of the assignment of a particular Employee to a particular Project, and it would be multivalued when characterizing either the Employee or the Project entity alone. Performance and storage utilization would be optimized at database implementation time by assigning these attributes to the relationship rather than the entities, because each instance of a task-assigned associated with an Employee must carry information about the Project with it, creating redundancy of data.

Attributes of relationships are typically assigned only to binary many-to-many relationships and to ternary relationships. Attributes are not normally assigned to one-to-one or one-to-many relationships because at least one side of the relationship is a single entity and there is no ambiguity in assigning the attribute to a particular entity instead of assigning it to the relationship. For example, in the one-to-many binary relationship between Department and Employee, an attribute start-date could be applied to Department to designate the start date for that department, or to Employee to be an attribute for each Employee instance to designate their start date in that department. If the relationship changes to many-to-many, so that an employee can belong to many departments, then the attribute start-date must shift to the relationship, so each instance of the relationship that matches one employee with one department can have a unique start date for that employee in that department.

2.1.5 Existence of an Entity in a Relationship

Some enterprises have entities whose existence depends on the existence of another entity. This is called existence dependency, or just existence. Existence of an entity in a relationship is defined as either mandatory or optional. If an occurrence of either the "one" or "many" side entity must always exist for the entity to be included in the relationship, then it is mandatory. When an occurrence of that entity need not exist, it is considered optional. For example, in Figure 2.2 the entity Employee may or may not be the manager of any Department, thus making the entity Department in the is-managed-by relationship between Employee and Department optional.

Optional existence, defined by a 0 on the connection line between an entity and a relationship, defines a minimum cardinality of zero. *Mandatory existence,* defined by a line perpendicular to the connection line between an entity and a relationship, defines a minimum cardinality of one. If neither a 0 nor a perpendicular line are shown on the connection line between a relationship and an entity, then the type of existence, optional or mandatory, is unknown. For example, in Figure 2.2 it is not known whether all employees at a given instant are allocated a telephone, but normally each employee has one. When existence is unknown, we assume the minimum cardinality is one.

Maximum cardinalities are defined explicitly on the ER diagram as a constant (if a number is shown on the ER diagram next to an entity) or variable (by default if no number is shown on the ER diagram next to an entity). For example, in Figure 2.2 the relationship is-occupied-by between the entity Office and Employee implies that an Office may house from zero to some variable maximum (N) number of Employees, but an Employee must be housed in exactly one Office, that is, mandatory.

Existence is often implicit in the real world. For example, an entity Employee associated with a dependent (weak) entity, Dependent, cannot be optional, but the weak entity is usually optional. Using the concept of optional existence, an entity instance may be able to exist in other relationships even though it is not participating in this particular relationship.

2.1.6 Alternative ER Notations

At this point we need to digress briefly to look at other ER notations that are commonly used today and compare them with the Chen approach selected for this book. A popular alternative form for one-to-many and many-to-many relationships uses "crow's foot" notation for the "many" side (see Figure 2.3a). This form was popularized by Gordon Everest [Ever86] and used by some CASE tools such as Knowledgeware's Information Engineering Workbench (IEW). Relationships have no explicit construct, but are implied by the connection line between entities and a relationship name on the connection line. Minimum cardinality is specified by either a 0 (for zero) or perpendicular line (for one) on the connection lines between entities. The term "intersection" entity is used to designate a weak entity, especially an entity which is equivalent to a many-to-many relationship.

Connectivity in the ER model is sometimes expressed by the relationship shading approach in [Rein85,TYF86]. The shaded side of the relationship diamond implies "many" and the unshaded side implies "one." The circle on the connection line between a relationship and entity denotes optional existence of a particular entity instance; mandatory existence is implied by the absence of the optional symbol. The constructs for entities, weak entities, and attributes are basically the same as the Chen notation (see Figure 2.3b). Another popular form used today is the IDEF1X notation, conceived by Robert G. Brown [Bruc92]. The similarities with the Chen notation are obvious from Figure 2.3c.

Fortunately, any of these forms is reasonably easy to learn and read, and the equivalence for the basic ER concepts is obvious from the diagrams.

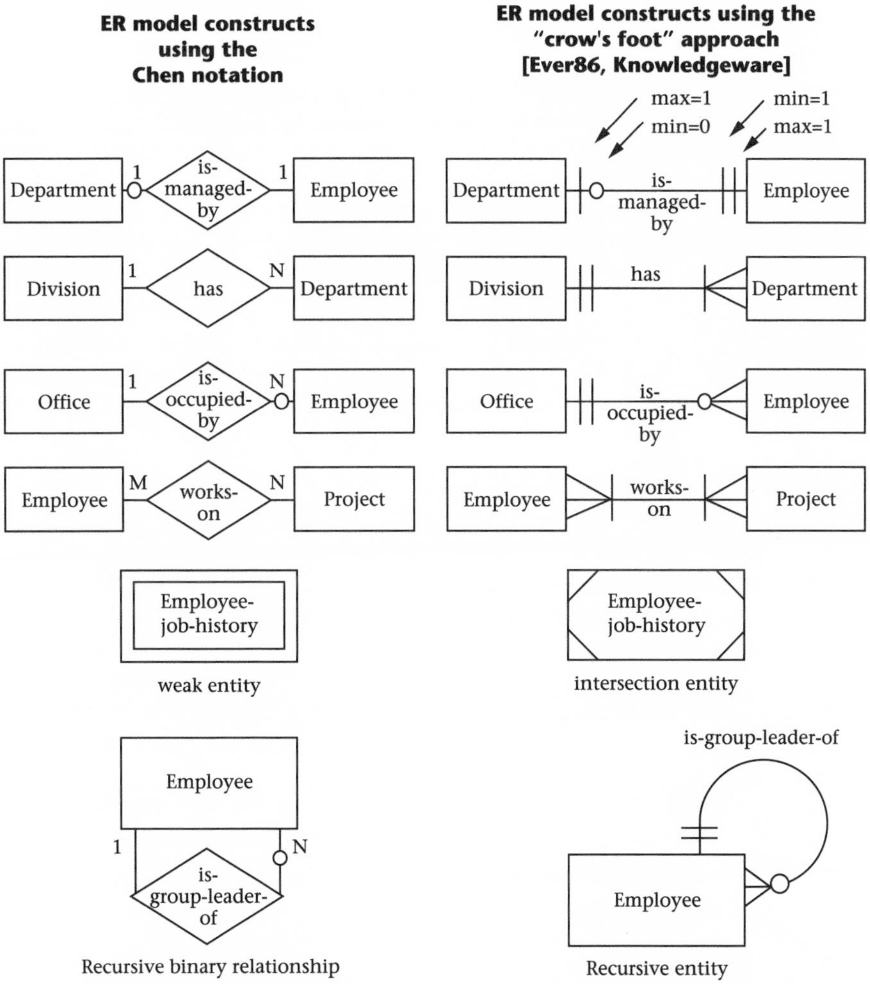

Figure 2.3a Comparison of ER construct conventions: Chen versus crowsfoot

Without a standard for the ER model, however, many other constructs are being used today in addition to the three types shown here. Although standards efforts are currently underway, it will be years before standardization will be achieved, if ever. Developers of new CASE tools would certainly benefit from standardization, and in turn most database developers should welcome it.

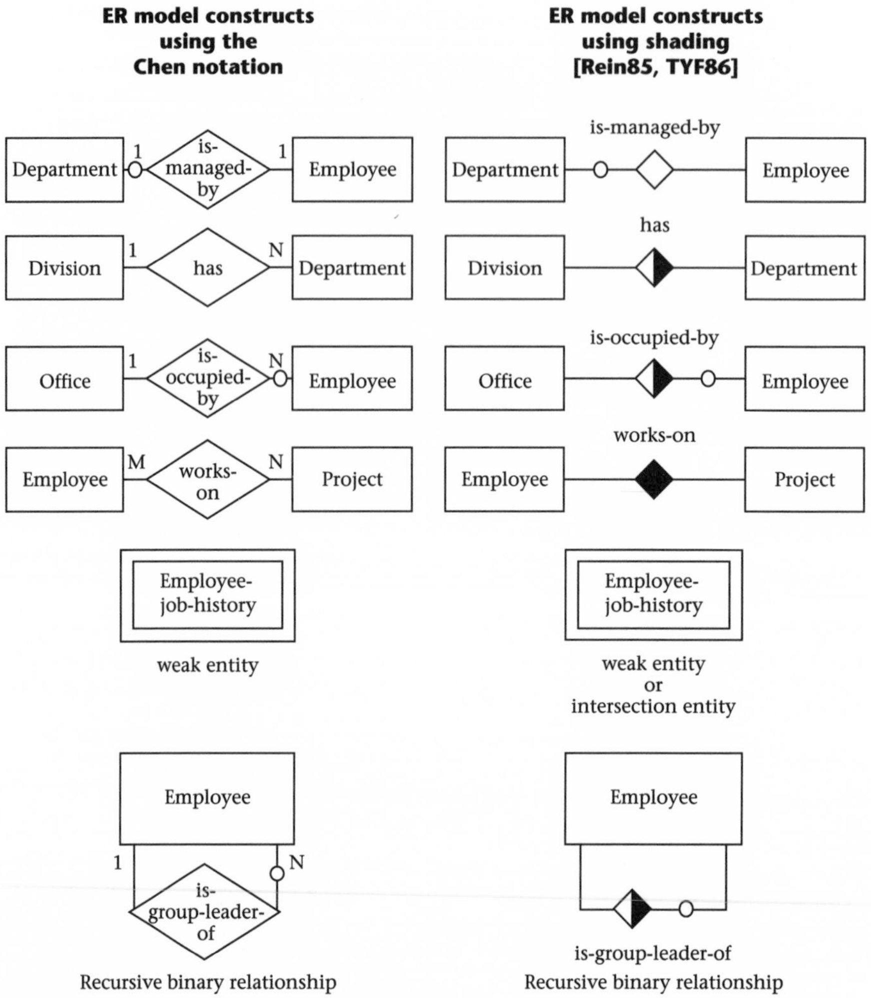

Figure 2.3b Comparison of ER construct conventions: Chen versus solid diamonds

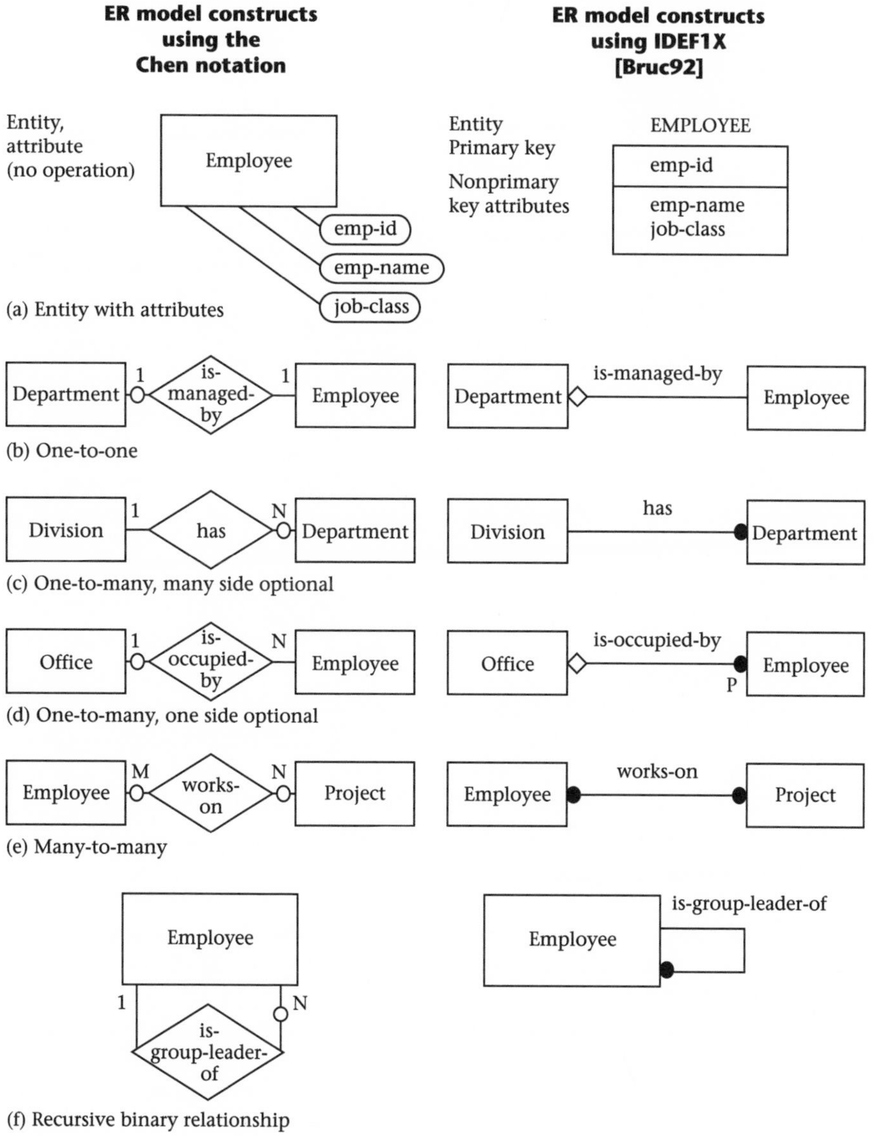

Figure 2.3c Comparison of ER construct conventions: Chen versus IDEF1X

2.2 Advanced ER Constructs

2.2.1 Generalization: Supertypes and Subtypes

The original ER model has been effectively used for communicating fundamental data and relationship definitions with the end user for a long time. However, using it to develop and integrate conceptual models with different end user views was severely limited until it could be extended to include database abstraction concepts such as *generalization*. The generalization relationship specifies that several types of entities with certain common attributes can be generalized into a higher level entity type: a generic or superclass entity, which is more commonly known as a supertype entity. The lower levels of entities—subtypes in a generalization hierarchy—can be either disjoint or overlapping subsets of the supertype entity. As an example, in Figure 2.4 the entity Employee is a higher level abstraction of Manager, Engineer, Technician, and Secretary—all of which are disjoint types of Employee. The ER model construct for the generalization abstraction is the connection of a supertype entity with its subtypes using a circle and the subset symbol on the connecting lines from the circle to the subtype entities. The circle contains a letter specifying a disjointness constraint (see below). *Specialization* is the same concept, but the reverse of generalization; it indicates that subtypes specialize the supertype.

A supertype entity in one relationship may be a subtype entity in another relationship. When a combination of supertype/subtype relationships comprise a structure, the structure is called a *supertype/subtype hierarchy*, or *generalization hierarchy*. Generalization can also be described in terms of inheritance, which specifies that all the attributes of a supertype are propagated down the hierarchy to entities of a lower type. Generalization may occur when a generic entity, which we call the supertype entity, is partitioned by different values of a common attribute. For example, in Figure 2.4 the entity Employee is a generalization of Manager, Engineer, Technician, and Secretary over the attribute job-title in Employee.

Generalization can be further classified by two important constraints on the subtype entities: *disjointness* and *completeness*. The disjointness constraint requires the subtype entities to be mutually exclusive. We denote this type of constraint by the letter "d" written inside the generalization circle (Figure 2.4a). Subtypes that are not disjoint—that is, are overlapping—are designated by using the letter "o" inside the circle. As an example, a supertype entity Individual which has two subtype entities, Employee and Customer, the subtypes could be described as overlapping or not mutually exclusive (Figure 2.4b). Regardless of whether the subtypes are disjoint or overlapping, they may have additional special attributes in addition to the generic (inherited) attributes from the supertype.

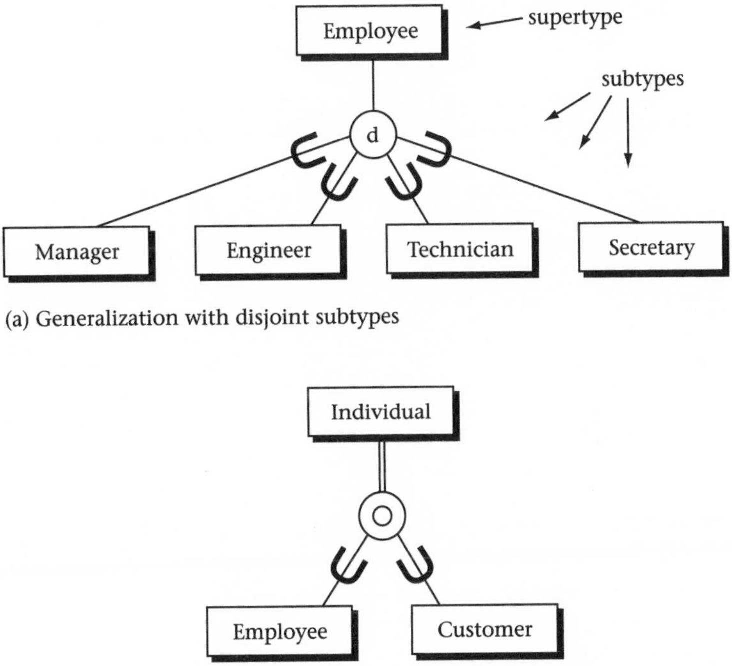

(a) Generalization with disjoint subtypes

(b) Generalization with overlapping subtypes and completeness constraint

Figure 2.4 Generalization

The completeness constraint requires the subtypes to be all-inclusive of the supertype. Thus subtypes can be defined as either total or partial coverage of the supertype. For example, in a generalization hierarchy with supertype Individual and subtypes Employee and Customer, the subtypes may be described as all-inclusive or total. We denote this type of constraint by a double line between the supertype entity and the circle. This is indicated in Figure 2.4b, which implies that the only types of individuals to be considered in the database are employees and customers.

2.2.2 Aggregation

Aggregation is a form of abstraction between a supertype and subtype entity that is somewhat different from the generalization abstraction. Generalization is often described in terms of an "is-a" relationship between the subtype and the supertype—for example, an Employee is an Individual. Similarly,

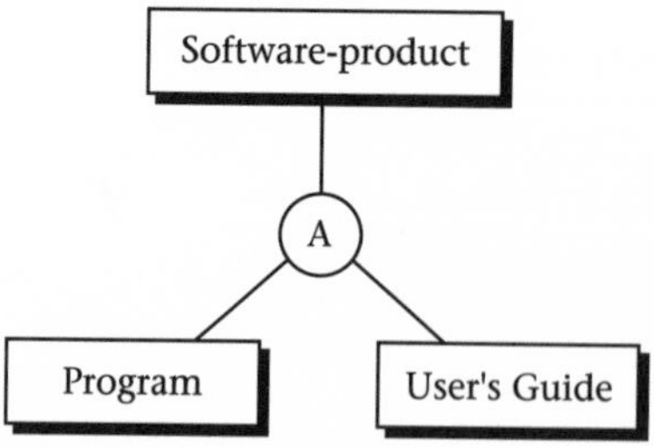

Figure 2.5 Aggregation

aggregation is described as a "part-of" relationship; for example, a report and a prototype software package are both parts of a deliverable for a contract. Thus, in Figure 2.5 the entity Software-Product is seen to consists of component parts Program and User's Guide. The construct for aggregation is similar to generalization in that the supertype entity is connected with the subtype entities with a circle, and the letter "A" is shown in the circle. However, there are no subset symbols because the "part-of" relationship is not a subset. Furthermore, there are no inherited attributes in aggregation; each entity has its own unique set of attributes.

2.2.3 Ternary Relationships

Ternary relationships are required when binary relationships are not sufficient to accurately describe the semantics of an association among three entities. Ternary relationships are somewhat more complex than binary relationships, however. The ER notation for a ternary relationship is shown in Figure 2.2 with three entities attached to a single relationship diamond, and the cardinality of each entity designated as either one or many. An entity in a ternary relationship is considered to be "one" if only one instance of it can be associated with one instance of each of the other two associated entities. It is "many" if more than one instance of it can be associated with one instance of each of the other two associated entities. In either case, one instance of each of the other entities is assumed to be given.

As an example, the relationship "manages" in Figure 2.6c associates the entities Manager, Engineer, and Project. The entities Engineer and Project are considered "many;" the entity Manager is considered "one." This is represented by the following assertions:

> ***Assertion 1:*** One engineer, working under one manager, could be working on many projects.

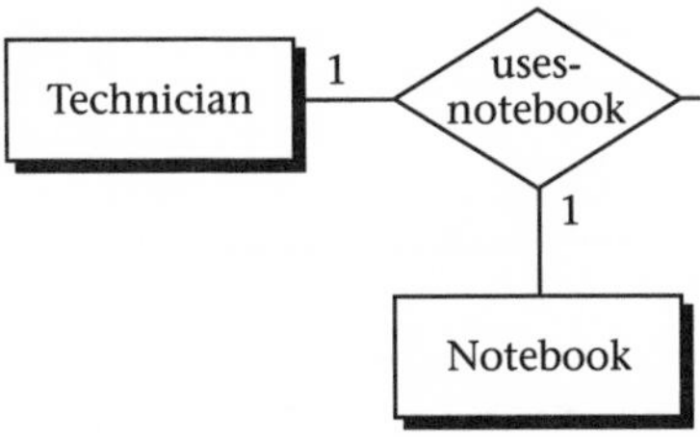

A technician uses exactly one notebook for each project. Each notebook belongs to one technician for each project. Note that a technician may still work on many projects and maintain different notebooks for different projects.

Functional dependencies

emp-id, project-name → notebook-no
emp-id, notebook-no → project-name
project-name, notebook-no → emp-id

(a) one-to-one-to-one ternary relationship

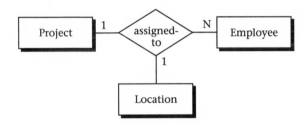

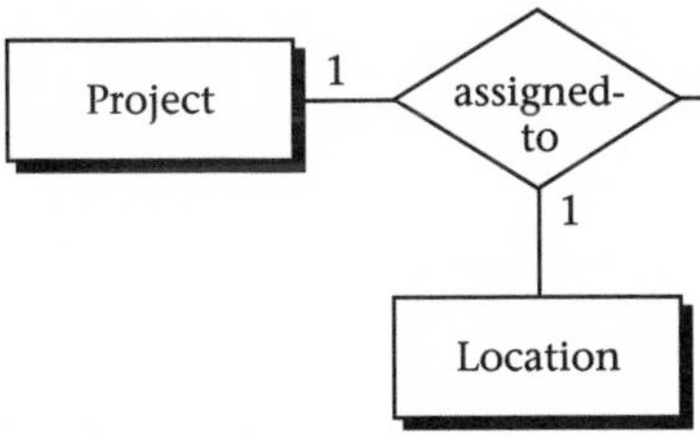

Each employee assigned to a project works at only one location for that project, but can be at different locations for different projects. At a particular location, an employee works on only one project. At a particular location, there can be many employees assigned to a given project.

Functional dependencies

emp-id, loc-name → project-name
emp-id, project-name → loc-name

(b) one-to-one-to-many ternary relationship

Figure 2.6 Types and properties of ternary relationships (Figure continues on the following page)

Assertion 2: One project, under the direction of one manager, could have many engineers.

Assertion 3: One engineer, working on one project, must have only a single manager.

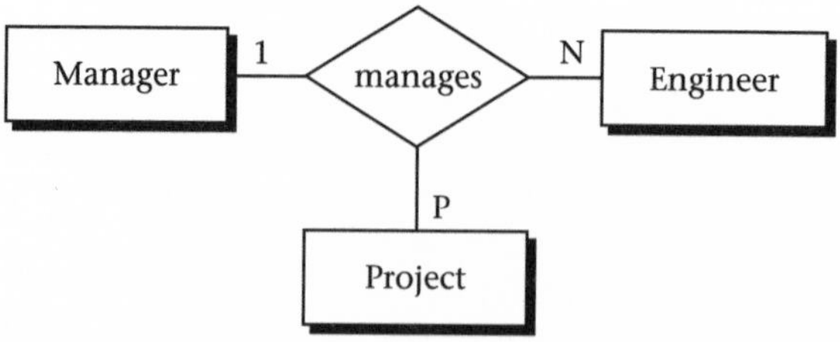

Each engineer working on a particular project has exactly one manager, but each manager of a project may manage many engineers, and each manager of an engineer may manage that engineer on many projects.

Functional dependencies
project-name, emp-id → mgr-id

(c) one-to-many-to-many ternary relationship

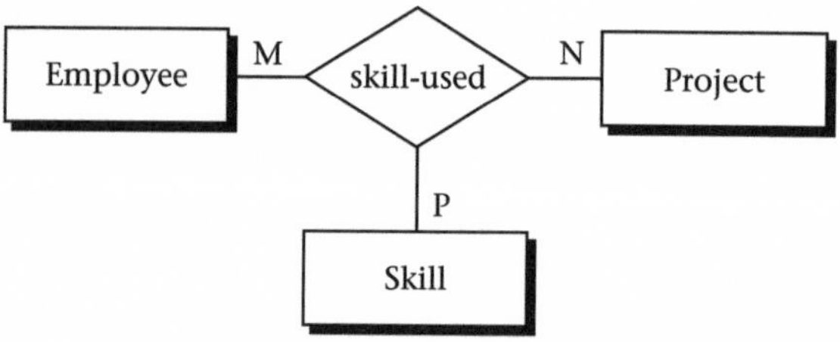

Employees can use many skills on any one of many projects, and each project has many employees with various skills.

Functional dependencies
none

(d) many-to-many-to-many ternary relationship

Figure 2.6 Continued

Assertion 3 could also be written in another form, using an arrow (→) in a kind of shorthand form called a *functional dependency*. For example:

emp-id, project-name → mgr-id

where emp-id is the primary key associated with the entity Engineer, project-name is the primary key associated with the entity Project, and mgr-id is the primary key of the entity Manager. In general, for an n-ary relationship, each entity considered to be a "one" has its key appearing on the right side of

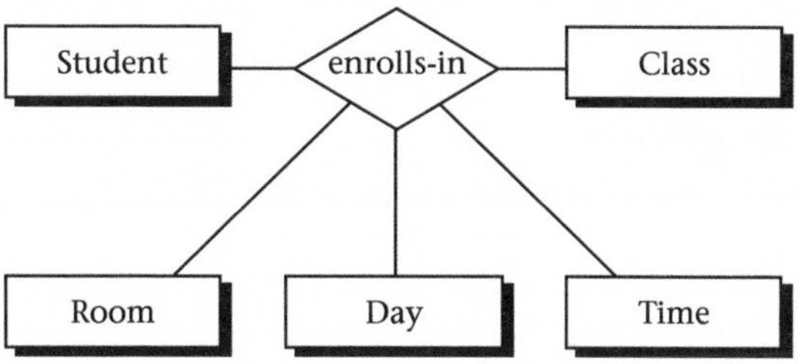

Figure 2.7 An n-ary relationship

exactly one functional dependency (FD). No entity considered "many" ever has its key appear on the right side of an FD.

All four forms of ternary relationships are illustrated in Figure 2.6. In each case the number of "one" entities implies the number of FDs used to define the relationship semantics, and the key of each "one" entity appears on the right side of exactly one FD for that relationship.

Ternary relationships can have attributes in the same way as many-to-many binary relationships. These are attributes whose values are uniquely determined by some combination of the keys of the entities associated with the relationship. For example, in Figure 2.6d the relationship skill-used might have the attribute tool associated with a given employee using a particular skill on a certain project, indicating that a value for tool is uniquely determined by the combination of employee, skill, and project.

2.2.4 General n-ary Relationships

Generalizing the ternary form to higher degree relationships, an n-ary relationship that describes some association among n entities is represented by a single relationship diamond with n connections, one to each entity (see Figure 2.7). The meaning of this form can be best described in terms of the functional dependencies among the keys of the n associated entities. There can be anywhere from zero to n FDs, depending on the number of "one" entities. The collection of FDs that describe an n-ary relationship must have n components: n-1 on the left side (determinant) and 1 on the right side. A ternary relationship (n=3), for example, has two components on the left and one on the right, as we saw in the example in Figure 2.6. In a more complex database, other types of FDs may also exist within an n-ary relationship. When this occurs, the ER model does not provide enough semantics by itself, and it must be supplemented with a narrative description of these dependencies.

2.2.5 ER Constraints: Extensions from the NIAM Model

Conceptual modeling of databases is by no means confined to the ER approach. A number of other schools of thought have received attention, and some offer a richer semantic base than the ER model. The binary relationship approach is the basis of the information analysis method called *Nijssens Information Analysis Method (NIAM)* [VeVa82]. This approach, which develops normalized (fifth normal form) tables from basic semantic constructs, provides low-level primitive constructs such as lexical object type, nonlexical object type, and role. These roughly correspond to the attribute, entity, and relationship concepts, respectively, in the ER model. However, unlike the ER approach, the binary relationship model tries to avoid making entity-attribute decisions early in the conceptual modeling process. The binary relationship model also includes the semantic concepts of subtyping (generalization), relationship connectivity, and membership class (mandatory or optional existence).

One obvious difference between the binary relationship model and the ER approach is that role names in the binary relationship model are directional between two lexical object types (attributes) and between a lexical (attribute) and nonlexical object type (entity). In fact, directional role names could easily be added to the ER model, but the designer would have to consider whether or not the added role names would degrade the readability of the ER diagram.

One of the most interesting aspects of the binary relationship model is the inclusion of integrity constraints on role occurrences. Some of the NIAM constraints such as exclusion and uniqueness can be easily adapted to the ER model. In the following paragraphs we illustrate how this could be done with some nonstandard ER notation.

Exclusion constraint

The normal, or default, treatment of multiple relationships is the *inclusive OR*, which allows any or all of the entities to participate. In some situations, however, multiple relationships may be affected by the exclusion (*disjoint* or *exclusive OR*) constraint, which allows at most one entity instance among several entity types, to participate in the relationship with a single root entity. For example, in Figure 2.8, suppose the root entity Work-task has two associated entities, External-project and Internal-project. At most one of the associated entity instances could apply to an instance of Work-task.

Uniqueness constraint

The uniqueness constraint in the NIAM model combines three or more entities such that the combination of roles for the two entities in one direction uniquely determines the value of the single entity in the other

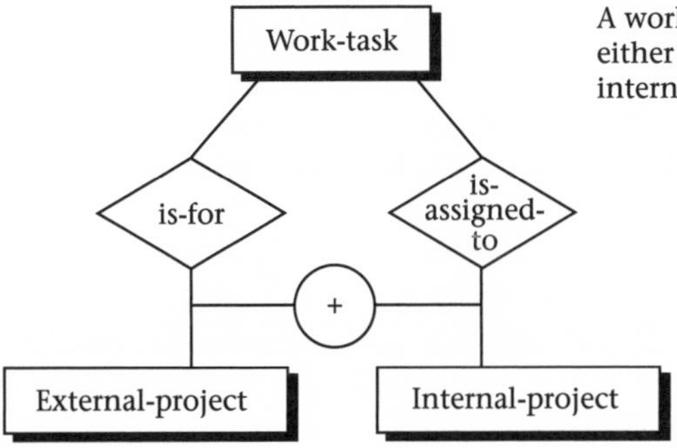

A work task can be assigned to either an external project or an internal project, but not both.

Figure 2.8 Exclusion constraint

direction. This, in effect, defines an FD from the composite keys of the entities in the first direction to the key of the entity in the second direction, and thus partly defines a ternary relationship. The ER constructs for ternary relationships are equivalent to the uniqueness constraint in NIAM.

2.2.6 Entity Integrity, Referential Integrity, and ID Dependency

Entity integrity, as defined in the relational model, requires that if an entity exists and it has a primary key, then its primary key must also exist. *Referential integrity* requires that for every foreign key instance that exists in a table, the row (and thus the primary key instance) of the parent table associated with that foreign key instance must also exist. Both the entity integrity and referential integrity constraints have become so common in relational systems that they are not explicitly described in the ER model; they are usually implied as requirements for the resulting relational database implementation. (Chapter 4 will discuss the SQL implementation of integrity constraints).

ID dependency is a special case of existence dependency in which there is an additional constraint that the primary key of the weak entity must include the key of the associated strong (parent) entity. This could be indicated by including the letters "id" in the corner of the box for the weak entity.

2.3 Object-Oriented Data Modeling

Object-oriented programming languages and database systems are rapidly becoming a major part of the information systems industry. They have incorporated many new ideas and other well-established concepts such as information hiding into a coherent set of rules for data structure and data operations: data abstraction, encapsulation of data structure and behavior (operations) into the same object, and sharing of data structure and code. The object-oriented (OO) approach views classes (or types) as collections of methods, that is, operations on specific classes of objects. The ER model, on the other hand, is limited to viewing classes (supertypes and subtypes) as relationships among objects (entities), and ignores the dynamic behavior of the objects. Thus, to compare ER and object modeling, we need to understand both the differences and the similarities. In this section we first look at the basic OO concepts and then compare the data-modeling constructs of the two approaches.

2.3.1 Object-Oriented Concepts

The object-oriented approach generally includes the following four characteristics [Rumb91]: identity, classification, polymorphism, and inheritance. *Identity* means that data is composed of discrete things called objects; objects can be things in the real world in the same way entities can be, but they can also be operations, or processes, on other objects. *Classification* is the grouping of objects with the same structure (attributes) and behavior (operations) into a class. Each object is then considered an instance of a class, and each instance of a class has its own value for each attribute but shares attribute names and operation names with other objects in that class. Operations that pertain to a particular class are called *methods*. Classification includes the concepts of data abstraction and encapsulation, the separation of the object's identity and function from the implementation details of that function.

Polymorphism is the characteristic that a given operation may behave differently on different object classes. For instance, a copy command has different implementations for buffers, disk files, and tape files. Finally, *inheritance* is the characteristic that attributes and operations among object classes can be shared in a hierarchical relationship. Each class can be divided into subclasses; each subclass inherits all the properties of the superclass in addition to defining its own unique properties. In OO programming, inheritance is often referred to in terms of code reuse because similar classes can be made to use common code in certain situations.

Some of the most popular object-oriented analysis (OOA) and design (OOD) techniques are OOA by Shlaer and Mellor [ShMe88] and by Coad and Yourdon [CoYo90], OOD by Booch [Booc91], object-oriented structured design (OOSD) by Wasserman [WPM89], object modeling technique (OMT) by Rumbaugh et al. [Rumb91], Jacobsen [Jaco87], Meyer [Meye88], and others. OMT, for instance, is a methodology for object-oriented system development and a notation for representing OO concepts. It includes details for object analysis, system design, object design, and implementation. A good summary and comparison of techniques can be found in [Fike92].

2.3.2 Object Modeling Versus ER Modeling

Object modeling is a necessary discipline for object-oriented databases in the same way ER modeling is needed as a front end for designing relational databases. The object model describes the individual objects in the system, their identity, attributes, behavior, and their relationships to other objects. The object diagram is a conceptual representation of the object model in the same way an ER diagram represents an ER model. Let us look at the basic concepts of object-oriented database (OODB) structure and compare it to the ER concepts we have already introduced in this chapter.

An *object* is a concept or thing in the real world. It has meaning for the data-oriented environment we are studying, and it has identity [Rumb91]. An *object class* is a meta-object that describes a group of objects with similar properties (attributes), common behavior (operations), and common relationships (associations) to other objects. An *object instance* is a single instance of an object class; for example, Bill Clinton is an instance of the object class President. An *attribute* of an object is a descriptive property of an object in the same way an attribute describes an entity in the ER model. An attribute also has a specific value which has the same data type within an object class it describes. A *link* is a connection between object instances, and an *association* is an abstraction of this linkage at the level of object classes. A *method* is an implementation of an operation for an object class, denoting that an operation such as "sort data" may be applied to many classes, with potentially many possible implementations.

The correspondence between the ER model and an object model is easily illustrated by showing equivalent (or nearly equivalent) constructs side by side (Figure 2.9). In Figure 2.9a we see how an entity can be represented in an object model as an object class. Note that object classes in Rumbaugh's notation have names in boldface in the upper section of the box, a list of attributes and their data types in the middle section, and the names of operations on that object class in the lower section. The ER model only specifies data structure and not data behavior.

Associations in the object model are shown by straight lines between the object classes they connect, with the lower bound of zero and upper bound of one on connectivity shown with a zero at the end of the association line adjacent to the appropriate object class (Figure 2.9b). The absence of a zero (or any other symbol) on the association line represents a lower and upper bound of one (Figure 2.9b). The upper bound of many and lower bound of

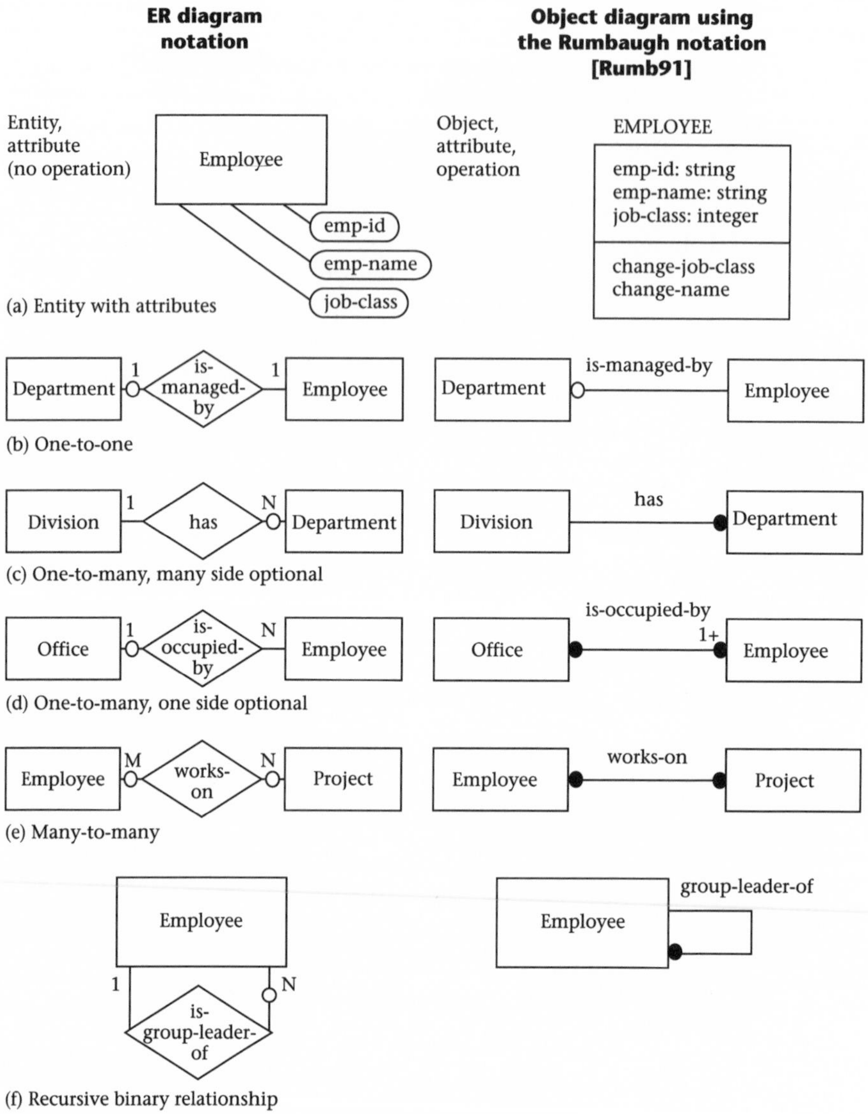

Figure 2.9 ER versus OO diagram notation: basic constructs

zero is normally shown by a darkened circle adjacent to the appropriate object class (Figure 2.9c and e), whereas an upper bound of many and a lower bound of one has the association line with a number "1+" adjacent to the appropriate object class (Figure 2.9d). A binary recursive relationship has the same connectivity notation as binary relationships, except that the two ends of the association line are connected to a single object class (Figure 2.9f).

Object diagrams represent a concept of *multiplicity*, similar to the ER concept of cardinality and connectivity of entities, in allowing the modeler to specify zero, one, many, an explicit range of values, or an explicit set of values for any object instance associated with another object instance. They also allow for the specification of association names when they are helpful to understanding the diagram, and for role names which specify the role of each object class in a particular association. The ER model does not include role names, but could easily be extended to do so.

Some of the more advanced ER constructs such as generalization, aggregation (an abstraction based on the "part-of" explosion idea), and ternary relationships are illustrated in Figure 2.10. The generalization hierarchy in an object model is similar to the ER model, except that the object model uses a triangle and states the name of the attribute in the superclass (supertype) object that is used to separate subclass (subtype) objects (Figure 2.10a). While generalization is used to refer to the "is-a" relationship among object classes, inheritance refers to the sharing of attributes and operations among classes using the generalization relationship.

The aggregation abstraction is modeled in the same way for entities and objects, however (Figure 2.10b). Ternary associations for objects do not have semantics as strong as the ER ternary relationships defined in this book (Figure 2.10c), but the object model does allow you to specify the candidate keys of the ternary association, which has the same semantics in most cases (see Chapter 5 for the subtleties of semantics for higher normal forms associated with ternary relationships).

Object model concepts that have similarities in the ER model, but not shown explicitly here include link attributes (such as attributes of many-to-many relationships in the ER model), constraints based on the NIAM model, and grouping (see clustering in Section 3.4). Object concepts that do not have ER equivalencies include role names, link attributes for one-to-many associations, ordering, derived objects, and homomorphisms [see Rumb91].

The Rumbaugh et al. approach (OMT) uses two other types of models in addition to object models to describe OO systems. One is the dynamic model, which specifies the dynamic aspects of a system such as events and the changing states of objects through state diagrams. The other type of model is the functional model which describes the data value transformations that occur during execution of a system through the use of data flow diagrams. Neither of these types of models are included in the ER model, but they represent useful information in the OO approach needed to capture the correspondence between data objects and their behavior. Triggers, or the propagation of operations to one or multiple objects based on the application of an operation to a starting object, are also defined in this methodology.

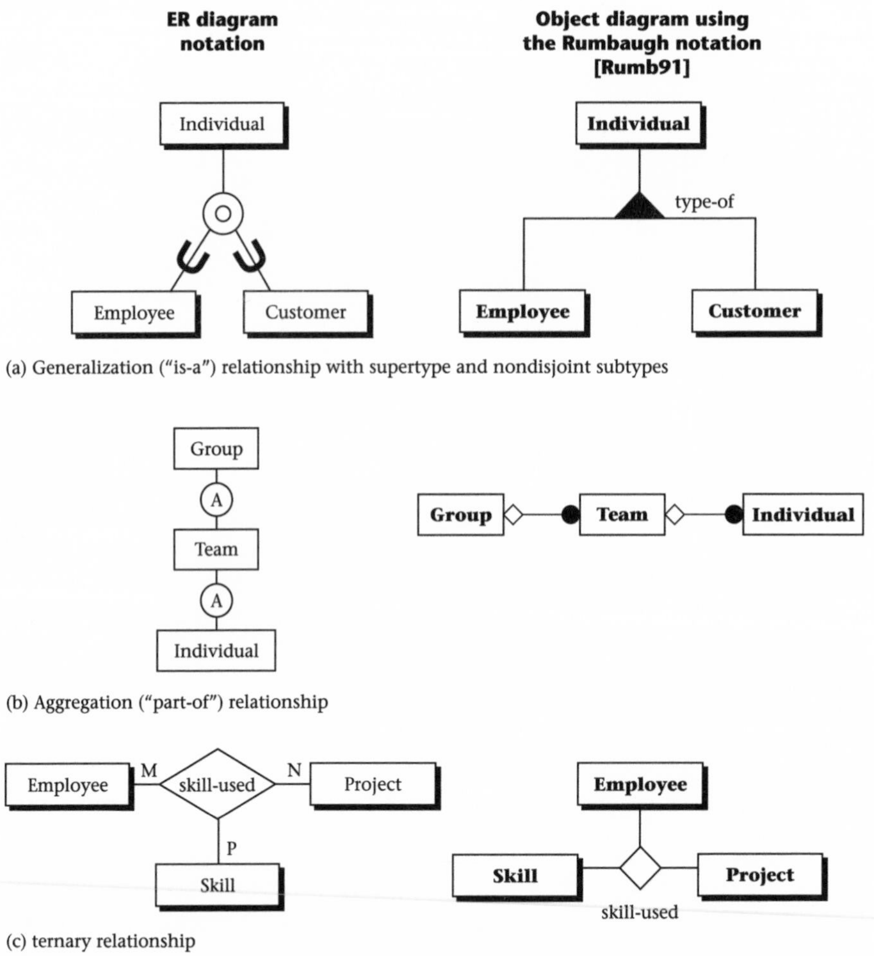

Figure 2.10 ER versus OO diagram notation: advanced constructs

2.4 Summary

The basic concepts of the entity-relationship model and their constructs are described in this chapter. An entity is a person, place, thing, or event of informational interest. Attributes are objects that provide descriptive information about entities. Attributes may be unique identifiers or nonunique descriptors. Relationships describe the connectivity between entity instances:

one-to-one, one-to-many, or many-to-many. The degree of a relationship is the number of associated entities: two (binary), three (ternary), or any n (n-ary). The role (name), or relationship name, defines the function of an entity in a relationship.

The concept of existence in a relationship determines whether an entity instance must exist (mandatory) or not (optional). So, for example, the minimum cardinality of a binary relationship—that is, the number of entity instances on one side that are associated with one instance on the other side—can either be zero if optional or one if mandatory. The concept of generalization allows for the implementation of supertype and subtype abstractions.

The more advanced constructs in ER diagrams are sporadically used and have no generally accepted construct as yet. They include ternary relationships, which we define in terms of the FD concept of relational databases; constraints borrowed from the NIAM model (exclusion and uniqueness); and the implicit constraints from the relational model such as referential integrity and primary key integrity.

There exists a very close relationship between the ER modeling concepts and the object-oriented approach, with the major exception that objects must include the encapsulation of data operations as well as data structure, which is expressed as part of the object class definition. Constructs such as entities, attributes, binary and ternary relationships, and the generalization abstraction are shown to be very similar in the two approaches.

We are now ready to apply the basic ER concepts to the life cycle database design steps.

Literature Summary

Most of the notation in this book is taken from the original ER definition by Chen [Chen76], with the shaded relationship coming from the Database Design and Evaluation Workbench project at CCA [Rein85]. The concept of data abstraction was first proposed by Smith and Smith [SmSm77] and applied to the ER model by [SSW80, NaCh83, TYF86, ElNa94, Shee89, Bruc92] among others. The application of the semantic network model to conceptual schema design was shown by [Bach77, McKi79, PoKe86, HuKi87, PeMa88], and the binary relationship model concepts, including the NIAM model, were studied by [Abri74, BPP76, NvS79, ISO82, VeVa82, Kent84, Mark87]. Other extensions to the original ER model such as the inclusion of the time dimension have also been described elsewhere [Bube77, ClWa83, Ferg85, Aria86, Ever86, MTM91]. Object-oriented data-modeling schemes and issues are discussed in [Booc86, Bane87, Jaco87, Meye88, ShMe88, WPM89, CoYo90, Booc91, Rumb91, CACM92, IEEE92, FiKe92].

[Abri74] Abrial, J. "Data Semantics," Data Base Management, *Proc. IFIP TC2 Conf.*, Cargese, Corsica, North-Holland, Amsterdam, 1974.

[Aria86] Ariav, G. "A Temporally Oriented Data Model," *ACM Trans. Database Systems* 11,4 (Dec. 1986), pp. 499–527.

[Bach77] Bachman, C.W. "The Role Concept in Data Models," *Proc. 3rd Intl. Conf. on Very Large Data Bases*, Tokyo, Oct. 6–8, 1977, IEEE, New York, pp. 464–476.

[Bane87] Banerjee, J., Chou, H.T., Garza, J.F., Kim, W., Woelk, B., and Ballou, N. "Data Model Issues for Object-Oriented Applications," *ACM Trans. on Office Information Systems* 5,1 (Jan. 1987), pp. 3–26.

[Booc86] Booch, G. "Object-Oriented Development," *IEEE Trans. on Software Engineering* SE-12,2 (Feb. 1986), pp. 211–221.

[Booc91] Booch, G. *Object Oriented Design with Appications*, Benjamin/Cummings, Redwood City, CA, 1991.

[BPP76] Bracchi, G., Paolini, P., and Pelagatti, G. "Binary Logical Associations in Data Modelling," Modelling in Data Base Management Systems, *Proc. IFIP TC2 Conf.*, Freudenstadt, North-Holland, Amsterdam, 1976.

[Bruc92] Bruce, T.A. *Designing Quality Databases with IDEF1X Information Models*, Dorset House, New York, 1992.

[Bube77] Bubenko, J. "The Temporal Dimension in Information Modelling," *Architecture and Models in Data Base Management Systems*, G. Nijssen (editor), North-Holland, Amsterdam, 1977.

[CACM92] Special Issue: Analysis and Modeling in Software Development, *Comm. ACM* 35,9 (Sept. 1992), pp. 35–171.

[Chen76] Chen, P.P. "The Entity-Relationship Model—Toward a Unified View of Data," *ACM Trans. Database Systems* 1,1 (March 1976), pp. 9–36.

[Chen87] Chen and Associates, Inc. ER Designer (user manual), 1987.

[ClWa83] Clifford, J. and Warren, D. "Formal Semantics for Time in Databases," *ACM Trans. Database Systems* 8,2 (1983), pp. 214–254.

[CoYo90] Coad, P. and Yourdon, E. *Object-Oriented Analysis*, Prentice-Hall, Englewood Cliffs, NJ, 1990.

[ElNa94] Elmasri, R. and Navathe, S.B. *Fundamentals of Database Systems* (2nd Ed.), Addison-Wesley/Benjamin/Cummings, Redwood City, CA, 1994.

[Ever86] Everest, G.C. *Database Management: Objectives, System Functions, and Administration*, McGraw-Hill, New York, 1986.

[Ferg85] Ferg, S. "Modeling the Time Dimension in an Entity-Relationship Diagram," *Proc. 4th Intl. Conf. on the Entity-Relationship Approach*, Chicago, IEEE Computer Society Press, Silver Spring, MD, 1985, pp. 280–286.

[FiKe92] Fichman, R.G. and Kemerer, C.F. "Object-Oriented and Conventional Analysis and Design Methodologies," *IEEE Computer* 25,10 (Oct. 1992), pp. 22–39.

[HuKi87] Hull, R. and King, R. "Semantic Database Modeling: Survey, Applications, and Research Issues," *ACM Computing Surveys* 19,3 (Sept. 1987), pp. 201–260.

[IEEE92] *IEEE Computer* (Special Issue: Inheritance and Classification in Object-Oriented Computing) 25,10 (Oct. 1992), pp. 6–90.

[ISO82] ISO/TC97/SC5/WG3-N695 Report "Concepts and Terminology for the Conceptual Schema and the Information Base," J. van Griethuysen (editor), ANSI, New York, 1982.

[Jaco87] Jacobsen, I. "Object Oriented Development in an Industrial Environment," OOPSLA'87 as *ACM SIGPLAN* 22, 12 (Dec. 1987), pp. 183–191.

[Kent84] Kent, W. "Fact-Based Data Analysis and Design," *J. Systems and Software* 4 (1984), pp. 99–121.

[Mark87] Mark, L. "Defining Views in the Binary Relationship Model," *Inform. Systems* 12,3 (1987), pp. 281–294.

[McKi79] McLeod, D. and King, R. "Applying a Semantic Database Model," *Proc. 1st Intl. Conf. on the Entity-Relationship Approach to Systems Analysis and Design,* Los Angeles, North-Holland, Amsterdam, 1979, pp. 193–210.

[Meye88] Meyer, B. *Object-Oriented Software Construction,* Prentice-Hall Int'l., Hertfordshire, England, 1988.

[MTM91] Moyne, J.R., Teorey, T.J., and McAfee, L.C. "Time Sequence Ordering Extensions to the Entity Relationship Model and Their Application to the Automated Manufacturing Process," *Data and Knowledge Engr.* 6,5 (Sept. 1991), pp. 421–433.

[NaCh83] Navathe, S. and Cheng, A. "A Methodology for Database Schema Mapping from Extended Entity Relationship Models into the Hierarchical Model," *The Entity-Relationship Approach to Software Engineering,* G.C. Davis et al. (editors), Elsevier, North-Holland, Amsterdam, 1983.

[NvS79] Nijssen, G., van Assche, F., and Snijders, J. "End User Tools for Information Systems Requirement Definition," *Formal Models and Practical Tools for Information System Design,* H. Schneider (editor), North-Holland, Amsterdam, 1979.

[PeMa88] Peckham, J. and Maryanski, F. "Semantic Data Models," *ACM Computing Surveys* 20,3 (Sept. 1988), pp. 153–190.

[PoKe86] Potter, W.D. and Kerschberg, L. "A Unified Approach to Modeling Knowledge and Data," *IFIP WG 2.6 Working Conf. on Knowledge and Data,* University of South Carolina, Elsevier, North-Holland, New York, Sept. 1986.

[Rein85] Reiner, D., Brodie, M., Brown, G., Friedell, M., Kramlich, D., Lehman, J., and Rosenthal, A. "The Database Design and Evaluation Workbench (DDEW) Project at CCA," *Database Engineering* 7,4 (1985), pp. 10–15.

[Rumb91] Rumbaugh, J., Blaha, M., Premerlani, W., Eddy, F., and Lorensen, W. *Object-Oriented Modeling and Design*, Prentice-Hall, Englewood Cliffs, NJ, 1991.

[SSW80] Scheuermann, P., Scheffner, G., and Weber, H. "Abstraction Capabilities and Invariant Properties Modelling within the Entity-Relationship Approach," *Entity-Relationship Approach to Systems Analysis and Design*, P. Chen (editor), Elsevier, North-Holland, Amsterdam, 1980, pp. 121–140.

[Shee89] Sheer, A. W. *Enterprise-Wide Data Modeling*, Springer-Verlag, Berlin, 1989.

[ShMe88] Shlaer, S. and Mellor, S. *Object-Oriented Systems Analysis: Modeling the World in Data*, Yourdon Press, Englewood Cliffs, NJ, 1988.

[SmSm77] Smith, J. and Smith, D. "Database Abstractions: Aggregation and Generalization," *ACM Trans. Database Systems* 2,2 (June 1977), pp. 105–133.

[TYF86] Teorey, T.J., Yang, D., and Fry, J.P. "A Logical Design Methodology for Relational Databases Using the Extended Entity-Relationship Model," *ACM Computing Surveys* 18,2 (June 1986), pp. 197–222.

[VeVa82] Verheijen, G. and Van Bekkum, J. "NIAM: An Information Analysis Method," *Information Systems Design Methodologies*, Olle, Sol, and Verryn-Stuart (editors). North-Holland, Amsterdam, 1982, pp. 537–590.

[WPM89] Wasserman, A.I., Pircher, P.A., and Muller, R.J. "An Object-Oriented Structured Design Method for Code Generation," *Software Eng. Notices* 14,1 (Jan. 1989), pp. 32–55.

EXERCISES

Problem 2-1

Construct an ER diagram (including important attributes) for a bank database that shows the basic relationships among customers, checking accounts, savings accounts, loans, and the bank branches where various accounts and loans are taken out. You also want to keep track of transactions on accounts and loans, and maintain the current balance in each account and the balance of the loan. Remember that each entity in the ER diagram represents a simple file of data of which you want to keep track.

Problem 2-2

Construct an ER diagram (including important attributes) for a car insurance database that includes data about customers (car owners), cars, accidents, drivers involved in accidents, and injured drivers and/or passengers. Note that any customer can insure many cars, each car may have different drivers at different times, and accidents typically involve one or more cars.

For this problem, show at least one use of generalization and at least one use of a ternary or higher n-ary relationship. Also, show two separate ER diagrams (without attributes), where the concept "accident" is an entity and a relationship, respectively. One of these two ER diagrams may be satisfied with the first diagram with attributes.

Problem 2-3

There is a business that owns a softball complex. It organizes league and tournament play over several seasons per year. The people associated with this business are represented as players or employees. An employee may also be a player. Most of these people play for teams that compose the leagues of this organization. These teams are not allowed to register into multiple leagues. Each season consists of several leagues and teams, with each team playing several games each season. Once a team and a league have entered the organization, they are invited to participate in each season thereafter.

CHAPTER 3

ER MODELING IN LOGICAL DATABASE DESIGN

This chapter shows how the ER approach can be applied to the database life cycle, particularly in Steps I through IIb (as defined in Section 1.3), which include the requirements analysis and conceptual modeling stages of logical database design. The example introduced in Chapter 2 is used again to illustrate the ER modeling principles developed in this chapter.

3.1 Introduction

Logical database design is accomplished with a variety of approaches, including the top-down, bottom-up, and combined methodologies. The traditional approach, particularly for relational databases, has been a low-level, bottom-up activity, synthesizing individual data elements into normalized relations (tables) after careful analysis of the data element interdependencies defined by the requirements analysis. Although the traditional process has had some success for small- to medium-sized databases, its complexity for large databases can be overwhelming to the point where practicing designers do not bother to use it with any regularity. In practice, a combination of the top-down and bottom-up approaches is used; in some cases, tables can be defined directly from the requirements analysis. A new form of the combined approach has recently become popular because of the introduction of the ER model into the process.

The ER model has been most successful as a tool for communication between the designer and the end user during the requirements analysis and logical design phases. Its success is due to the fact that the model is easy to understand and convenient to represent. Another reason for its effectiveness is that it is a top-down approach using the concept of abstraction. The number of entities in a database is typically an order of magnitude less than the number of data elements, because data elements usually represent the attributes. Therefore, using entities as an abstraction for data elements and focusing on the interentity relationships greatly reduces the number of objects under consideration and simplifies the analysis. Though it is still necessary to represent data elements by attributes of entities at the conceptual level, their dependencies are normally confined to the other attributes within the entity or, in some cases, to those attributes associated with other entities that have a direct relationship to their entity.

The major interattribute dependencies that occur in data models are the dependencies between the entity keys, the unique identifiers of different entities that are captured in the ER modeling process. Special cases such as dependencies among data elements of unrelated entities can be handled when they are identified in the ensuing data analysis.

The logical database design approach defined here uses both the ER model and the relational model in successive stages. It benefits from the simplicity and ease of use of the ER model and the structure and associated formalism of the relational model. In order to facilitate this approach, it is necessary to build a framework for transforming the variety of ER constructs into tables that are already normalized or can be normalized with the minimum of transformation. Before we do this, however, we need to first define the major steps of the relational design methodology in the context of the database life cycle.

3.2 Requirements Analysis and ER Modeling

Requirements analysis is the most important step (Step I) of the database life cycle, and is typically the most labor-intensive. The database designer must interview the end user population and determine exactly what the database is to be used for and what it must contain. The basic objectives of requirements analysis are

- to delineate the data requirements of the enterprise in terms of primitive objects;
- to describe the information about the objects and the relationships among objects needed to model these data requirements;
- to determine the types of transactions that are intended to be executed on the database and the interaction between the transactions and the data objects;
- to define any performance, integrity, security, or administrative constraints that must be imposed on the resulting database;
- to specify the hardware and software platform for the database implementation; and

- to thoroughly document all of the above in a detailed requirements specification. The data objects can also be defined in a data dictionary system, often provided as an integral part of the database management system.

The ER model helps the designer accurately capture the real data requirements because it requires him or her to focus on semantic detail in the data relationships, which is greater than the detail that would be provided by FDs alone. The semantics of ER allow for direct transformations of entities and relationships to at least first normal form tables. They also provide clear guidelines for integrity constraints. In addition, abstraction techniques such as generalization provide useful tools for integrating end user views to define a global conceptual schema.

Let us now look more closely at the basic objects and relationships that should be defined during requirements analysis and conceptual design. These two life-cycle steps are often done simultaneously.

Consider the substeps in Step IIa, ER modeling:

- Classify entities and attributes.
- Identify the generalization hierarchies.
- Define relationships.

The remainder of this section will discuss the tasks involved in each substep.

3.2.1 Classify Entities and Attributes

Though it is easy to define entity, attribute, and relationship constructs, it is not as easy to distinguish their roles in modeling the database. What makes an object an entity, an attribute, or even a relationship? For example, project headquarters are located in cities. Should city be an entity or an attribute? A vita is kept for each employee. Is vita an entity or a relationship?

The following guidelines for classifying entities and attributes will help the designer's thoughts converge to a normalized relational database design.

- Entities should contain descriptive information.
- Classify multivalued attributes as entities.
- Attach attributes to the entities they most directly describe.

Now we will examine each guideline in turn.

Entity Contents

Entities should contain descriptive information. If there is descriptive information about an object, the object should be classified as an entity. If an object requires only an identifier, the object should be classified as an attribute. With city, for example, if there is some descriptive information such as country and population for cities, then city should be classified as an entity. If only the city name is needed to identify a city, then city should be classified as an attribute associated with some entity, such as Project. Examples of objects in the real world that are typically classified as entities are employee, task, project, department, company, customer, and so on.

Multivalued Attributes

Classify multivalued attributes as entities. If more than one value of a descriptor attribute corresponds to one value of an identifier, the descriptor should be classified as an entity instead of an attribute, even though it does not have descriptors itself. A large company, for example, could have many offices, some of them possibly in different cities. In that case, office could be classified as a multivalued attribute of company, but it would be better to be classified as an entity, with office-address as its identifier. If attributes are restricted to be single-valued only, the later design and implementation decisions will be simplified.

Attribute Attachment

Attach attributes to the entities they most directly describe. For example, attribute office-building-name should normally be an attribute of the entity Department instead of the entity Employee.

The procedure of identifying entities and attaching attributes to entities is iterative: Classify some objects as entities and attach identifiers and descriptors to them. If you find some violation of the preceding guidelines, change some objects from entity to attribute (or from attribute to entity), attach attributes to the new entities, and so forth.

3.2.2 Identify the Generalization Hierarchies

If there is a generalization hierarchy among entities, then put the identifier and generic descriptors in the generic or supertype entity and put the same identifier and specific descriptors in the subtype entities.

For example, suppose three entities were identified in the ER model shown in Figure 2.4b:

- Individual, with identifier indiv-id and descriptors indiv-name, address, and date-of-birth
- Employee, with identifier emp-id and descriptors emp-name and job-title
- Customer, with identifier cust-no and descriptors cust-name, and organization

We determine, through our analysis, that Individual is a generalization of Employee and Customer. Then we put identifier indiv-id and generic descriptors indiv-name, address, and date-of-birth in the generic entity Individual; put identifier emp-id and specific descriptor job-title in the entity Employee; and put identifier cust-no and specific descriptor organization in entity Customer. Later, if we decide to eliminate **Individual** as a table, the generic attributes can be redistributed to the subtype tables, **Employee** and **Customer**. (Note that we put table names in boldface throughout the book for readability.)

3.2.3 Define Relationships

We now deal with objects that represent associations among entities, which we call relationships. Examples of typical relationships are works-in, works-for, purchases, drives, or any verb that connects entities. For every relationship the following should be specified: degree (binary, ternary, and so on), connectivity (one-to-many, and so on), optional or mandatory, and any attributes that are associated with the relationship and not the entities. The following are some guidelines for defining the more difficult types of relationships.

Redundant Relationships

Analyze redundant relationships carefully. Two or more relationships that are used to represent the same concept are considered to be redundant. Redundant relationships are more likely to result in unnormalized tables when transforming the ER model into relational schemas. Note that two or more relationships are allowed between the same two entities as long as the two relationships have different meanings. In this case they are not considered redundant.

One important case of nonredundancy is shown in Figure 3.1a. If belongs-to is a one-to-many relationship between Employee and Professional-association, if located-in is a one-to-many relationship between Professional-association and City, and if lives-in is a one-to-many relationship between Employee and City, then lives-in is not redundant because the relationships are unrelated. However, consider the situation shown in Figure 3.1b. Employee works-on a

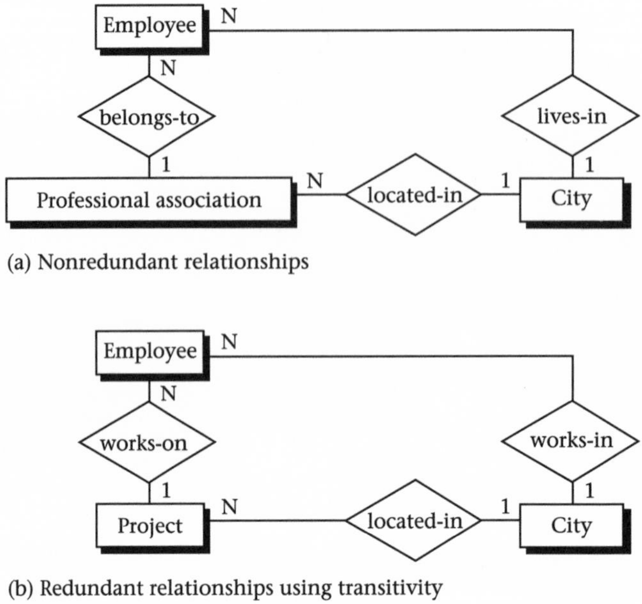

Figure 3.1 Redundant and nonredundant relationships

Project located in a City, so the works-in relationship between Employee and City is redundant and can be eliminated.

Ternary Relationships

Define ternary relationships carefully. We define a ternary relationship among three entities only when the concept cannot be represented by several binary relationships among those entities. For example, let us assume there is some association among entities Technician, Project, and Notebook. If each technician can be working on any of several projects and using the same notebooks on each project, then three many-to-many binary relationships can be defined (see Figure 3.2a). If, however, each technician is constrained to use exactly one notebook for each project and that notebook belongs to only one technician, then a one-to-one-to-one ternary relationship must be defined (see Figure 3.2b). The approach to take in ER modeling is to first attempt to express the associations in terms of binary relationships; if this is impossible because of the constraints of the associations, then try to express them in terms of a ternary.

The meaning of connectivity for ternary relationships is important. Figure 3.2b shows that for a given pair of instances of Technician and Project, there

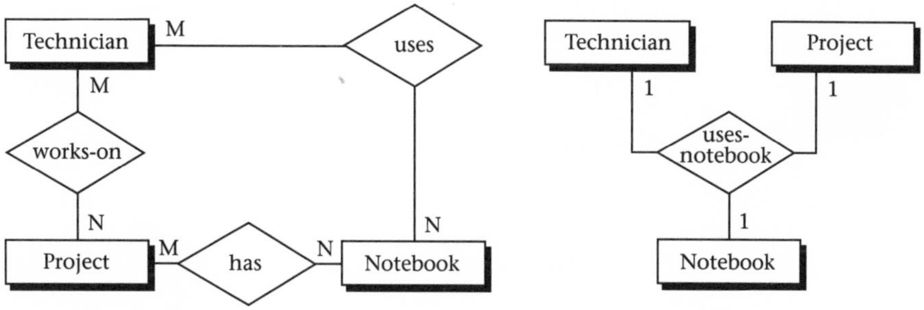

(a) Binary relationships

(b) Different meaning using a ternary relationship

Figure 3.2 Comparison of binary and ternary relationships

is only one corresponding instance of Notebook; for a given pair of instances of Technician and Notebook, there is only one corresponding instance of Project; and for a given pair of instances of Project and Notebook, there is only one instance of Technician. In general, we know by our definition of ternary relationships that if a relationship among three entities can be expressed by a functional dependency involving the keys of all three entities, then it cannot be expressed by binary relationships, which only apply to associations between two entities.

3.2.4 Example of ER Modeling: Company Personnel and Project Database

Requirements Analysis and ER Modeling of Individual Views

Let us suppose it is desirable to build a companywide database for a large engineering firm that keeps track of all full-time personnel, their skills and projects assigned, department (and division) worked in, engineer professional associations belonged to, and engineer desktop computers allocated. During the requirements collection process—that is, interviewing the end users—we obtain three views of the database.

The first view, a management view, defines each employee as working in a single department and a division as the basic unit in the company, consisting of many departments. Each division and department has a manager, and we want to keep track of each manager. The ER model for this view is shown in Figure 3.3a.

The second view defines each employee as having a job title: engineer, technician, secretary, manager, and so on. Engineers typically belong to

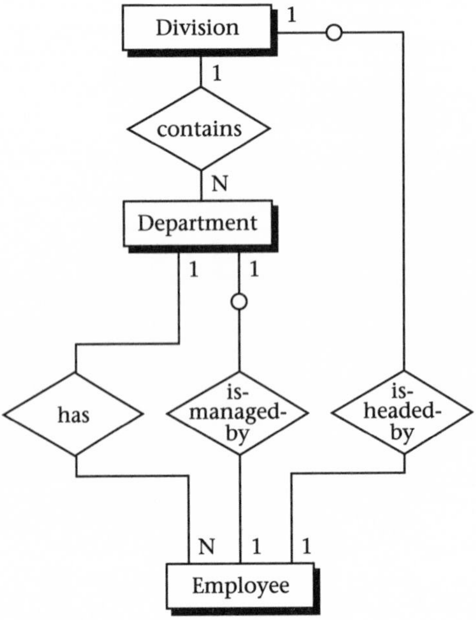

(a) Management view

Figure 3.3 Global ER schema: company personnel and project database (Figure continues on next two pages)

professional associations and might be allocated an engineering workstation (or computer). Secretaries and managers are each allocated a desktop computer. A pool of desktops and workstations is maintained for potential allocation to new employees and for loans while an employee's computer is being repaired. Any employee may be married to another employee, and we want to keep track of this relationship to avoid assigning an employee to be managed by his or her spouse. This view is illustrated in Figure 3.3b.

The third view, shown in Figure 3.3c, involves the assignment of employees, mainly engineers and technicians, to projects. Employees may work on several projects at one time, and each project could be headquartered at different locations (cities). However, each employee at a given location works on only one project at that location. Employee skills can be individually selected for a given project, but no individual has a monopoly on skills, projects, or locations.

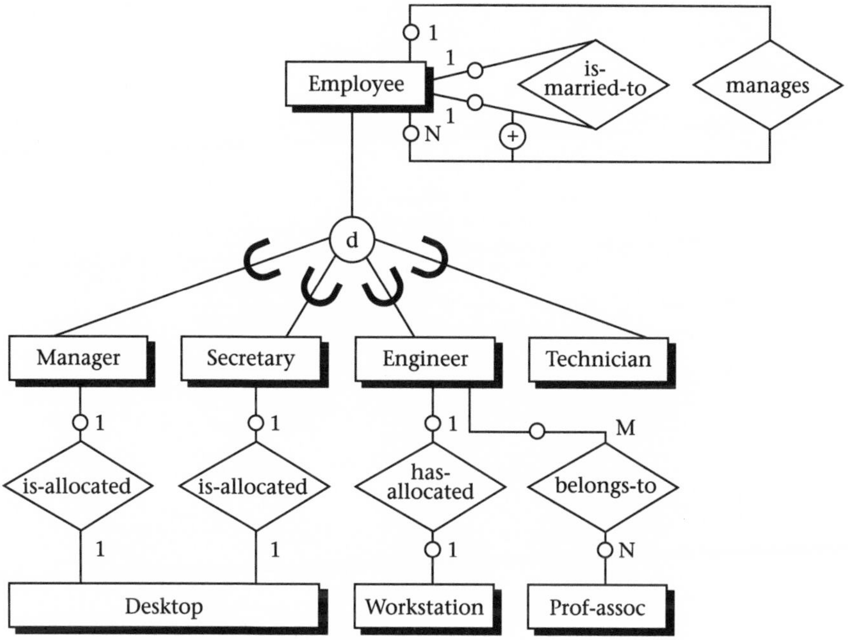

(b) Employee view

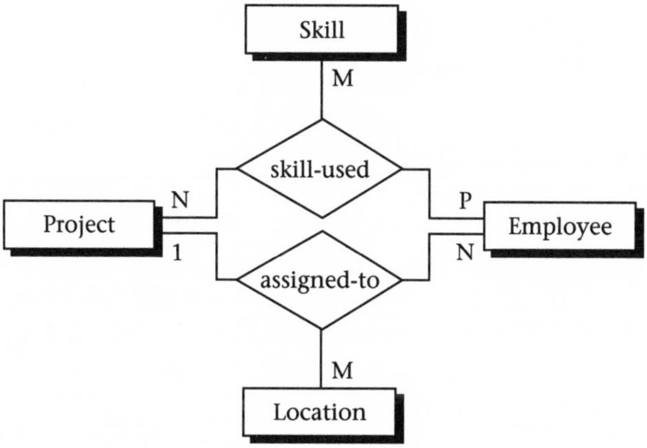

(c) Employee assignment view

Figure 3.3 Continued

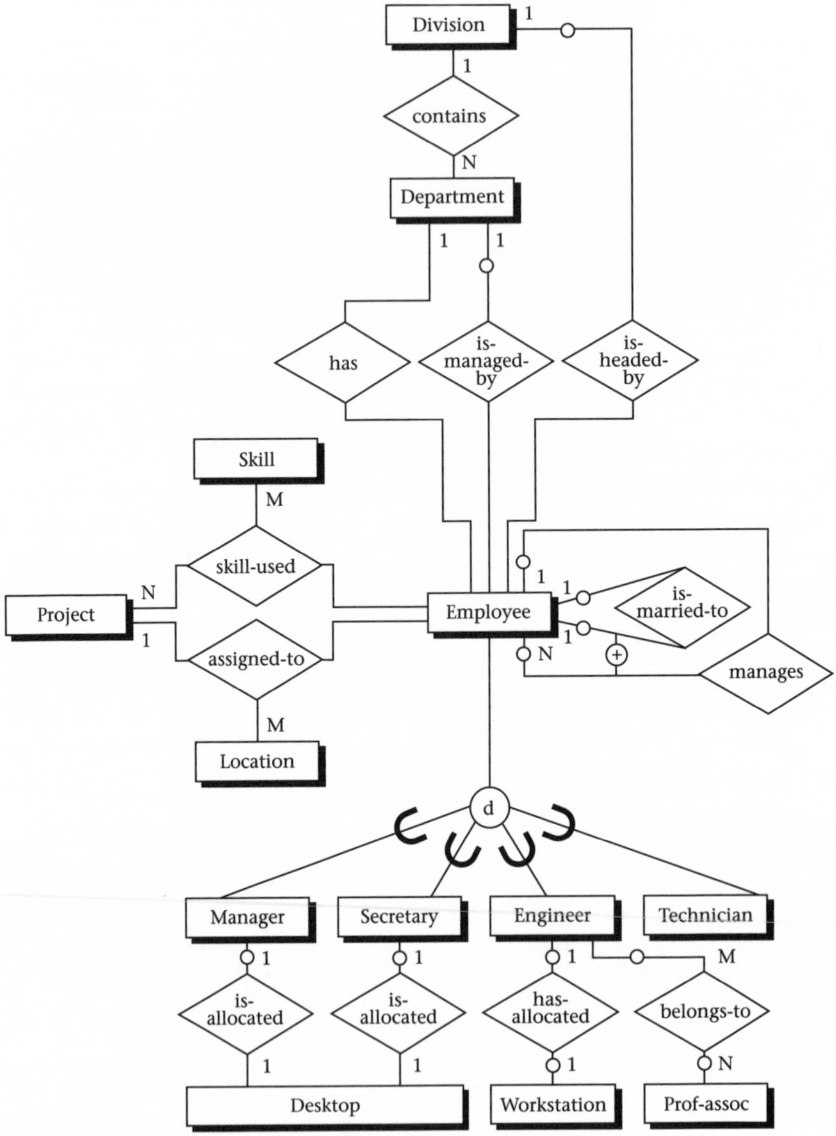

(d) Global ER schema

Figure 3.3 Continued

Global ER Schema

A simple integration of the three views defined above results in the global ER schema (diagram) in Figure 3.3d, which becomes the basis for developing the normalized tables. Each relationship in the global schema is based upon a verifiable assertion about the actual data in the enterprise, and analysis of those assertions leads to the transformation of these ER constructs into candidate SQL tables, as Chapter 4 will show.

The diagram shows examples of binary, ternary, and binary recursive relationships; optional and mandatory existence in relationships; and generalization with the disjointness constraint. Ternary relationships skill-used and assigned-to are necessary because binary relationships cannot be used for the equivalent notions. For example, one employee and one location determines exactly one project (a functional dependency). In the case of skill-used, selective use of skills to projects cannot be represented with binary relationships (see Section 5.5).

The use of optional existence, for instance between Employee and Division or between Employee and Department, is derived from our general knowledge that most employees will not be the manager of any division or department. In another example of optional existence, we show that the allocation of a desktop to an engineer may not always occur, nor will all desktops be necessarily allocated to someone at all times. In general, all relationships, optional existence constraints, and generalization constructs need to be verified with the end user before the ER model is transformed to SQL tables.

In summary, the application of the ER model to relational database design offers the following benefits:

- Use of an ER approach focuses end user discussions on important relationships between entities. Some applications are characterized by counter-examples affecting a small number of instances, and lengthy consideration of these instances can divert attention from basic relationships.
- A diagrammatic syntax conveys a great deal of information in a compact, readily understandable form.
- Extensions to the original ER model, such as optional and mandatory membership classes, are important in many relationships. Generalization allows entities to be grouped for one functional role or to be seen as separate subtypes when other constraints are imposed.
- A complete set of rules transforms ER constructs into candidate SQL tables, which follow easily from real-world requirements.

3.3 View Integration

A most critical part of the database design process is Step IIb, the integration of different user views into a unified, nonredundant conceptual schema. The individual end user views are represented by ER conceptual models, and the integrated conceptual schema results from sufficient analysis of the end user views to resolve all differences in perspective and terminology. Experience has shown that nearly every situation can be resolved in a meaningful way through integration techniques.

Schema diversity occurs when different users or user groups develop their own unique perspectives of the world, or at least of the enterprise to be represented in the database. For instance, marketing tends to have the whole product as a basic unit for sales, but engineering may concentrate on the individual parts of the whole product. In another case, one user may view a project in terms of its goals and progress toward meeting those goals over time; another user may view a project in terms of the resources it needs and the personnel involved. Such differences cause the conceptual models to seem to have incompatible relationships and terminology. These differences show up in ER conceptual models as different levels of abstraction, connectivity of relationships (one-to-many, many-to-many, and so on), or as the same concept being modeled as an entity, attribute, or relationship, depending on the user's perspective.

As an example of the latter case, in Figure 3.4 we see three different perspectives of the same real-life situation, the placement of an order for a certain product. The result is a variety of schemas. The first schema (Figure 3.4a) depicts Customer, Order, and Product as entities and places and for-a as relationships. The second schema (Figure 3.4b), however, defines orders as a relationship between Customer and Product and omits Order as an entity altogether. Finally, in the third case (Figure 3.4c), the relationship orders has been replaced by another relationship, purchases; order-no, the identifier (key) of an order, is designated as an attribute of the relationship purchases. In other words, the concept order has been variously represented as an entity, a relationship, and an attribute, depending on perspective.

The resolution of different views is part of a view integration methodology defined by Batini, Lenzerini, and Navathe [BaLe84, BLN86]. They defined four basic steps needed for conceptual schema integration:

1. preintegration analysis;
2. comparison of schemas;
3. conformation of schemas; and
4. merging and restructuring of schemas.

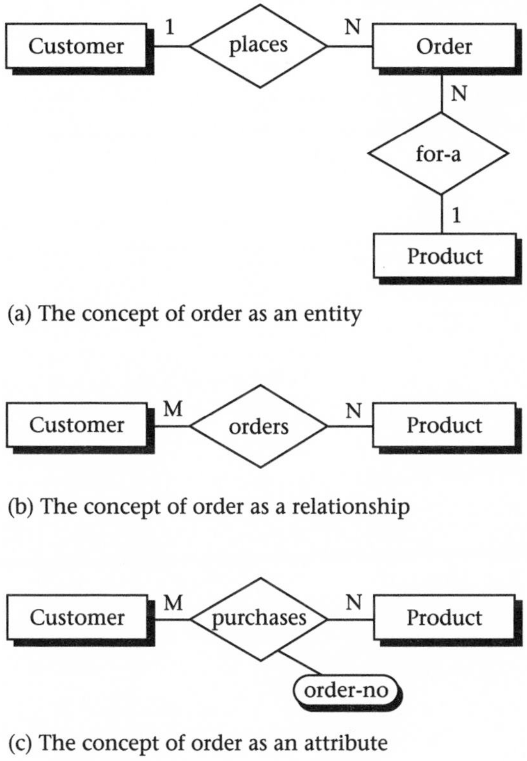

Figure 3.4 Concept of "order" as an entity, relationship, and attribute

3.3.1 Preintegration Analysis

The first step, preintegration analysis, involves choosing an integration strategy. Typically, the choice is between a binary approach with two schemas merged at one time and an n-ary approach with n schemas merged at one time, where n is between 2 and the total number of schemas developed in the conceptual design. The binary approach is attractive because each merge involves a small number of ER constructs and is easier to conceptualize. The n-ary approach may require one grand merge only, but the number of constructs may be so large that it is not humanly possible to organize the transformations properly.

3.3.2 Comparison of Schemas

In the second step, comparison of schemas, the designer looks at how entities correspond and detects conflicts arising from schema diversity—that is, from user groups adopting different viewpoints in their respective schemas. Naming conflicts include synonyms and homonyms. Synonyms occur when different names are given for the same concept. These can be detected by scanning the data dictionary, if one has been established for the database. Homonyms occur when the same name is used for different concepts. These can only be detected by scanning the different schemas and looking for common names.

Structural conflicts occur in the schema structure itself. Type conflicts involve using different ER constructs to model the same concept. In Figure 3.4, for example, an entity, a relationship, or an attribute can be used to model the concept of order in a business database. Dependency conflicts result when users specify different levels of connectivity for similar or even the same concepts. One resolution of such conflicts might be to use only the most general connectivity—for example, many-to-many. If that is not semantically correct, change the names of entities so that each type of connectivity has a different set of entity names. Key conflicts occur when different keys are assigned to the same entity in different views. For example, a key conflict occurs if an employees full name, employee ID number, and social security number are all assigned as keys. Behavioral conflicts result from different integrity constraints, particularly on nulls and insert/delete rules.

3.3.3 Conformation of Schemas

The resolution of conflicts often requires user and designer interaction. The basic goal is to align or conform schemas to make them compatible for integration. The entities as well as the primary key attributes may need to be renamed. Conversion may be required so that concepts that are modeled as entities, attributes, or relationships are conformed to only one primitive data model type. Relationships with equal degree, roles, and cardinality constraints are easy to merge. Those with differing characteristics are more difficult and, in some cases, impossible to merge. Also, relationships that are not consistent—for example, a relationship using generalization in one place and the exclusive OR in another—must be resolved. Finally, assertions may need to be modified so that integrity constraints are consistent.

Techniques used for view integration include abstraction, such as generalization and aggregation, to create new supertypes or subtypes, or even the introduction of new relationships. As an example, the generalization of Individual over different values of the descriptor attribute job-title could represent the consolidation of two views of the database, one based on an individual as the basic unit of personnel in the organization and another based on the classification of individuals by job-titles and special characteristics within those classifications. An example of a special characteristic is the allocation of personal computers to reviewers.

3.3.4 Merging and Restructuring of Schemas

Step 4 consists of the merging and restructuring of schemas. This step is driven by the goals of completeness, minimality, and understandability. Completeness requires all component concepts to appear semantically intact in the global schema. Minimality requires the designer to remove all redundant concepts in the global schema. Examples of redundant concepts are overlapping entities, redundant hierarchies, and truly semantically redundant relationships. Understandability requires that the global schema make sense to the user.

Component schemas are first merged by superimposing the same concepts and then restructuring the resulting integrated schema for understandability. For instance, if a supertype/subtype combination is defined as a result of the merging operation, the properties of the subtype can be dropped from the schema because they are automatically provided by the supertype entity or object.

3.3.5 Example of View Integration

Let us look at two different views of overlapping data. The views are based on two separate interviews of end users. We adapt the interesting example cited by Batini, Lenzerini, and Navathe to a hypothetical situation related to our example. In Figure 3.5a we have a view that focuses on reports and includes data on departments that publish the reports, topic areas in reports, and contractors for whom the reports are written. Figure 3.5b shows another view, with publications as the central focus and keywords on publication as the secondary data. Our objective is to find meaningful ways to integrate the two views and maintain completeness, minimality, and understandability.

We first look for synonyms and homonyms, particularly among the entities. Note that a synonym exists between the entities Topic-area in schema 1 and Keyword in schema 2, even though the attributes do not match. However, we find that the attributes are compatible and can be consolidated. This is shown in Figure 3.6a, which presents a revised schema, schema 2.1. In schema 2.1 Keyword has been replaced by Topic-area.

Next we look for structural conflicts between schemas. A type conflict is found to exist between the entity Department in schema 1 and the attribute

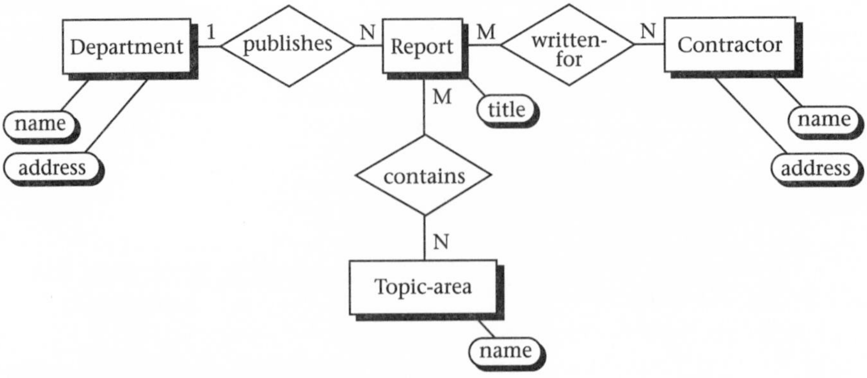

(a) Original schema 1, focused on reports

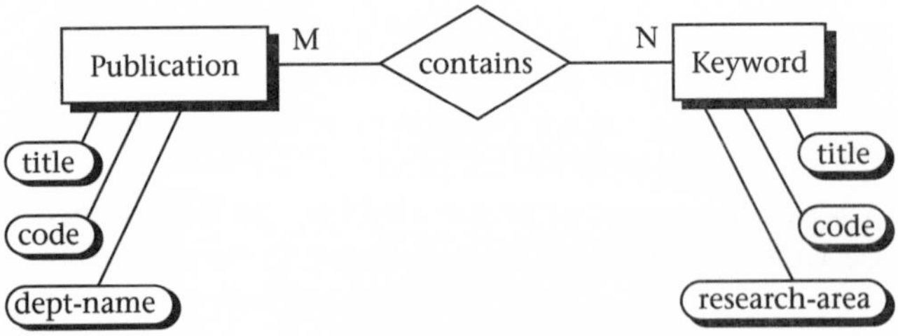

(b) Original schema 2, focused on publications

Figure 3.5 Example of two views and corresponding ER schemas

dept-name in schema 2.1. The conflict is resolved by keeping the stronger entity type, Department, and moving the attribute type dept-name under Publication in schema 2 to the new entity, Department, in schema 2.2 (see Figure 3.6b).

At this point we have sufficient commonality between schemas to attempt a merge. In schemas 1 and 2.2 we have two sets of common entities, Department and Topic-area. Other entities do not overlap and must appear intact in the superimposed, or merged, schema. The merged schema, schema 3, is shown in Figure 3.7a. Because the common entities are truly equivalent, there are no bad side effects of the merge due to existing relationships involving those entities in one schema and not in the other. (Such a relationship that remains intact exists in schema 1 between Topic-area and Report, for example.) If true equivalence cannot be established, the merge may not be possible in the existing form.

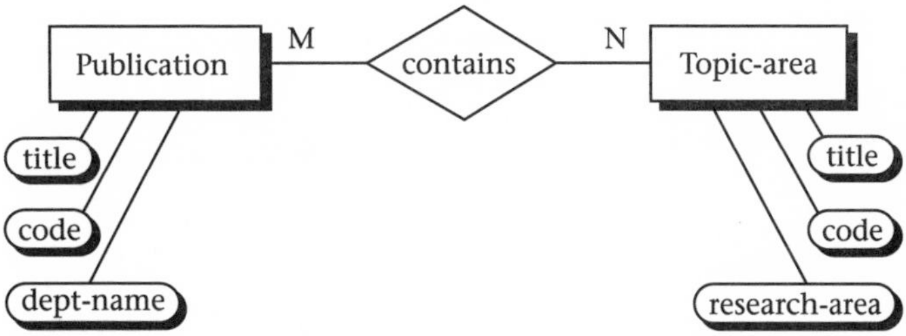

(a) Schema 2.1, in which Keyword has changed to Topic-area

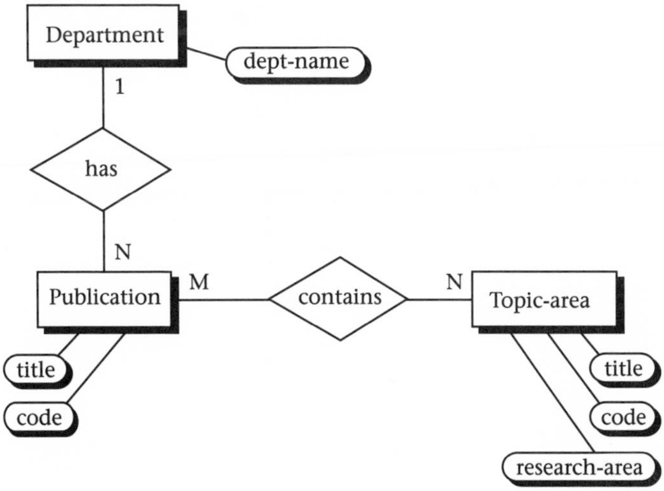

(b) Schema 2.2, in which the attribute dept-name has changed to an attribute and an entity

Figure 3.6 View integration: synonyms and structural conflicts

In Figure 3.7, there is some redundancy between Publication and Report in terms of the relationships with Department and Topic-area. Such a redundancy can be eliminated if there is a supertype/subtype relationship between Publication and Report, which does in fact occur in this case because Publication is a generalization of Report. In schema 3.1 (Figure 3.7b) we see the introduction of this generalization from Report to Publication. Then in schema 3.2 (Figure 3.7c) we see that the redundant relationships between Report and Department and Topic-area have been dropped. The attribute title has been eliminated as an attribute of Report in Figure 3.7c because title

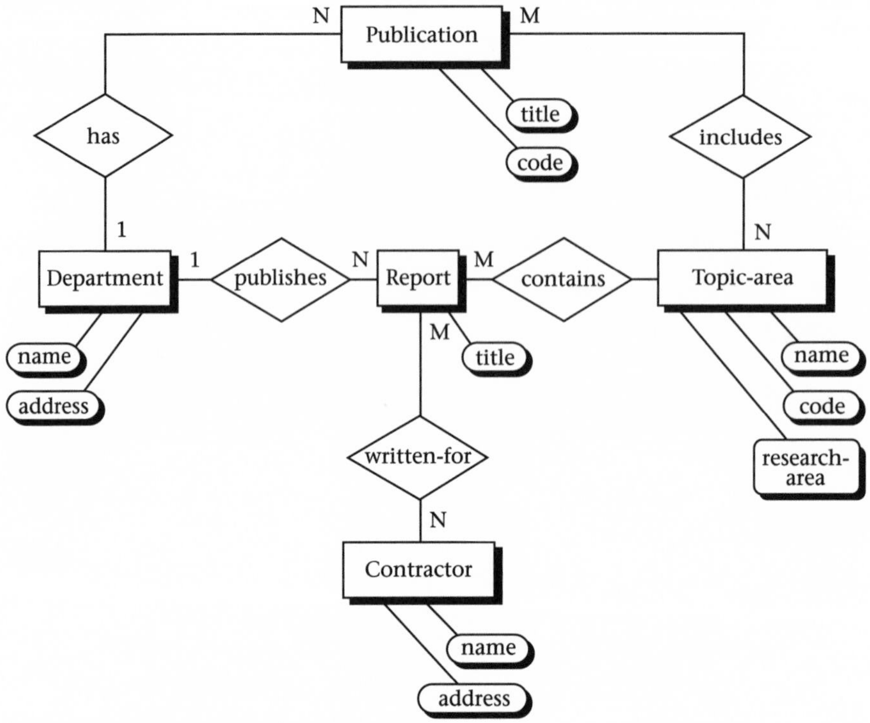

(a) Schema 3, the result of merging schemas 1 and 2.2

Figure 3.7 View integration: merging and restructuring of schemas (Figure continues next 2 pages)

already appears as an attribute of Publication, at a higher level of abstraction; title is inherited by the subtype Report.

The final schema, in Figure 3.7c, expresses completeness because all the original concepts (report, publication, topic area, department, and contractor) are kept intact. It expresses minimality because of the transformation of dept-name from attribute in schema 1 to entity and attribute in schema 2.2, and the merger between schema 1 and schema 2.2 to form schema 3, and also because of the elimination of title as an attribute of Report and of Report relationships with Topic-area and Department. Finally, it expresses understandability in that the final schema actually has more meaning than the individual original schemas. The view integration process is one of continual refinement and reevaluation. It has therefore been difficult to automate, although some semiautomatic algorithms, with some designer interaction, can be used.

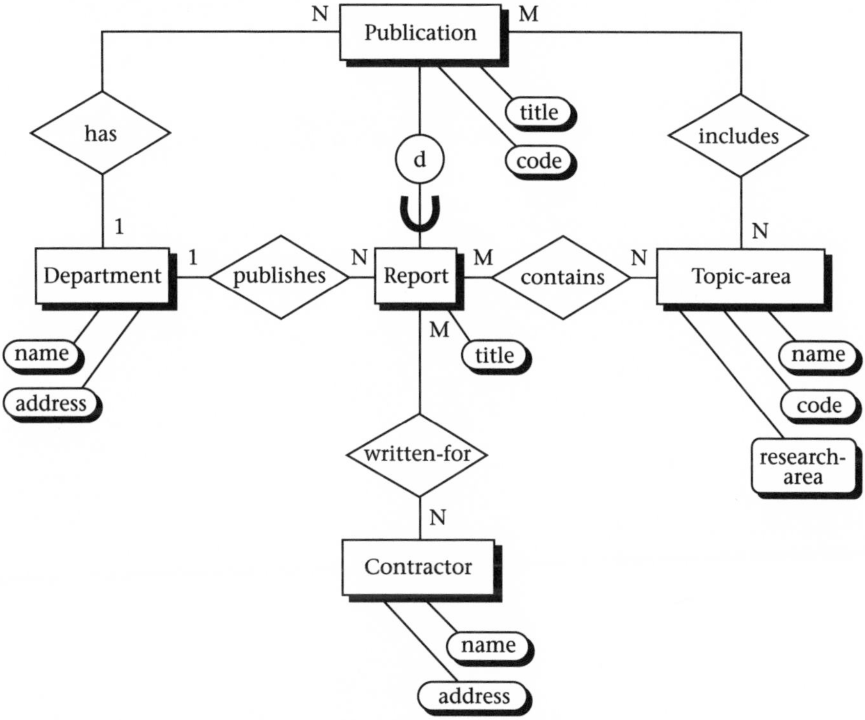

(b) Schema 3.1: creation of a generalization relationship

Figure 3.7 Continued

3.4 Entity Clustering

This section presents the concept of entity clustering, which abstracts the ER schema to such a degree that the entire schema can appear on a single sheet of paper or a single computer screen. This has happy consequences for the end user and database designer in terms of developing a mutual understanding of the database contents and formally documenting the conceptual model.

An entity cluster is the result of a grouping operation on a collection of entities and relationships. Clustering can be applied repeatedly, resulting in layered levels of abstraction with manager and end user views at the top level, database designer views at middle levels, and both designer and programmer views at the bottom level.

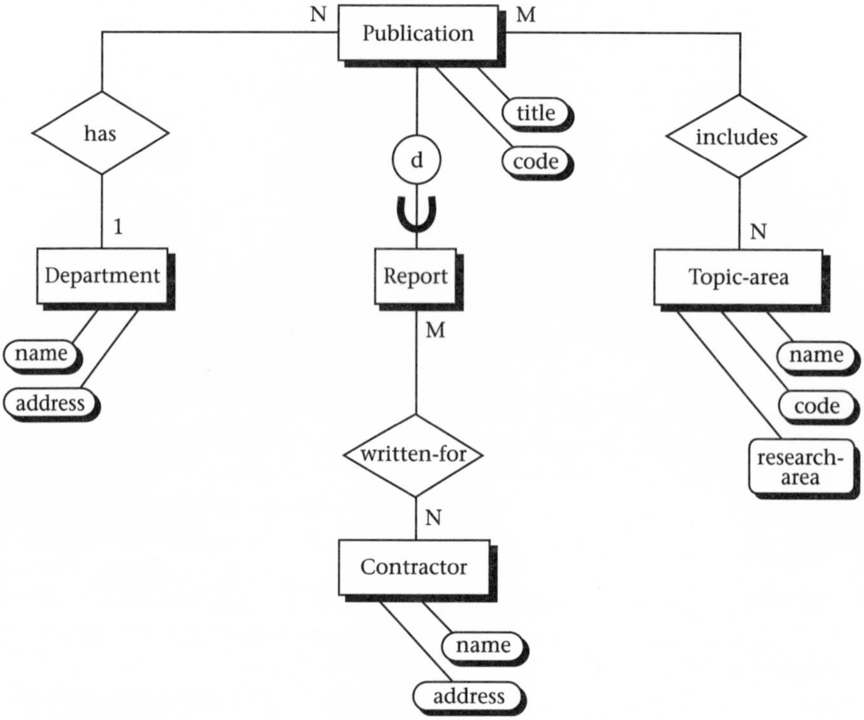

(c) Schema 3.2: elimination of redundancy

Figure 3.7 Continued

Entity clustering is potentially useful for designing large databases. When the scale of a database or information structure is large and includes a large number of interconnections among its different components, it may be very difficult to understand the semantics of such a structure and to manage it, especially for the end users or managers. In an ER diagram with 1,000 entities, the overall structure will probably not be very clear, even to a well-trained database analyst. Clustering is therefore important because it provides a method to organize a conceptual database schema into layers of abstraction, and it supports the different views of a variety of end users.

3.4.1 Clustering Concepts

The entity clustering technique integrates object clustering concepts with the traditional design of ER models to produce bottom-up abstraction of natural groupings of entities. Think of grouping as an operation that combines entities and their relationships to form a higher level construct. The result of a grouping operation on purely elementary entities is called an *entity cluster.* A grouping operation on entity clusters or on combinations of elementary entities and entity clusters results in a higher level entity cluster. The highest level entity cluster, representing the entire database conceptual schema, is called the *root entity cluster.*

Figure 3.8a illustrates the concept of entity clustering in a simple case where (elementary) entities R-sec (report section), R-abbr (report abbreviation), and Author are naturally bound to (dominated by) the entity Report; and entities Department, Contractor, and Project are not dominated. (Note that to avoid unnecessary detail, we do not include the attributes of entities in the diagrams.) In Figure 3.8b the dark-bordered box around entity Report and the entities it dominates defines the entity cluster Report. The dark-bordered box will be called the EC box to represent the idea of entity cluster. In general, the name of the entity cluster need not be the same as the name of any internal entity; however, when there is a single dominant entity, the names are often the same. The EC box number in the lower right is a clustering level number used to keep track of the sequence in which clustering is done. The number 2.1 signifies that the entity cluster Report is the first entity cluster at level 2. Note that all the original entities are considered to be at level 1.

The higher level abstraction, the entity cluster, must maintain the same relationships between entities inside and outside the entity cluster as occur between the same entities in the lower level diagram. Thus, the entity names inside the entity cluster should appear just outside the EC box along the path of their direct relationship to the appropriately related entities outside the box, maintaining consistent interfaces (relationships) as shown in Figure 3.8b. For simplicity, we modify this rule slightly: If the relationship is between an external entity and the dominant internal entity (for which the entity cluster is named), the entity cluster name need not be repeated outside the EC box. Thus, in Figure 3.8b, we could drop the name Report both places it occurs outside the Report box, but we must retain the name Author, which is not the name of the entity cluster.

Relationships in entity diagrams used here are not restricted to current ER model implementations and commercial tools, but they may include n-ary as well as binary-degree relationships; optional/mandatory existence dependencies; abstractions; and, possibly, the role concept and integrity constraints of the NIAM model.

3.4.2 Grouping Operations

The grouping operations are the fundamental components of the entity clustering technique. They define what collections of entities and relation-

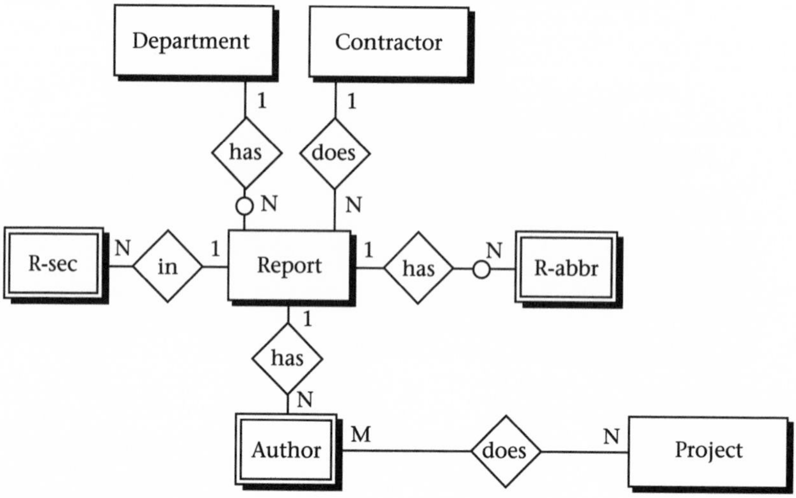

(a) ER model before clustering

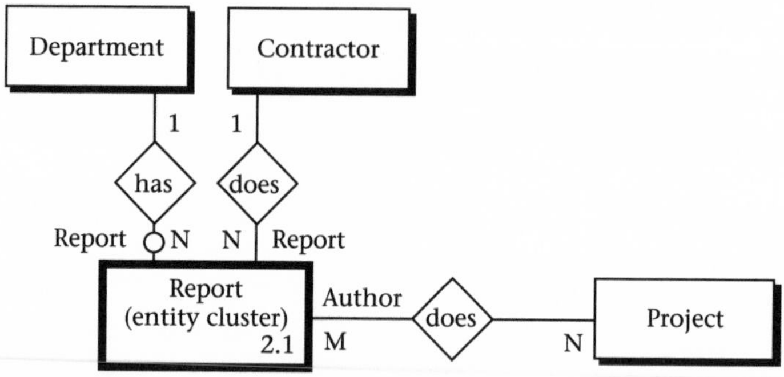

(b) ER model after clustering

Figure 3.8 Format of an entity cluster

ships comprise higher level objects, the entity clusters. The operations are heuristic in nature and include:

- dominance grouping
- abstraction grouping
- constraint grouping
- relationship grouping

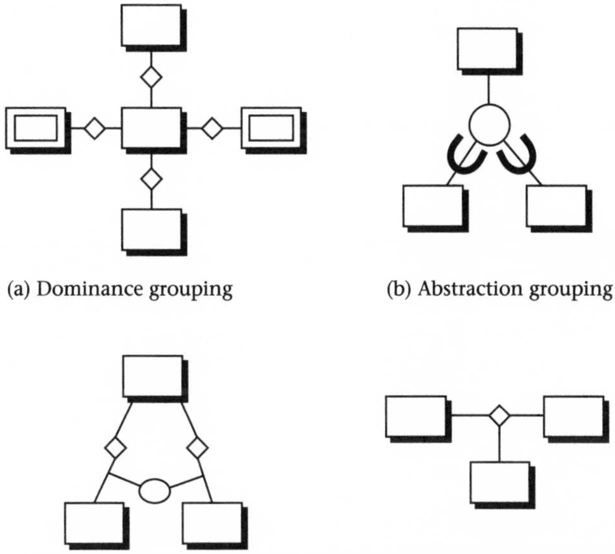

(a) Dominance grouping (b) Abstraction grouping

(c) Constraint grouping (d) Relationship grouping

Figure 3.9 Grouping operations (generic forms)

These grouping operations can be applied recursively or used in a variety of combinations to produce higher level entity clusters, that is, clusters at any level of abstraction. An entity or entity cluster may be an object that is subject to combinations with other objects to form the next higher level. That is, entity clusters have the properties of entities and can have relationships with any other objects at any equal or lower level. The original relationships among entities are preserved after all grouping operations, as illustrated in Figure 3.8.

A cluster level number is given as x.y, where x is the next level above the highest level of entities and entity clusters being grouped. Elementary entities are considered to be at level 0. The y value represents a unique identification number given to each cluster at level x (see Figure 3.9 for the generic forms of grouping).

Dominant objects or entities normally become obvious from the ER diagram or the relationship definitions. Each dominant object is grouped with all its related nondominant objects to form a cluster. Weak entities can be attached to an entity to make a cluster.

Multilevel data objects using such abstractions as generalization, subset generalization, and aggregation can be grouped into an entity cluster. The supertype or aggregate entity name is used as the entity cluster name.

Constraint-related objects that extend the ER model to incorporate the integrity constraints of NIAM can be grouped into an entity cluster.

The n-ary relationships of degree 3 or more can potentially be grouped into an entity cluster. The cluster represents the relationship as a whole, such as the relationship table that would be defined when transforming the n-ary relationship into a set of equivalent normalized tables.

3.4.3 Clustering Technique

The grouping operations and their order of precedence determine the individual activities needed for clustering. We now learn how to build a root entity cluster from the elementary entities and relationships defined in the ER modeling process. This technique assumes that a top-down analysis has been performed as part of the database requirement analysis and that it has been documented so that the major functional areas and subareas are identified. Functional areas are often defined by an enterprises important organizational units, business activities, or, possibly, by dominant applications for processing information. As an example, recall Figure 3.3 (reconstructed in Figure 3.10), which can be thought of as having three major functional areas: company organization (division, department), project management (project, skill, location, employee), and employee data (employee, manager, secretary, engineer, technician, prof-assoc, and desktop). Note that the functional areas are allowed to overlap. Using an ER diagram resulting from the database requirement analysis as shown in Figure 3.10, clustering involves a series of bottom-up steps using the basic grouping operations. The list that follows explains these steps.

1. *Define points of grouping within functional areas.* Locate the dominant entities in a functional area through the natural relationships, local n-ary relationships, integrity constraints, abstractions, or just the central focus of many simple relationships. If such points of grouping do not exist within an area, consider a functional grouping of a whole area.
2. *Form entity clusters.* Use the basic grouping operations on elementary entities and their relationships to form higher level objects, or entity clusters. Because entities may belong to several potential clusters, we need to have a set of priorities for forming entity clusters. The following set of rules, listed in priority order, defines the set that is most likely to preserve the clarity of the conceptual model.
   a. Entities to be grouped into an entity cluster should exist within the same functional area; that is, the entire entity cluster should occur within the boundary of a functional area. For example, in Figure 3.10, the relationship between Department and Employee should

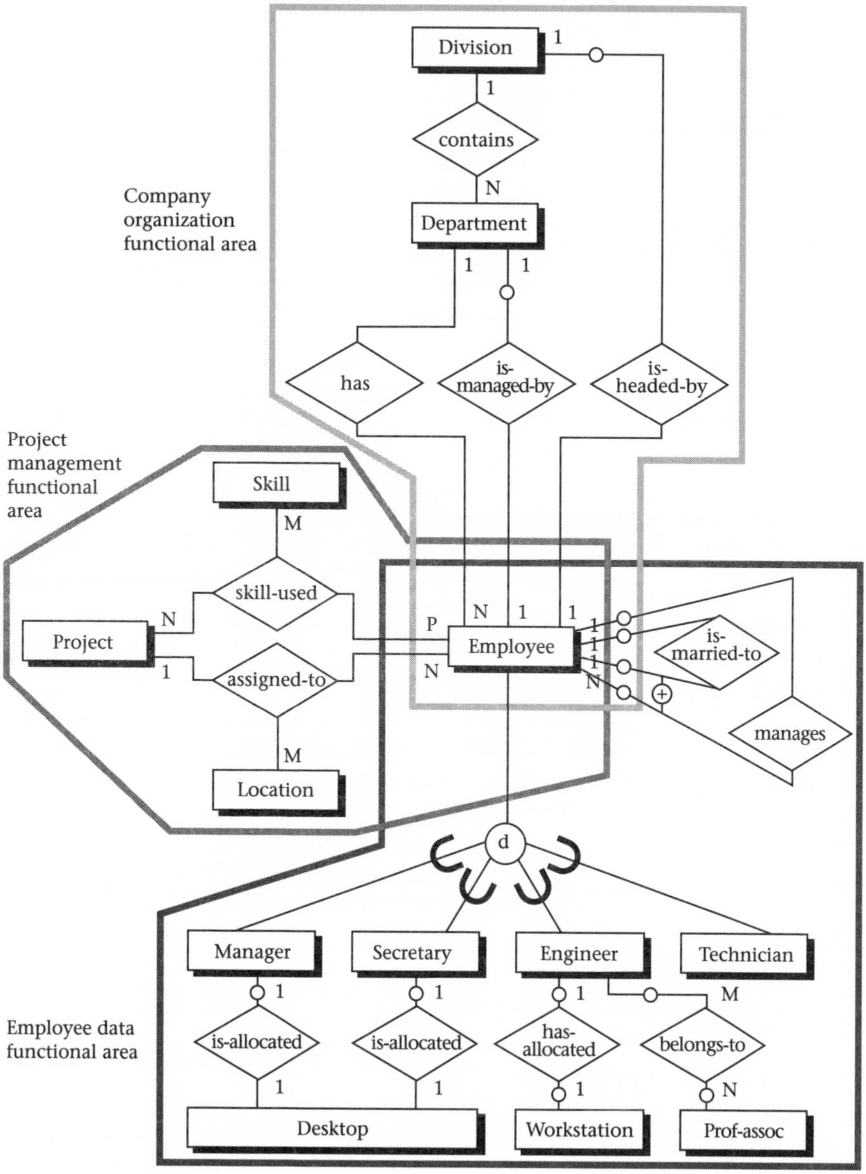

Figure 3.10 Global ER schema with functional areas defined

not be clustered unless Employee is included in the company organization functional area with Department and Division. In another example, the relationship between the supertype Employee and its subtypes could be clustered within the employee data functional area.

b. If a conflict in choice between two or more potential entity clusters cannot be resolved (e.g., between two constraint groupings at the same level of precedence), then leave these entity clusters ungrouped within their functional area. If that functional area remains cluttered with unresolved choices, then define functional subareas in which to group unresolved entities, entity clusters, and their relationships.

3. *Form higher level entity clusters.* Apply the grouping operations recursively to any combination of elementary entities and entity clusters to form new levels of entity clusters (higher level objects). Resolve conflicts using the same set of priority rules given in Step 2. Continue the grouping operations until all the entity representations fit on a single page without undue complexity. The root entity cluster is then defined.
4. *Validate the cluster diagram.* Check for consistency of the interfaces (relationships) between objects at each level of the diagram. Verify the meaning of each level with the end users.

The result of one round of clustering is shown in Figure 3.11, where each of the clusters is shown at level 2. The root entity cluster for this database would be a single box at level 3. This technique could feasibly be implemented with software whose diagrams are created and accessed with the simple open, close, group, and ungroup operations found in available object-oriented drawing packages.

3.5 Summary

The ER approach is particularly useful in the early steps of the database life cycle, which involve requirements analysis and logical design. These two steps are often done simultaneously, particularly when requirements are determined from end user interviews and modeled in terms of data-to-data relationships and process-to-data relationships. The ER modeling step involves the classification of entities and attributes first, then identification of generalization hierarchies and other abstractions, and finally the definition of all relationships among entities. Relationships may be binary (the most common), ternary, and higher level n-ary.

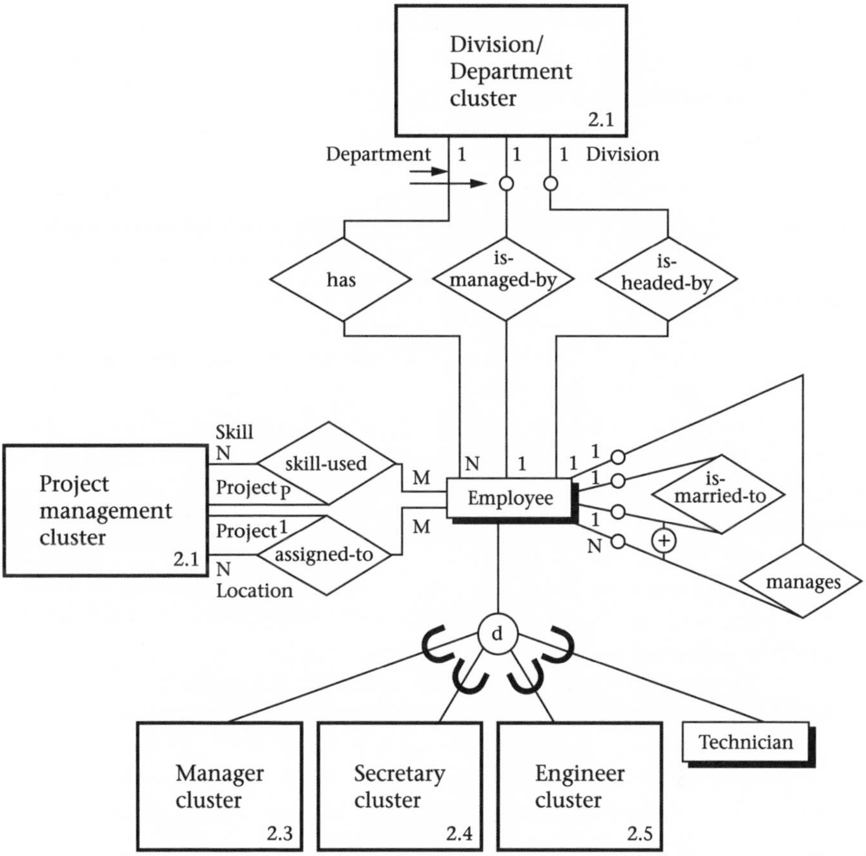

Figure 3.11 Entity clusters at the second (root) level

ER modeling of individual requirements typically involves creating a different view for each end users requirements. Then the designer must integrate those views into a global schema so that the entire database is pictured as an integrated whole. This helps to eliminate needless redundancy—such elimination is particularly important in logical design. Controlled redundancy can be created later, at the physical design level, to enhance database performance.

Finally, entity clustering promotes the simplicity that is vital for fast end user comprehension, as well as the complexity at a more detailed level to satisfy the database designers need for extended semantic expression in the conceptual model. An entity cluster is a grouping of entities and their corresponding relationships into a higher level abstract object.

In the next chapter we take the global schema produced from the ER modeling and view integration steps and transform it into SQL tables. The SQL format is the end product of logical design, which is still independent of a database management system.

Literature Summary

Conceptual modeling is defined in [TsLo82, BMS84, NiHa89, BCN92]. At the theoretical level a top-down approach to database design was investigated with regard to the universal relation assumption [BBG78, Kent81] and the combined top-down and bottom-up approach was discussed in [Date86, Swee85]. Discussion of the requirements data collection process can be found in [Mart82, TeFr82, Yao85].

Recent research has advanced view integration from a representation tool [SmSm77] to heuristic algorithms [ElWi79, NaGa82, NSE84, BaLe84, EHW85, NEL86, BLN86]. These algorithms are typically interactive, allowing the database designer to make decisions based on suggested alternative integration actions. Adopting an ER extension called the Entity-Category-Relationship model [EHW85], Navathe and others organized the different classes of objects and relationships into forms that are either compatible or incompatible for view integration [NEL86].

An entity cluster is also known in the literature as a complex object [Su83, DGL86, StRo86, PoKe86], molecular aggregation [BaBu84], or subject area [FeMi86]. The entity or object cluster concept can already be found in some database systems [BaBu84, MSOP86, Wied86]. Clustering models have been recently defined that provide a useful foundation for the proposed clustering technique [Ossh84, FeMi86, DGL86, TWBK89].

[BCN92] Batini, C., Ceri, S., and Navathe, S. *Conceptual Database Design: An Entity-Relationship Approach,* Benjamin/Cummings, Redwood City, CA, 1992.

[BaLe84] Batini, C. and Lenzerini, M. "A Methodology for Data Schema Integration in the Entity Relationship Model," *IEEE Trans. on Software Eng.* SE-10,6 (Nov. 1984), pp. 650–664.

[BLN86] Batini, C., Lenzerini, M., and Navathe, S.B. "A Comparative Analysis of Methodologies for Database Schema Integration," *ACM Computing Surveys* 18,4 (Dec. 1986), pp. 323–364.

[BaBu84] Batory, D.S. and Buchmann, A.P. "Molecular Objects, Abstract Data Types, and Data Models: A Framework," *Proc. 10th Intl. Conf. on Very Large Data Bases,* Singapore, Aug. 1984, pp. 172–184.

[BBG78] Beeri, C., Bernstein, P., and Goodman, N. "A Sophisticates Introduction to Database Normalization Theory," *Proc. 4th Intl. Conf. on Very Large Data Bases,* Berlin, Sept. 13–15, 1978, IEEE, New York, 1978, pp. 113–124.

[BMS84] Brodie, M.L., Mylopoulos, J., and Schmidt, J. (editors). *On Conceptual Modeling: Perspectives from Artificial Intelligence, Databases, and Programming Languages,* Springer-Verlag, New York, 1984.

[Date86] Date, C.J. *An Introduction to Database Systems, Vol. 1* (4th Ed.), Addison-Wesley, Reading, MA, 1986.

[DGL86] Dittrich, K.R., Gotthard, W., and Lockemann, P.C. "Complex Entities for Engineering Applications," *Proc. 5th ER Conf.,* North-Holland, Amsterdam, 1986.

[ElWi79] Elmasri, R. and Wiederhold, G. "Data Model Integration Using the Structural Model," *Proc. ACM SIGMOD Conf.,* Boston, 1979, ACM, New York, pp. 319–326.

[EHW85] Elmasri, R., Hevner, A., and Weeldreyer, J. "The Category Concept: An Extension to the Entity-Relationship Model," *Data and Knowledge Engineering*1,1 (1985), pp. 75–116.

[FeMi86] Feldman, P. and Miller, D. "Entity Model Clustering: Structuring a Data Model by Abstraction," *Computer Journal*29,4 (Aug. 1986), pp. 348–360.

[Kent81] Kent, W. "Consequences of Assuming a Universal Relation," *ACM Trans. Database Systems* 6,4 (1981), pp. 539–556.

[MSOP86] Maier, D., Stein, J., Otis, A., and Purdy, A. "Development of an Object-Oriented DBMS," *OOPSLA 1986 Proc.,* Sept. 1986, pp. 472–482.

[Mart82] Martin, J. *Strategic Data-Planning Methodologies,* Prentice-Hall, Englewood Cliffs, NJ, 1982.

[NaGa82] Navathe, S. and Gadgil, S. "A Methodology for View Integration in Logical Database Design," *Proc. 8th Intl. Conf. on Very Large Data Bases,* Mexico City, 1982, pp. 142–152.

[NEL86] Navathe, S., Elmasri, R., and Larson, J. "Integrating User Views in Database Design," *IEEE Computer* 19,1 (1986), pp. 50–62.

[NSE84] Navathe, S., Sashidhar, T., and Elmasri, R. "Relationship Merging in Schema Integration," *Proc. 10th Intl. Conf. on Very Large Data Bases,* Singapore, 1984, pp. 78–90.

[NiHa89] Nijssen, G.M. and Halpin, T.A. *Conceptual Schema and Relational Database Design: A Fact Oriented Approach,* Prentice-Hall, New York, 1989.

[Ossh84] Ossher, H.L. "A New Program Structuring Mechanism Based on Layered Graphs," *Proc. 11th Annual ACM SIGACT-SIGPLAN POPL,* Salt Lake City, Utah, Jan. 15–18, 1984, pp. 11–22.

[PoKe86] Potter, W.D. and Kerschberg, L. "A Unified Approach to Modeling Knowledge and Data," *IFIP WG 2.6 Working Conf. on Knowledge and Data,* University of South Carolina, Elsevier, North-Holland, New York, Sept. 1986.

[SmSm77] Smith, J. and Smith, D. "Database Abstractions: Aggregation and Generalization," *ACM Trans. Database Systems* 2,2 (June 1977), pp. 105–133.

[StRo86] Stonebraker, M. and Rowe, L.A. "The Design of Postgres," *Proc. ACM-SIGMOD Intl. Conf. on Management of Data,* May 1986, pp. 340–355.

[Su83] Su, S.Y.W. "SAM*: A Semantic Association Model for Corporate and Scientific Statistical Databases," *Inform. Sciences* 29, 2–3 (May–June 1983), pp. 151–199.

[Swee85] Sweet, F. "Process-Driven Data Design," *Datamation* 31,16 (1985), pp. 84–85, first of a series of 14 articles.

[TeFr82] Teorey, T. and Fry, J. *Design of Database Structures,* Prentice-Hall, Englewood Cliffs, NJ, 1982.

[TYF86] Teorey, T.J., Yang, D., and Fry, J.P. "A Logical Design Methodology for Relational Databases Using the Extended Entity-Relationship Model," *ACM Computing Surveys* 18,2 (June 1986), pp. 197–222.

[TWBK89] Teorey, T.J., Wei, G., Bolton, D.L., and Koenig, J.A. "ER Model Clustering as an Aid for User Communication and Documentation in Database Design," *Comm. ACM* 32, 8 (Aug. 1989), pp. 975–987.

[TsLo82] Tsichritzis, D. and Lochovsky, F. *Data Models,* Prentice-Hall, Englewood Cliffs, NJ, 1982.

[Wied86] Wiederhold, G. "Views, Objects, and Databases," *IEEE Computer* (Dec. 1986), pp. 37–44.

[Yao85] Yao, S.B. (editor). *Principles of Database Design,* Prentice-Hall, Englewood Cliffs, NJ, 1985.

EXERCISES

Problem 3-1

An ER diagram that satisfies the following assertions is shown on the following page. For this diagram, fill in the missing relationship connectivities, optionalities, and entities (or weak entities).

Publishers publish many different types of professional journals and books. Some publishers only publish books, some journals, and some both. No book or journal is published by more than one publisher. An author many write either books, journal articles, or both. A journal typically contains several articles, each one written by one or more authors. No article appears in more than one journal. Any journal may have one or more abbreviations, or none.

Every book and article is reviewed by several professionals in the field who may or may not be authors as well. Of course, an author never reviews his or

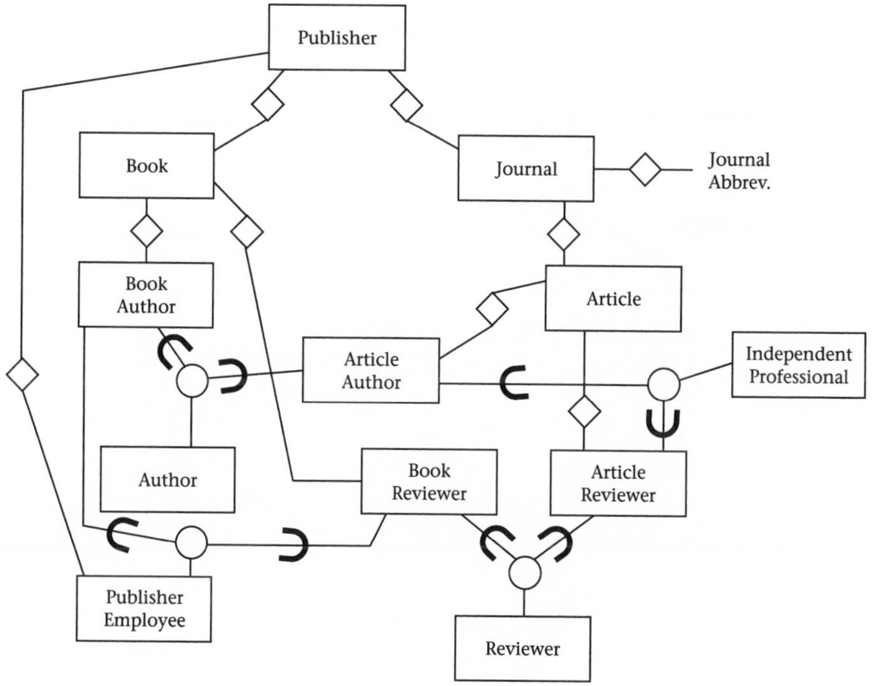

her own book or article. Each book reviewer and author works for and is paid by a single publisher. Article authors and reviewers are not paid, however, and thus article reviewers are never book reviewers. Authors and reviewers who are not paid by a publisher are known as independent professionals.

Problem 3-2

Given the assertions below for a relational database that represents the current term enrollment at a large university, draw an ER diagram for this schema that takes into account *all* the assertions given. There are 2,000 instructors, 4,000 courses, and 30,000 students. Use as many ER constructs as you can to represent the true semantics of the problem.

Assertions:

a. An instructor may teach none, one, or more courses in a given term (average is 2.0 courses).

b. An instructor must direct the research of at least one student (average = 2.5 students).

c. A course may have none, one, or two prerequisites (average = 1.5 prerequisites).

d. A course may exist even if no students are currently enrolled.

e. All courses are taught by only one instructor.

f. The average enrollment in a course is 30 students.

g. A student must select at least one course per term (average = 4.0 course selections).

Problem 3-3

Create an ER diagram for the database that satisfies the following assertions about a general purpose community medical facility. What questions about this enterprise's environment do these assertions leave unanswered?

A person is represented as either a patient or a medical worker. A medical worker is either a doctor, nurse, paramedic, clerk, or administrator. Medical workers work in a medical facility which has a name, address, possibly a specialty area, and the name of an administrator.

A patient visits a medical facility for a diagnosis of a health problem, and then may come for additional visits for treatment if so designated as a result of the diagnosis and if the facility has the expertise to treat the problem. Each visit is called an encounter and it must involve a patient, a medical worker, and a service. The service could be a diagnosis, treatment, checkup, or payment. A patient may be eligible for his or her company health benefits or must pay-as-you-go. Patients who are unable to pay are not turned away, but are registered as indigent citizens and are given short-term care. Patient data includes name, ID number (ssn), address (street, city, state, zip), phone (day and evenings), employer (company) name, employer address, type of benefits eligible for, and method of payment.

A medical worker must hold one or more credentials that are granted to work in a particular medical facility. Doctors are allowed to perform any kind of diagnosis and give treatment based on their specialty. Paramedics are allowed to give only emergency diagnoses and treatment, but for any type of life-threatening problem. Nurses do not do diagnoses, but participate in treatment, particularly if the patient must be prepared for surgery or remain at the facility overnight.

The facility administrator is concerned with personnel needs and assignments. Each medical worker must have at least one and possibly more assignments at a facility. Each assignment partially or completely fills an authorized slot specified by the personnel needs; thus an authorization may involve many assignments. Medical workers have certain skills that must be recorded and accessed for a new assignment.

CHAPTER 4

TRANSFORMATION OF THE ER MODEL TO SQL

This chapter focuses on the database life-cycle step that is of particular interest when designing relational databases: transformation of the ER model to candidate tables and their definition in SQL (Step IIc). We will see a natural evolution from the ER model to a relational schema. The evolution is so natural, in fact, that it supports the contention that ER modeling is an effective early step in relational database development. This contention has been proven to some extent by the widespread commercialization and use of CASE tools that support not only ER modeling, but also the automatic conversion of ER models to vendor-specific SQL table definitions and integrity constraints.

4.1 Transformation Rules and SQL Constructs

We now look at each ER modeling construct in detail to see how the rules about transforming the ER model to relational (SQL-92) schemas are defined and applied. Our example is drawn from the company personnel and project ER schemas illustrated in Figure 3.3.

The basic transformations can be described in terms of the three types of tables they produce:

- *An entity table with the same information content as the original entity.* This transformation always occurs for entities with binary relationships that are many-to-many, one-to-many on the "one" (parent) side, or one-to-one on one side; entities with binary recursive relationships that are many-to-many; and entities with any ternary or higher-degree relationship, or a generalization hierarchy.
- *An entity table with the embedded foreign key of the parent entity.* This transformation always occurs for entities with binary relationships

that are one-to-many for the entity on the "many" (child) side, for one-to-one relationships for one of the entities, and for each entity with a binary recursive relationship that is one-to-one or one-to-many. This is one of the two most common ways CASE tools handle relationships, by prompting the user to define a foreign key in the child table that matches a primary key in the parent table.

- *A relationship table with the foreign keys of all the entities in the relationship*. This transformation always occurs for relationships that are binary and many-to-many, relationships that are binary recursive and many-to-many, and all relationships that are of ternary or higher degree. This is other most common way CASE tools handle relationships in the ER model. A many-to-many relationship can only be defined in terms of a table that contains foreign keys that match the primary keys of the two associated entities. This new table may also contain attributes of the original relationship—for example, a relationship enrolled-in between two entities Student and Course might have the attributes term and grade, which are associated with a particular student enrolled in a particular course.

The following rules apply to handling SQL null values in these transformations:

- Nulls are allowed in an entity table for foreign keys of associated (referenced) optional entities.
- Nulls are not allowed in an entity table for foreign keys of associated (referenced) mandatory entities.
- Nulls are not allowed for any key in a relationship table because only complete row entries are meaningful in the table.

In some relational systems, rules for nulls are different. These rules can be modified to be consistent with such systems. Figures 4.1 through 4.4 show standard SQL statements needed to define each type of ER model construct. Note that table names are shown in boldface for readability.

4.1.1 Binary Relationships

A one-to-one binary relationship between two entities is illustrated in Figure 4.1, parts a through c. When both entities are mandatory (Figure 4.1a), each entity becomes a table and the key of either entity can appear in the other entitys table as a foreign key. One of the entities in an optional relationship (see Department in Figure 4.1b) should contain the foreign key of the other entity in its transformed table. Employee, the other entity in Figure 4.1b, could also contain a foreign key (dept_no) with nulls allowed, but this would

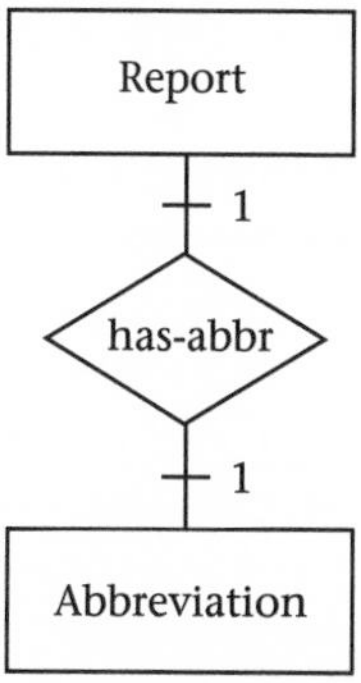

Every report has one abbreviation, and every abbreviation represents exactly one report.

```
create table report
        (report_no integer,
        report_name varchar(256),
        primary key(report_no);
create table abbreviation
        (abbr_no char(6),
        report_no integer not null unique,
        primary key (abbr_no),
        foreign key (report_no) references report
            on delete cascade on update cascade);
```

(a) one-to-one, both entities mandatory

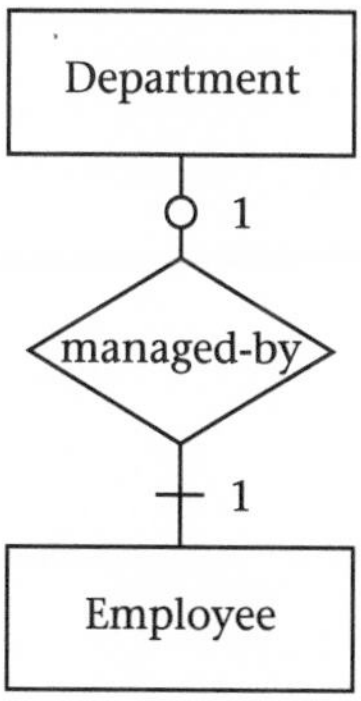

Every department must have a manager, but an employee can be a manager of at most one department.

```
create table department
        (dept_no integer,
        dept_name char(20),
        mgr_id char(10) not null unique,
        primary key (dept_no),
        foreign key (mgr_id) references employee
            on delete set default on update cascade);
create table employee
        (emp_id char(10),
        emp_name char(20),
        primary key (emp_id));
```

(b) one-to-one, one entity optional, one mandatory

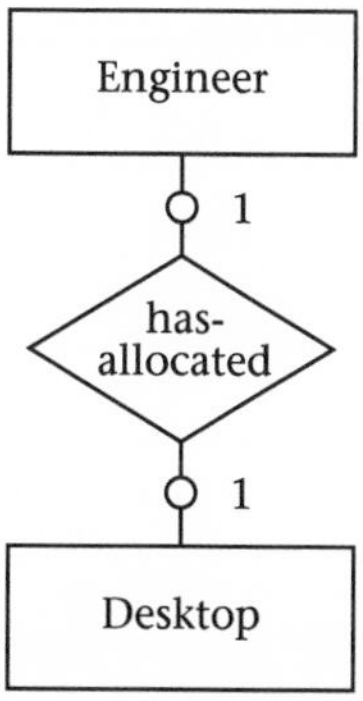

Some desktop computers are allocated to engineers, but not necessarily to all engineers.

```
create table engineer
        (emp_id char(10),
        desktop_no integer,
        primary key (emp_id),
        foreign key (desktop_no) references desktop
            on delete set null on update cascade);
create table desktop
        (desktop_no integer,
        emp_id char(10),
        primary key (desktop_no),
        foreign key (emp_id) references engineer
            on delete set null on update cascade);
```

(c) one-to-one, both entities optional

Figure 4.1 Binary relationship transformation rules
(Figure continues on the following page)

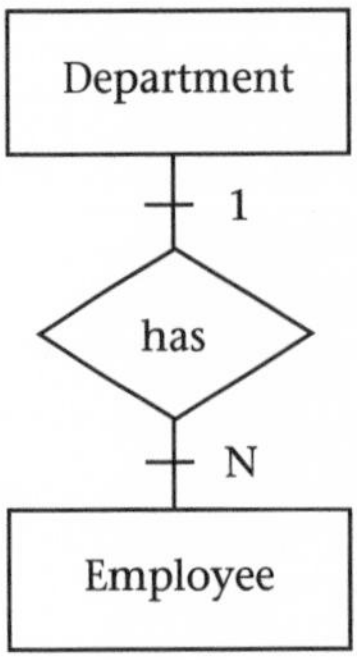

Every employee works in exactly one department, and each department has at least one employee.

```
create table department
      (dept_no integer,
      dept_name char(20),
      primary key (dept_no));
create table employee
      (emp_id char(10),
      emp_name char(20),
      dept_no integer not null,
      primary key (emp_id),
      foreign key (dept_no) references department
         on delete set default on update cascade);
```

(d) one-to-many, both entities mandatory

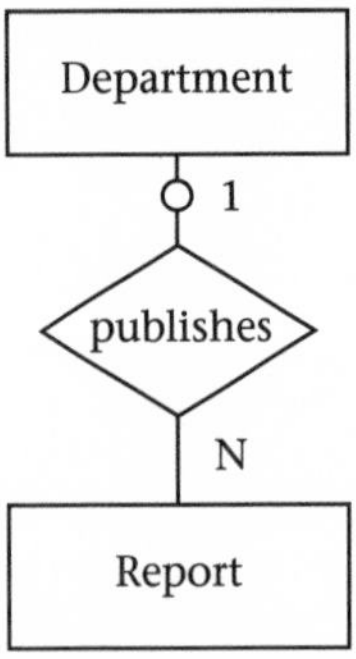

Each department publishes one or more reports. A given report may not necessarily be published by a department.

```
create table department
      (dept_no integer,
      dept_name char(20),
      primary key (dept_no));
create table report
      (report_no integer,
      dept_no integer,
      primary key (report_no),
      foreign key (dept_no) references department
         on delete set null on update cascade);
```

(e) one-to-many, one entity optional, one unknown

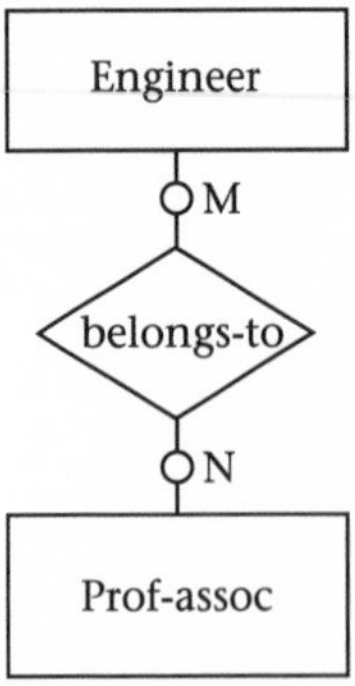

Every professional association could have none, one, or many engineer members. Each engineer could be a member of none, one, or many professional associations.

```
create table engineer
      (emp_id char(10),
      primary key (emp_id));
create table prof_assoc
      (assoc_name varchar(256),
      primary key (assoc_name));
create table belongs_to
      (emp_id char(10),
      assoc_name varchar(256),
      primary key (emp_id, assoc_name),
      foreign key (emp_id) references engineer
         on delete cascade on update cascade,
      foreign key (assoc_name) references prof_assoc
         on delete cascade on update cascade);
```

(f) many-to-many, both entities optional

Figure 4.1 Continued

require more storage space because of the much greater number of Employee entity instances than Department instances. When both entities are optional (Figure 4.1c), either entity can contain the embedded foreign key of the other entity, with nulls allowed in the foreign keys.

The one-to-many relationship can be shown as either mandatory or optional on the "many" side, without affecting the transformation. On the "one" side it may be either mandatory (Figure 4.1d) or optional (Figure 4.1e). In all cases the foreign key must appear on the "many" side, which represents the child entity, with nulls allowed for foreign keys only in the optional "one" case. Foreign key constraints are set according to the specific meaning of the relationship and may vary from one relationship to another.

The many-to-many relationship, shown in Figure 4.1f as completely optional, requires a relationship table with primary keys of both entities. The same transformation applies to either the optional or mandatory case, including the fact that the not null clause must appear for the foreign keys in both cases. Foreign key constraints on delete and update must always be *cascade* because each entry in the SQL table depends on the current value or existence of the referenced primary key.

4.1.2 Binary Recursive Relationships

A single entity with a one-to-one relationship implies some form of entity occurrence pairing, as indicated by the relationship name. This pairing may be completely optional, completely mandatory, or neither. In all of these cases (Figure 4.2a), the pairing entity key appears as a foreign key in the resulting table. The two key attributes are taken from the same domain but are given different names to designate their unique use. The one-to-many relationship requires a foreign key in the entity table (Figure 4.2b). The foreign key constraints can vary with the particular relationship.

The many-to-many relationship is shown as optional (Figure 4.2c) and uses a relationship table; it could also be defined as mandatory (using the word "must" instead of "may"); both cases have the foreign keys defined as "not null." In many-to-many relationships, foreign key constraints on delete and update must always be cascade because each entry in the SQL table depends on the current value, or existence of the referenced primary key.

4.1.3 Ternary and n-ary Relationships

An n-ary relationship has n+1 possible variations of connectivity: all n sides with connectivity "one;" n-1 sides with connectivity "one," and one side with connectivity "many;" n-2 sides with connectivity "one" and two sides with "many;" and so on until all sides are "many."

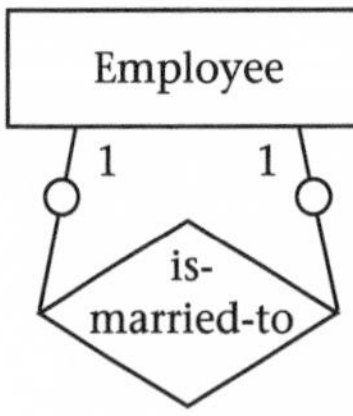

Any employee is allowed to be married to another employee in this company.

```
create table employee
        (emp_id char(10),
        emp_name char(20),
        spouse_id char(10),
        primary key (emp_id),
        foreign key (spouse_id) references employee
            on delete set null on update cascade);
```

(a) one-to-one, both sides optional

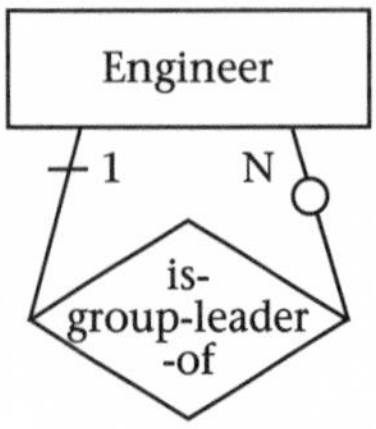

Engineers are divided into groups for certain projects. Each group has a leader.

```
create table engineer
        (emp_id char(10),
        leader_id char(10) not null,
        primary key (emp_id),
        foreign key (leader_id) references engineer
            on delete set default on update cascade);
```

(b) one-to-many, one side mandatory, many side optional

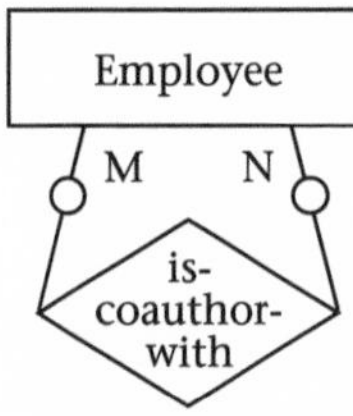

Each employee has the opportunity to coauthor a report with one or more other employees, or to write the report alone.

```
create table employee
        (emp_id char(10),
        emp_name char(20),
        primary key (emp_id));
create table coauthor
        (author_id char(10),
        coauthor_id char(10),
        primary key (author_id, coauthor_id),
        foreign key (author_id) references employee
            on delete cascade on update cascade,
        foreign key (coauthor_id) references employee
            on delete cascade on update cascade);
```

(c) many-to-many, both sides optional

Figure 4.2 Binary recursive relationship transformation rules

The four possible varieties of a ternary relationship are shown in Figure 4.3. All variations are transformed by creating a relationship table containing the primary keys of all entities; however, in each case the meaning of the keys is different. When all relationships are "one" (Figure 4.3a), the relationship table consists of three possible distinct candidate keys. This represents the fact

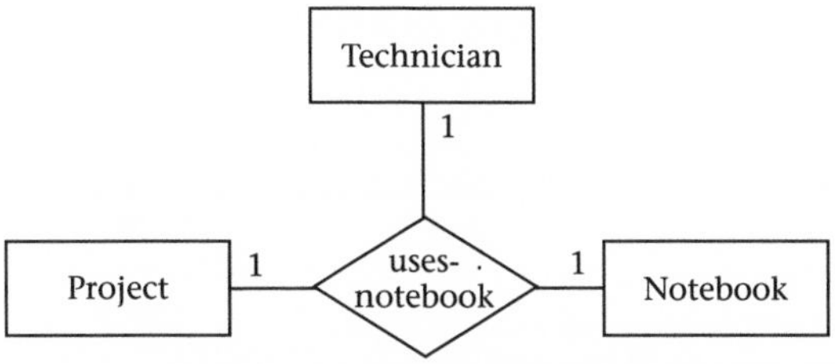

A technician uses exactly one notebook for each project. Each notebook belongs to one technician for each project. Note that a technician may still work on many projects and maintain different notebooks for different projects.

```
create table technician (emp_id char(10),
                         primary key (emp_id));
create table project (project_name char(20),
                      primary key (project_name));
create table notebook (notebook_no integer,
                       primary key (notebook_no));
create table uses_notebook (emp_id char(10),
                            project_name char(20),
                            notebook_no integer not null,
                            primary key (emp_id, project_name),
                            foreign key (emp_id) references technician
                               on delete cascade on update cascade,
                            foreign key (project_name) references project
                               on delete cascade on update cascade,
                            foreign key (notebook_no) references notebook
                               on delete cascade on update cascade);
```

uses_notebook

emp_id	project_name	notebook_no
35	alpha	5001
35	gamma	2008
42	delta	1004
42	epsilon	3005
81	gamma	1007
93	alpha	1009
93	beta	5001

Functional dependencies

emp_id, project_name → notebook_no
emp_id, notebook_no → project_name
project_name, notebook_no → emp_id

(a) one-to-one-to-one ternary relationship

Figure 4.3 Ternary relationship transformation rules
(Figure continues on the following 3 pages)

that there are three FDs needed to describe this relationship. The optionality constraint is not used here because all n entities must participate in every instance of the relationship to satisfy the FD (or multivalued dependency) constraints. (See Chapter 5 for more discussion of functional and multivalued dependencies.)

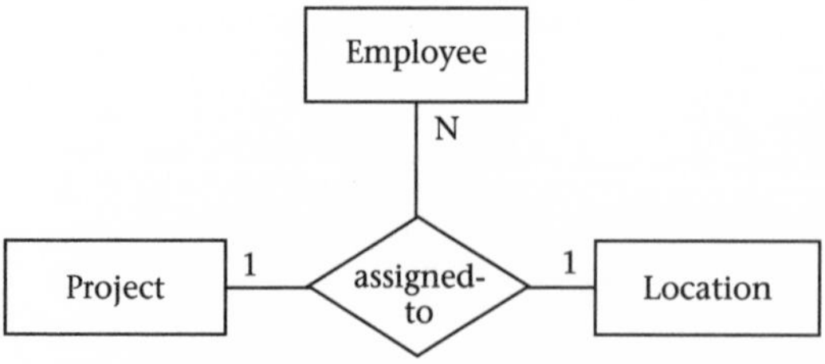

Each employee assigned to a project works at only one location for that project, but can be at a different location for a different project. At a given location, an employee works on only one project. At a particular location, there can be many employees assigned to a given project.

```
create table employee (emp_id char(10),
                       emp_name Char(20),
                       primary key (emp_id));
create table project (project_name char(20),
                      primary key (project_name));
create table location (loc_name char(15),
                       primary key (loc_name));
create table assigned_to (emp_id char(10),
                          project_name char(20),
                          loc_name char(15) not null,
                          primary key (emp_id, project_name),
                          foreign key (emp_id) references employee
                            on delete cascade on update cascade,
                          foreign key (project_name) references project
                            on delete cascade on update cascade,
                          foreign key (loc_name) references location
                            on delete cascade on update cascade);
```

assigned_to

emp_id	project_name	loc_name
48101	forest	B66
48101	ocean	E71
20702	ocean	A12
20702	river	D54
51266	river	G14
51266	ocean	A12
76323	hills	B66

Functional dependencies

emp_id, loc_name → project_name
emp_id, project_name → loc_name

(b) one-to-one-to-many ternary relationships

Figure 4.3 Continued

In general the number of entities with connectivity "one" determines the lower bound on the number of FDs. Thus, in Figure 4.3b, which is one-to-one-to-many, there are two FDs; in Figure 4.3c, which is one-to-many-to-many, there is only one FD. When all relationships are "many" (Figure 4.3d), the relationship table is all one composite key unless the relationship has its own

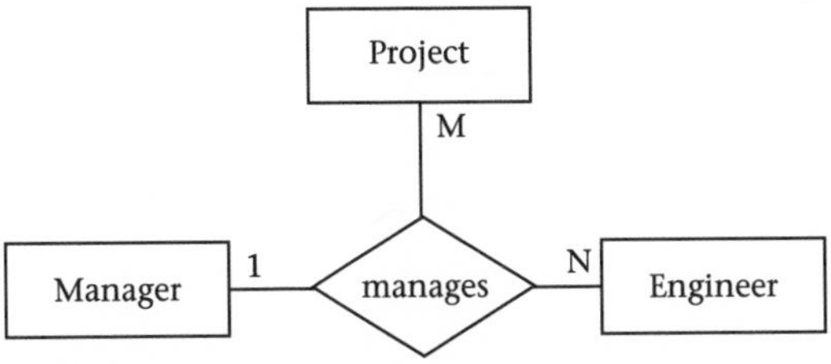

Each engineer working on a particular project has exactly one manager, but a project may have many managers and an engineer may have many managers and many projects. A manager may manage several projects.

```
create table project (project_name char(20),
                      primary key (project_name));
create table manager (mgr_id char(10),
                      primary key (mgr_id));
create table engineer (emp_id char(10),
                       primary key (emp_id));
create table manages (project_name char(20),
                      mgr_id char(10) not null,
                      emp_id char(10),
                      primary key (project_name, emp_id),
                      foreign key (project_name) references project
                         on delete cascade on update cascade,
                      foreign key (mgr_id) references manager
                         on delete cascade on update cascade,
                      foreign key (emp_id) references engineer
                         on delete cascade on update cascade);
```

manages

project_name	emp_id	mgr_id
alpha	4106	27
alpha	4200	27
beta	7033	32
beta	4200	14
gamma	4106	71
delta	7033	55
delta	4106	39
iota	4106	27

Functional dependencies

project_name, emp_id → mgr_id

(c) one-to-many-to-many ternary relationships

Figure 4.3 Continued

attributes. In that case the key is the composite of all three keys from the three associated entities.

Foreign key constraints on delete and update for ternary relationships transformed to SQL tables must always be cascade because each entry in the SQL table depends on the current value of, or existence of, the referenced primary key.

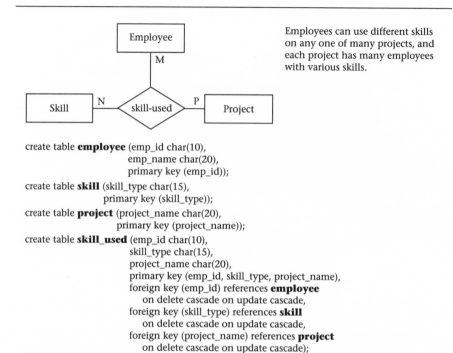

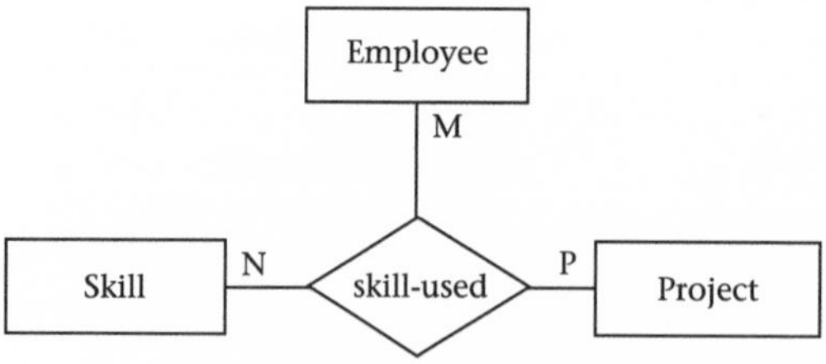

Employees can use different skills on any one of many projects, and each project has many employees with various skills.

```
create table employee (emp_id char(10),
                       emp_name char(20),
                       primary key (emp_id));
create table skill (skill_type char(15),
                    primary key (skill_type));
create table project (project_name char(20),
                      primary key (project_name));
create table skill_used (emp_id char(10),
                         skill_type char(15),
                         project_name char(20),
                         primary key (emp_id, skill_type, project_name),
                         foreign key (emp_id) references employee
                           on delete cascade on update cascade,
                         foreign key (skill_type) references skill
                           on delete cascade on update cascade,
                         foreign key (project_name) references project
                           on delete cascade on update cascade);
```

skill_used

emp_id	skill_type	project_name
101	algebra	electronics
101	calculus	electronics
101	algebra	mechanics
101	geometry	mechanics
102	algebra	electronics
102	set-theory	electronics
102	geometry	mechanics
105	topology	mechanics

Functional dependencies

none

(d) many-to-many-to-many ternary relationships

Figure 4.3 Continued

4.1.4 Generalization and Aggregation

The transformation of a generalization abstraction produces a separate table for the generic or supertype entity and each of the subtypes (Figure 4.4). The supertype entity table contains the supertype entity key and all common attributes. Each subtype entity table contains the supertype entity key and

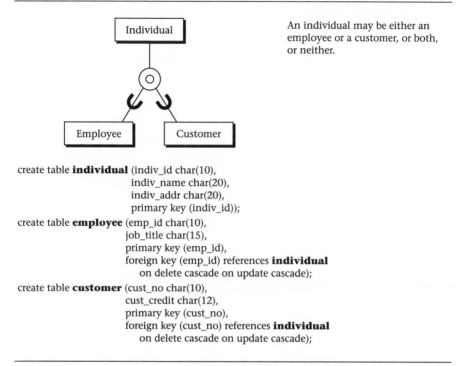

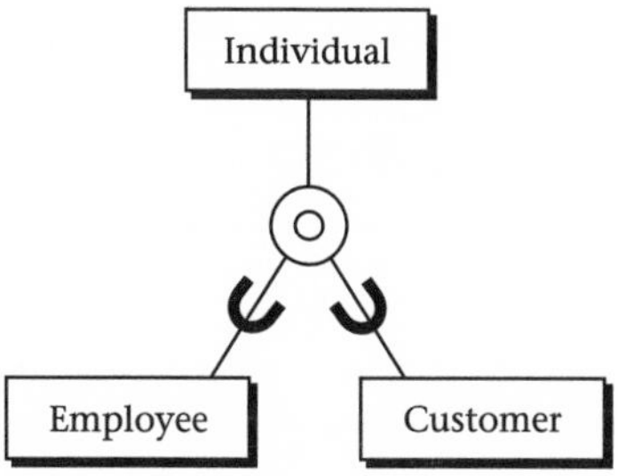

An individual may be either an employee or a customer, or both, or neither.

```
create table individual (indiv_id char(10),
                         indiv_name char(20),
                         indiv_addr char(20),
                         primary key (indiv_id));
create table employee (emp_id char(10),
                       job_title char(15),
                       primary key (emp_id),
                       foreign key (emp_id) references individual
                          on delete cascade on update cascade);
create table customer (cust_no char(10),
                       cust_credit char(12),
                       primary key (cust_no),
                       foreign key (cust_no) references individual
                          on delete cascade on update cascade);
```

Figure 4.4 Generalization abstraction transformation rules

only the attributes that are specific to that subtype. Update integrity is maintained by requiring all insertions and deletions to occur in both the supertype entity table and relevant subtype table—that is, the foreign key constraint cascade must be used. If the update is to the primary key of the supertype entity table, then all subtype tables as well as the supertype table must be updated. An update to a nonkey attribute affects either the supertype or one subtype table, but not both. The transformation rules (and integrity rules) are the same for both the disjoint and overlapping subtype generalizations.

The transformation of an aggregation abstraction also produces a separate table for the supertype entity and each subtype entity. However, there are no common attributes and no integrity constraints to maintain. The main function of aggregation is to provide an abstraction to aid the view integration process during ER modeling.

4.1.5 Multiple Relationships

Multiple relationships among n entities are alway considered to be completely independent. One-to-one or one-to-many binary or binary recursive relationships that result in entity tables that are either equivalent or differ only in the addition of a foreign key can simply be merged into a single entity table containing all the foreign keys. Many-to-many or ternary relationships that result in relationship tables tend to be unique and cannot be merged.

4.1.6 Weak Entities

Weak entities differ from entities only in their need for keys from other entities to establish their uniqueness. Otherwise, they have the same transformation properties as entities, and no special rules are needed. When a weak entity is already derived from two or more entities in the ER diagram, it can be directly transformed into an entity table without further change.

4.2 Transformation Steps

The list that follows summarizes the basic transformation steps from an ER diagram to SQL.

- Transform each entity into a table containing the key and nonkey attributes of the entity.
- Transform every many-to-many binary or binary recursive relationship into a relationship table with the keys of the entities and the attributes of the relationship.
- Transform every ternary or higher level n-ary relationship into a relationship table.

Now we will study each step in turn.

4.2.1 Entity Transformation

If there is a one-to-many relationship between two entities, add the key of the entity on the "one" side (the parent) into the child table as a foreign key. If there is a one-to-one relationship between one entity and another entity, then add the key of one of the entities into the table for the other entity, thus changing it to a foreign key. The addition of a foreign key due to a one-to-one relationship can be made in either direction. One strategy is to maintain the most natural parent-child relationship by putting the parent key into the child table. Another strategy is based on efficiency: Add the foreign key to the table with fewer rows.

Every entity in a generalization hierarchy is transformed into a table. Each of these tables contains the key of the supertype entity; in reality, the subtype primary keys are foreign keys as well. The supertype entity table also contains nonkey values that are common to all the relevant entities; the other tables contain nonkey values specific to each subtype entity.

SQL constructs for these transformations may include constraints for not null, unique, and foreign key. A primary key must be specified for each table, either explicitly from among the candidate keys in the ER diagram or by taking the composite of all attributes as the default superkey. Note that the primary key designation implies that the attribute is not null unique. Check and default clauses are optional, depending on the narrative text associated with the ER diagram.

4.2.2 Many-to-Many Binary Relationship Transformation

In this step, every many-to-many binary (or binary recursive) relationship is transformed into a relationship table with the keys of the entities and the attributes of the relationship. A relationship table shows the correspondence between specific instances of one entity and those of another entity. Any attribute of this correspondence, such as the elected-office an engineer has in a professional association (Figure 4.1f), is considered intersection data and is added to the relationship table as a nonkey attribute.

SQL constructs for this transformation may include constraints for not null. The unique constraint is not used here because all candidate keys are composites of the participating primary keys of the associated entities in the relationship. The constraints for primary key and foreign key are required because of the definition of a relationship table as a composite of the primary keys of the associated entities.

4.2.3 Ternary Relationship Transformation

In this step, every ternary (or higher n-ary) relationship is transformed into a relationship table. Ternary or higher n-ary relationships are defined as a collection of the n primary keys in the associated entities in that relationship, with possibly some nonkey attributes that are dependent on the superkey formed by the composite of those n primary keys.

SQL constructs for this transformation must include constraints for not null, since optionality is not allowed. The unique constraint is not used for individual attributes, because all candidate keys are composites of the participating primary keys of the associated entities in the relationship. The constraints for primary key and foreign key are required because of the definition of a relationship table as a composite of the primary keys of the associated entities. The unique clause must also be used to define alternate candidate keys that often occur with ternary relationships. An n-ary relationship table has n foreign keys.

4.2.4 Example of ER-to-SQL Transformation

ER diagrams for the company personnel and project database (Figure 3.3) are transformed to candidate relational tables. A summary of the transformation of entities and relationships to candidate tables is illustrated in the list that follows.

SQL tables transformed directly from entities

division	**secretary**	**project**
department	**engineer**	**location**
employee	**technician**	**prof_assoc**
manager	**skill**	**desktop**

SQL tables transformed from many-to-many binary or binary recursive relationships

belongs_to

SQL tables transformed from ternary relationships

skill_used
assigned_to

4.3 Summary

Entities, attributes, and relationships can be transformed directly into SQL (SQL-92) relational table definitions with some simple rules. Entities are transformed into tables, with all attributes mapped one-to-one to table attributes. Tables representing entities that are the child ("many" side) of a parent-child (one-to-many or one-to-one) relationship must also include, as a foreign key, the primary key of the parent entity. A many-to-many relationship is transformed into a relationship table that contains the primary keys of the associated entities as its composite primary key; the components of that key are also designated as foreign keys in SQL.

A ternary or higher level n-ary relationship is transformed into a relationship table that contains the primary keys of the associated entities; these keys are designated as foreign keys in SQL. A subset of those keys can be designated as the primary key, depending on the functional dependencies associated with the relationship.

Rules for generalization require the inheritance of the primary key from the supertype to the subtype entities when transformed into SQL tables. Optionality constraints in the ER diagram translate into nulls allowed in the zrelational model when applied to the "one" side of a relationship. In SQL the lack of an optionality constraint determines the not null designation in the create table definition.

Literature Summary

Definition of the basic transformations from the ER model to tables is covered in [McGe74, Saka83, Mart83, Hawr84, JaNg84]. The ISO and ANSI standard for SQL-92 is given in [MeSi92].

[Hawr84] Hawryszkiewycz, I. *Database Analysis and Design,* SRA, Chicago, 1984.

[JaNg84] Jajodia, S. and Ng, P. "Translation of Entity-Relationship Diagrams into Relational Structures," *J. Systems and Software* 4,2–3 (1984), pp. 123–133.

[Mart83] Martin, J. *Managing the Data-Base Environment,* Prentice-Hall, Englewood Cliffs, NJ, 1983.

[McGe74] McGee, W. "A Contribution to the Study of Data Equivalence," *Data Base Management,* J.W. Klimbie and K.L. Koffeman (editors), North-Holland, Amsterdam, 1974, pp. 123–148.

[MeSi93] Melton, J. and Simon, A.R. *Understanding The New SQL: A Complete Guide,* Morgan Kaufmann Pub., San Francisco, 1993.

[Saka83] Sakai, H. "Entity-Relationship Approach to Logical Database Design," *Entity-Relationship Approach to Software Engineering,* C.G. Davis, S. Jajodia, P.A. Ng, and R.T. Yeh (editors), Elsevier, North-Holland, New York, 1983, pp. 155–187.

[TYF86] Teorey, T.J., Yang, D., and Fry, J.P. "A Logical Design Methodology for Relational Databases Using the Extended Entity-Relationship Model," *ACM Computing Surveys* 18,2 (June 1986), pp. 197–222.

EXERCISES

Problem 4-1

Define SQL tables for the ER diagram shown in Figure 3.7c on page 62.

Problem 4-2

Define SQL tables for the ER diagram you derived in Problem 3-2 on page 73.

Problem 4-3

Define SQL tables for the ER diagram you derived in Problem 3-3 on page 74.

Problem 4-4

Given the ER diagram below, define the appropriate SQL tables.

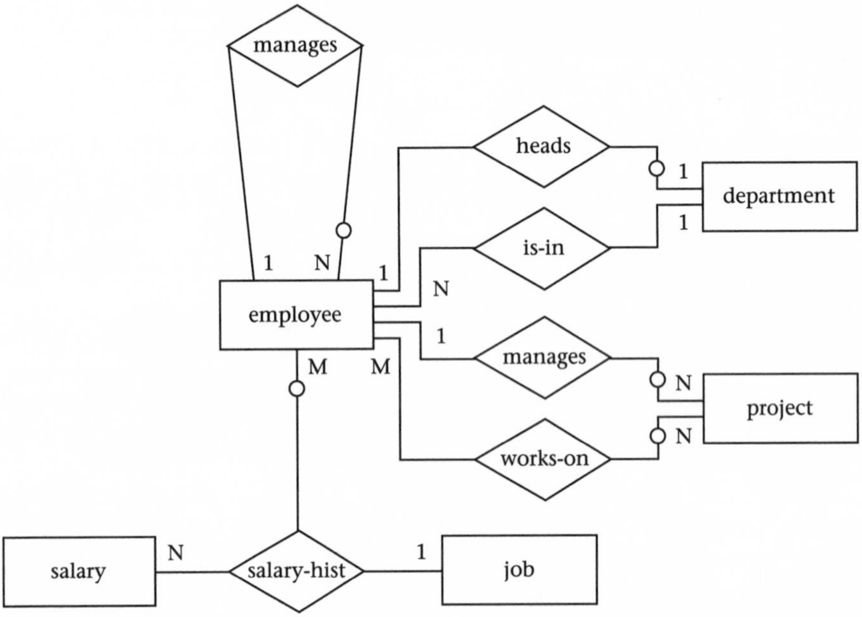

CHAPTER 5

NORMALIZATION

This chapter focuses on the fundamentals of normal forms for relational databases and the database design step that normalizes the candidate tables (Step IId of the database life cycle). It also investigates the equivalence between the ER model and normal forms for tables.

5.1 Fundamentals of Normalization

Relational database tables, whether they are derived from ER models or from some other design method, sometimes suffer from some rather serious problems in terms of performance, integrity, and maintainability. For example, when the entire database is defined as a single large table, it can result in a large amount of redundant data and lengthy searches for just a small number of target rows. It can also result in long and expensive updates, and deletions in particular can result in the elimination of useful data as an unwanted side effect.

Such a situation is shown in Figure 5.1, where products, salespersons, customers, and orders are all stored in a single table called **sales**. In this table we see that certain product and customer information is stored redundantly, wasting storage space. Queries such as "Which customers ordered vacuum cleaners last month?" would require a search of the entire table. Also, updates such as changing the address of the customer Dave Bachmann would require changing many rows. Finally, deleting the only outstanding order by a valued customer such as Elena Huang (who bought an expensive computer) also deletes the only copy of her address and credit rating as a side effect. Such information may be difficult (or sometimes impossible) to recover. These problems also occur for situations in which the database has already been set up as a collection of many tables, but some of the tables are still too large.

If we had a method of breaking up such a large table into smaller tables so that these types of problems would be eliminated, the database would be much more efficient and reliable. Classes of relational database schemes or table definitions, called *normal forms,* are commonly used to accomplish this goal. The creation of a normal form database table is called *normalization*. It is accomplished by analyzing the interdependencies among individual attributes associated with those tables and taking projections (subsets of columns) of larger tables to form smaller ones.

Let us first review the basic normal forms which have been well established in the relational database literature and in practice.

5.1.1 First Normal Form

Relational database tables such as the **Sales** table illustrated in Figure 5.1 have no columns that repeat themselves—that is, each column appears exactly once in the table definition. Such tables are considered to be in first normal form, the most basic level of normalized tables. Obviously, a table in first normal form suffers from many problems (as we have seen in Figure 5.1) and must be further normalized to be useful in practice. However, there are other tables that are unnormalized to even this extent, and these must be avoided if one wants to produce well-formatted business and personal databases. (On the other hand, there are some types of databases, particularly in scientific and engineering practice, where unnormalized data is actually good; we see this frequently in object-oriented databases.)

Before we give the definition for first normal form, we need to know the difference between a domain, an attribute, and a column. A *domain* is the set of all possible values for a particular type of attribute, but may be used for more than one attribute. For example, the domain of people's names is the underlying set of all possible names that could be used for either customer-name or salesperson-name in the database table in Figure 5.1. Each column in a relational table represents a single attribute, but in some cases more than one column may refer to the same attribute. When this occurs, the table is said to have a repeating group (repeating column), and is therefore unnormalized.

> ***Definition:*** A table is in *first normal form (1NF)* if and only if all columns contain only atomic values; that is, there are no repeating groups (columns) within a row.

A repeating group occurs in a relational table when a multivalued attribute is allowed to have more than one value represented within a single row. When this happens, rows must either be defined as variable length or defined with enough attribute positions to accommodate the maximum possible set of values. For example, the ER diagram in Figure 5.2a would be transformed into an unnormalized table as shown in Figure 5.2b with multiple attribute positions (repeating groups) for author_id, author_name, and author_address. Figure

Sales

product-name	order-no	cust-name	cust-addr	credit	date	sales-name
vacuum cleaner	1458	Dave Bachmann	Austin	6	5-5-92	Carl Bloch
computer	2730	Elena Huang	Mt.View	10	5-6-92	Ted Hanss
refrigerator	2460	Mike Stolarchuck	Ann Arbor	8	7-3-92	Dick Phillips
television	519	Peter Honeyman	Detroit	3	9-5-92	Fred Remley
radio	1986	Charles Antonelli	Chicago	7	9-18-92	R. Metz
CD-player	1817	C.V. Ravishankar	Bombay	8	1-3-93	Paul Basile
vacuum cleaner	1865	Charles Antonelli	Chicago	7	4-18-93	Carl Bloch
vacuum cleaner	1885	Betsy Blower	Detroit	8	5-13-93	Carl Bloch
refrigerator	1943	Dave Bachmann	Austin	6	6-19-93	Dick Phillips
television	2315	Dave Bachmann	Austin	6	7-15-93	Fred Remley

Figure 5.1 Example single table database

5.2c has the equivalent data defined in a normalized (1NF) table that puts each item of author information into a separate row.

The advantages of 1NF over unnormalized tables are its representational simplicity and the ease with which one can develop a query language for it. The disadvantage is the requirement of duplicate data. In this case, for instance, report_no appears in each row where there are multiple authors for a particular report.

5.1.2 Superkeys, Candidate Keys, and Primary Keys

A table in 1NF often suffers from data duplication, update performance, and update integrity problems. In order to understand these issues better, however, the concept of a key needs to be defined in the context of normalized tables. A *superkey* is a set of one or more attributes which, taken collectively, allows us to identify uniquely an entity or table. Any subset of the attributes of a superkey that is also a superkey and not reducible to another superkey is called a *candidate key*. A *primary* key is selected arbitrarily from the set of candidate keys to be used in an index for that table.

As an example, in Figure 5.2c a composite of all the attributes of the table forms a superkey because duplicate rows are not allowed in the relational model. Thus, a trivial superkey is formed from the composite of all attributes in a table. Assuming that each department address (dept_addr) in this table is single valued, we can conclude that the composite of all attributes except dept_addr is also a superkey. Looking at smaller and smaller composites of attributes and making realistic assumptions about which attributes are single

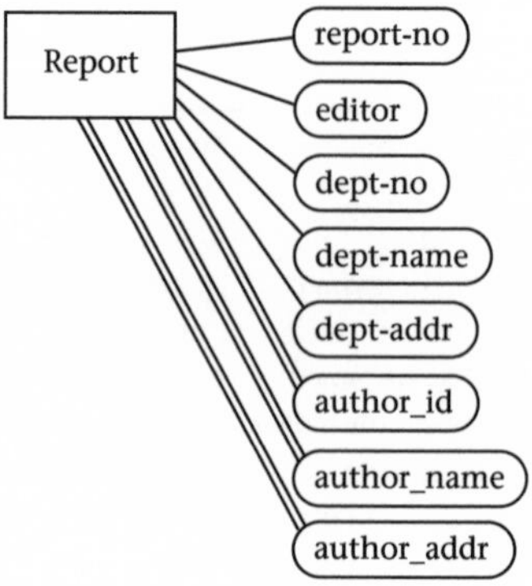

(a) ER diagram for Report

report_no	editor	dept_no	dept_name	dept_addr	author_id	author_name
4216	woolf	15	design	argus 1	53	mantei
5789	koenig	27	analysis	argus 2	26	fry

author_addr	author_id	author_name	author_addr	author_id	author_name	. . .
cs-tor	44	bolton	mathrev	71	koenig	
folkstone	38	umar	prise	71	koenig	

(b) Unnormalized table

Report

report_no	editor	dept_no	dept_name	dept_addr	author_id	author_name	author_addr
4216	woolf	15	design	argus 1	53	mantei	cs-tor
4216	woolf	15	design	argus 1	44	bolton	mathrev
4216	woolf	15	design	argus 1	71	koenig	mathrev
5789	koenig	27	analysis	argus 2	26	fry	folkstone
5789	koenig	27	analysis	argus 2	38	umar	prise
5789	koenig	27	analysis	argus 2	71	koenig	mathrev

(c) Normalized table (1NF)

Figure 5.2 ER diagram and transformation to unnormalized and normalized tables

valued, we find that the composite report_no, author_id uniquely determines all the other attributes in the table and is therefore a superkey. However, neither report_no nor author_id alone can determine a row uniquely, and the composite of these two attributes cannot be reduced and still be a superkey. Thus, the composite report_no, author_id becomes a candidate key. Since it is the only candidate key in this table, it also becomes the primary key.

A table can have more than one candidate key. If, for example, in Figure 5.2c, we had an additional column for author_ssn, and the composite of report_no and author_ssn uniquely determine all the other attributes of the table, then both (report_no, author_id) and (report_no, author_ssn) would be candidate keys. The primary key would then be an arbitrary choice between these two candidate keys.

Other examples of multiple primary keys can be seen in Figure 4.3. In Figure 4.3a the table **uses_notebook** has three candidate keys: (emp_id, project_name), (emp_id, notebook_no), and (project_name, notebook_no); and in Figure 4.3b the table **assigned_to** has two candidate keys: (emp_id, loc_name), and (emp_id, project_name). Figs. 4.3c and 4.3d each have only a single candidate key.

5.1.3 Second Normal Form

The goal of database normalization is to attain at least third normal form (3NF). Thus, first and second normal forms are merely intermediate stages to this goal. However, it helps to understand these stages as stepwise improvements of the database. In order to better understand the concept of second normal form and higher, we introduce the concept of functional dependence, which was briefly described in Chapter 2.

The property of one or more attributes that uniquely determines the value of one or more other attributes is called *functional dependence*. Given a table (R), a set of attributes (B) is functionally dependent on another set of attributes (A) if, at each instant of time, each A value is associated with only one B value. Such a functional dependence is denoted by A–B. In the preceding example from Figure 5.2c, let us assume we are given the following functional dependencies for the table **report:**

report: report_no -> editor, dept_no
dept_no -> dept_name, dept_addr
author_id -> author_name, author_addr

Definition: A table is in *second normal form (2NF)* if and only if it is in 1NF and every nonkey attribute is fully dependent on the primary key. An attribute is fully dependent on the primary key if it is only on the right-hand side of FDs for which the left side is either the primary key itself or something that can be derived from the primary key using the transitivity of FDs.

An example of a transitive FD in report is the following:

report_no -> dept_no
dept_no -> dept_name

Therefore we can derive the FD (report_no -> dept_name), since dept_name is transitively dependent on report_no.

Continuing our example, the composite key in Figure 5.2c, report_no, author_id, is the only candidate key and is therefore the primary key. However, there exist one FD (dept_no -> dept_name, dept_addr) that has no component of the primary key on the left side, and two FDs (report_no -> editor, dept_no and author_id->author_name, author_addr) that contain one component of the primary key on the left side, but not both components. As such, **report** does not satisfy the condition for 2NF for any of the FDs.

Consider the disadvantages of 1NF in table **report**. Report_no, editor, and dept_no are duplicated for each author of the report. Therefore, if the editor of the report changes, for example, several rows must be updated. This is known as the *update anomaly*, and it represents a potential degradation of performance due to the redundant updating. If a new editor is to be added to the table, this can only be done if the new editor is editing a report, since both the report number and editor number must be known to add a row to the table, because you cannot have a primary key with a null value in most relational databases. This is known as the *insert anomaly*. Finally, if a report is withdrawn, all rows associated with that report must be deleted. This has the side effect of deleting the information that associates an author_id with author_name and author_addr. Deletion side effects of this nature are known as *delete anomalies*. They represent a potential loss of integrity because the only way the data can be restored is to find the data somewhere outside the database and insert it back into the database. All three of these anomalies represent problems to database designers, but the delete anomaly is by far the most serious because you might lose data that cannot be recovered.

These disadvantages can be overcome by transforming the 1NF table into two or more 2NF tables by using the projection operator on the subset of the attributes of the 1NF table. In this example we project **report** over report_no, editor, dept_no, dept_name, and dept_addr to form **report1**; and project **report** over author_id, author_name, and author_addr to form **report2**; and finally project **report** over report_no and author_id to form **report3**. The projection of **report** into three smaller tables has preserved the FDs and the association between report_no and author_no that was important in the original table. Data for the three tables is shown in Figure 5.3. The FDs for these 2NF tables are:

Report 1

report_no	editor	dept_no	dept_name	dept_addr
4216	woolf	15	design	argus 1
5789	koenig	27	analysis	argus 2

Report 2

author_id	author_name	author_addr
53	mantei	cs-tor
44	bolton	mathrev
71	koenig	mathrev
26	fry	folkstone
38	umar	prise
71	koenig	mathrev

Report 3

report_no	author_id
4216	53
4216	44
4216	71
5789	26
5789	38
5789	71

Figure 5.3 2NF tables

report1: report_no –> editor, dept_no
dept_no –> dept_name, dept_addr

report2: author_id –> author_name, author_addr

report3: report_no, author_id is a candidate key (no FDs)

We now have three tables that satisfy the conditions for 2NF, and we have eliminated the worst problems of 1NF, especially integrity (the delete anomaly). First, editor, dept_no, dept_name, and dept_addr are no longer duplicated for each author of a report. Second, an editor change results in only an update to one row for **report1**. And third, the most important, the deletion of the report does not have the side effect of deleting the author information.

Not all performance degradation is eliminated, however. Report_no is still duplicated for each author and deletion of a report requires updates to two tables (**report1** and **report3**) instead of one. However, these are minor problems compared to those in the 1NF table **report**.

Note that these three report tables in 2NF could have been generated directly from an ER diagram that equivalently modeled this situation with entities Author and Report and a many-to-many relationship between them.

5.1.4 Third Normal Form

The 2NF tables we established in the previous section represent a significant improvement over 1NF tables; however, they still suffer from the same types of anomalies as the 1NF tables, but for different reasons associated with transitive dependencies. If a transitive (functional) dependency exists in a table, it means that two separate facts are represented in that table, one fact for each functional dependency involving a different left side. For example, if we delete a report from the database, which involves deleting the appropriate rows from **report1** and **report3** (see Figure 5.3), we have the side effect of deleting the association between dept_no, dept_name, and dept_addr as well. If we could project table **report1** over report_no, editor, and dept_no to form table **report11**, and project **report1** over dept_no, dept_name, and dept_addr to form table **report12**, we could eliminate this problem. Example tables for **report11** and**report12** are shown in Figure 5.4.

> ***Definition:*** A table is in *third normal form (3NF)* if and only if for every nontrivial functional dependency X–>A, where X and A are either simple or composite attributes, one of two conditions must hold. Either attribute X is a superkey, or attribute A is a member of a candidate key. If attribute A is a member of a candidate key, A is called a prime attribute. Note: A trivial FD is of the form YZ–>Z.

In the preceding example, after projecting **report1** into **report11** and **report12** to eliminate the transitive dependency report_no –> dept_no –> dept_name, dept_addr, we have the following 3NF tables and their functional dependencies (and example data in Figure 5.4):

report11: report_no –> editor, dept_no

report12: dept_no –> dept_name, dept_addr

report2: author_id –> author_name, author_addr

report3: report_no, author_id is a candidate key (no FDs)

Report 11

report_no	editor	dept_no
4216	woolf	15
5789	koenig	27

Report 12

dept_no	dept_name	dept_addr
15	design	argus 1
27	analysis	argus 2

Report 2

author_id	author_name	author_addr
53	mantei	cs-tor
44	bolton	mathrev
71	koenig	mathrev
26	fry	folkstone
38	umar	prise
71	koenig	mathrev

Report 3

report_no	author_id
4216	53
4216	44
4216	71
5789	26
5789	38
5789	71

Figure 5.4 3NF tables

5.1.5 Boyce-Codd Normal Form

Third normal form, which eliminates most of the anomalies known in databases today, is the most common standard for normalization in commercial databases and CASE tools. The few remaining anomalies can be eliminated by the Boyce-Codd normal form and higher normal forms defined here and in Section 5.5. Boyce-Codd normal form is considered to be a strong variation of 3NF.

> ***Definition:*** A table R is in *Boyce-Codd normal form (BCNF)* if for every nontrivial FD X–>A, X is a superkey.

BCNF is a stronger form of normalization than 3NF because it eliminates the second condition for 3NF, which allowed the right side of the FD to be a prime attribute. Thus, every left side of an FD in a table must be a superkey. Every table that is BCNF is also 3NF, 2NF, and 1NF, by the previous definitions.

The following example shows a 3NF table that is not BCNF. Such tables have delete anomalies similar to those in the lower normal forms.

> ***Assertion 1:*** For a given team, each employee is directed by only one leader. A team may be directed by more than one leader.
>
> emp_name, team_name –> leader_name

Assertion 2: Each leader directs only one team.

leader_name -> team_name

This table is 3NF with a composite candidate key emp_name, team_name:

team:

emp_name	team_name	leader_name
Sutton	Hawks	Wei
Sutton	Condors	Bachmann
Niven	Hawks	Wei
Niven	Eagles	Makowski
Wilson	Eagles	DeSmith

The **team** table has the following delete anomaly: If Sutton drops out of the Condors team, then we have no record of Bachmann leading the Condors team. As shown by Date [Date86], this type of anomaly cannot have a lossless decomposition and preserve all FDs. A lossless decomposition requires that when you decompose the table into two smaller tables by projecting the original table over two overlapping subsets of the scheme, the natural join of those subset tables must result in the original table without any extra unwanted rows. The simplest way to avoid the delete anomaly for this kind of situation is to create a separate table for each of the two assertions. These two tables are partially redundant, enough so as to avoid the delete anomaly. This decomposition is lossless (trivially) and preserves functional dependencies, but it also degrades update performance due to redundancy, and necessitates additional storage space. The trade-off is often worth it because the delete anomaly is avoided.

5.2 The Design of Normalized Tables: A Simple Example

The example in this section is based on the ER diagram in Figure 5.5 and the FDs given below. In general, FDs can be given explicitly, derived from the ER diagram or from intuition (that is, from experience with the problem domain).

1. emp_id, start_date -> job_title, end_date
2. emp_id -> emp_name, phone_no, office_no, proj_no, proj_name, dept_no
3. phone_no -> office_no
4. proj_no -> proj_name, proj_start_date, proj_end_date
5. dept_no -> dept_name, mgr_id
6. mgr_id -> dept_no

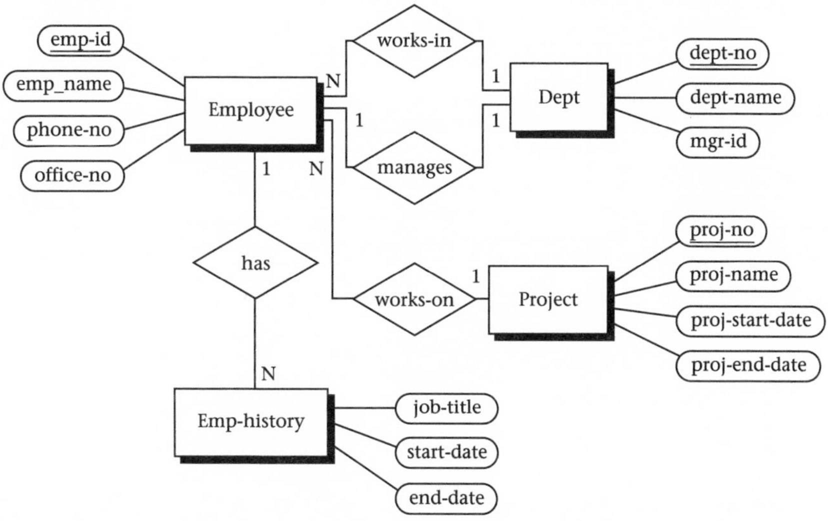

Figure 5.5 ER diagram for employee database example

Our objective is to design a relational database schema that is normalized to at least 3NF and, if possible, minimize the number of tables required. Our approach is to apply the definition of third normal form (3NF) in Section 5.1.3 to the FDs given above, and create tables that satisfy the definition.

If we try to put (1) through (6) into a single table with the composite candidate key (and primary key) emp_id, start_date we violate the 3NF definition because FDs (2) through (6) involve left sides of FDs that are not superkeys. Consequently, we need to separate (1) from the rest of the FDs. If we then try to combine (2) through (6), we have many transitivities. Intuitively, we know that (2), (3), (4), and (5) must be separated into different tables because of transitive dependencies. We then must decide whether (5) and (6) can be combined without loss of 3NF; this can be done because mgr_id and dept_no are mutually dependent and both attributes are superkeys in a combined table. Thus, we can define the following tables by appropriate projections from (1) through (6).

emp_hist:	emp_id, start_date –> job_title, end_date
employee:	emp_id –> emp_name, phone_no, proj_no, dept_no
phone:	phone_no –> office_no
project:	proj_no –> proj_name, proj_start_date, proj_end_date
department:	dept_no –> dept_name, mgr_id mgr_id –> dept_no

This solution, which is BCNF as well as 3NF, maintains all the original FDs. It is also a minimum set of normalized tables. In Section 5.4 we will look at a formal method of determining a minimum set that we can apply to much more complex situations.

Alternative designs may involve splitting tables into partitions for volatile (frequently updated) and passive (rarely updated) data, consolidating tables to get better query performance, or duplicating data in different tables to get better query performance without losing integrity. In summary, the measures we use to assess the trade-offs in our design are

- query performance (time),
- update performance (time),
- storage performance (space), and
- integrity (avoidance of delete anomalies).

Analysis of these trade-offs is discussed in detail in Chapters 6 and 7.

5.3 Normalization of Candidate Tables Derived from ER Diagrams

Normalization of candidate tables (Step IId in the database life cycle) is accomplished by analyzing the FDs associated with those tables: explicit FDs from the database requirements analysis (Section 5.2), FDs derived from the ER diagram, and FDs derived from intuition.

Primary FDs represent the dependencies among the data elements that are keys of entities—that is, the interentity dependencies. *Secondary FDs*, on the other hand, represent dependencies among data elements that comprise a single entity—that is, the intra-entity dependencies. Typically, primary FDs are derived from the ER diagram and secondary FDs are obtained explicitly from the requirements analysis. If the ER constructs do not include nonkey attributes used in secondary FDs, the data requirements specification or data dictionary must be consulted. Table 5.1 shows the types of primary FDs derivable from each type of ER construct, consistent with the derivable candidate tables in Figs. 4.1 through 4.4.

Each candidate table will typically have several primary and secondary FDs uniquely associated with it which determine the current degree of normalization of the table. Any of the well-known techniques for increasing the degree of normalization can be applied to each table, to the desired degree stated in the requirements specification. Integrity is maintained by requiring the normalized table schema to include all data dependencies existing in the candidate table schema.

Any table B that is subsumed by another table A can potentially be eliminated. Table B is subsumed by another table A when all the attributes in B are also contained in A, and all data dependencies in B also occur in A. As a trivial case, any table containing only a composite key and no nonkey attributes is automatically subsumed by any other table containing the same key attributes because the composite key is the weakest form of data dependency. If, however, tables A and B represent the supertype and subtype cases, respectively, of entities defined by the generalization abstraction, and A subsumes B because B has no additional specific attributes, the designer must collect and analyze additional information to decide whether or not to eliminate B.

A table can also be subsumed by the construction of a join of two other tables (a "join" table). When this occurs, the elimination of a subsumed table may result in the loss of retrieval efficiency, although storage and update costs will tend to be decreased. This trade-off must be further analyzed during physical design with regard to processing requirements, to determine whether elimination of the subsumed table is reasonable (see Chapter 6).

Table 5.1 Primary FDs derivable from ER relationship constructs

Degree	*Connectivity*	*Primary FD*
Binary or	one-to-one	2 ways: key(one side) –> key(one side)
Binary	one-to-many	key(many side) –> key(one side)
Recursive	many-to-many	none (composite key from both sides)
Ternary	one-to-one-to-one	3 ways: key(one), key(one) –> key(one)
	one-to-one-to-many	2 ways: key(one), key(many) –> key(one)
	one-to-many-to-many	1 way: key(many), key(many) –> key(one)
	many-to-many-to-many	none (composite key from all 3 sides)
Generalization	none	none(secondary FD only)

To continue our example company personnel and project database, we want to obtain the primary FDs by applying the rules in Table 5.1 to each relationship in the ER diagram in Figure 3.3. The results are shown in Table 5.2.

Table 5.2 Primary FDs derived from the ER diagram in Figure 3.3

dept_no –> div_no	in Department from relationship "contains"
emp_id –> dept_no	in Employee from relationship "has"
div_no –> emp_id	in Division from relationship "is-headed-by"
dept_no –> emp_id	from binary relationship "is-managed-by"
emp_id –> desktop_no	from binary relationship "has-allocated"
desktop_no –> emp_no	from binary relationship "has-allocated"
emp_id –> spouse_id	from binary recursive relationship "is-married-to"
spouse_id –> emp_id	from binary recursive relationship "is-married-to"
emp_id, loc_name –> project_name	from ternary relationship "assigned-to"

Next we want to determine the secondary FDs. Let us assume that the dependencies in Table 5.3 are derived from the requirements specification and intuition:

Table 5.3 Secondary FDs derived from the requirements specification

div_no –> div_name, div_addr	from entity Division
dept_no –> dept_name, dept_addr, mgr_id	from entity Department
emp_id –> emp_name, emp_addr, office_no, phone_no	from entity Employee
skill_type –> skill_descrip	from entity Skill
project_name –> start_date, end_date, head_id	from entity Project
loc_name –> loc_county, loc_state, zip	from entity Location
mgr_id –> mgr_start_date	beeper_phone_no
assoc_name –> assoc_addr, phone_no, start_date	from entity Prof-assoc
desktop_no –> computer_type, serial_no	from entity Desktop

Normalization of the candidate tables is accomplished next. In Table 5.4 we bring together the primary and secondary FDs that apply to each candidate table. We note that for each table except **employee**, all attributes are functionally dependent on the primary key (denoted by the left side of the FDs) and are thus BCNF. In the case of table **employee** we note that spouse_id determines emp_id and emp_id is the primary key; thus, spouse_id can be shown to be a superkey (see Superkey Rule 2 in Section 5.4). Therefore, **employee** is found to be BCNF.

In general we observe that candidate tables, like the ones shown in Table 4.1, are fairly good indicators of the final schema and normally require very little refinement to get to 3NF or BCNF.

Table 5.4 Candidate tables (and FDs) from ER diagram transformation

division	div_no -> div_name, div_addr div_no -> emp_id
department	dept_no -> dept_name, dept_addr, mgr_id dept_no -> div_no dept_no -> emp_id
employee	emp_id -> emp_name, emp_addr, office_no, phone_no emp_id -> dept_no emp_id -> spouse_id spouse_id -> emp_id
manager	mgr_id -> mgr_start_date, beeper_phone_no
secretary	none
engineer	emp_id -> desktop_no
technician	none
skill	skill_type -> skill_descrip
project	project_name -> start_date, end_date, head_id
location	loc_name -> loc_county, loc_state, zip
prof_assoc	assoc_name -> assoc_addr, phone_no, start_date
desktop	desktop_no -> computer_type, serial_no desktop_no -> emp_no
assigned_to	emp_id, loc_name -> project_name
skill_used	none

5.4 Determining the Minimum Set of 3NF Tables

A minimum set of 3NF tables can be obtained from a given set of FDs by using the well-known synthesis algorithm developed by Bernstein [Bern76]. This process is particularly useful when you are confronted with a list of hundreds or thousands of FDs that describe the semantics of a database. In practice, the ER modeling process automatically decomposes this problem into smaller subproblems: the attributes and FDs of interest are restricted to those attributes within an entity (and its equivalent table) and any foreign keys that might be imposed upon that table. Thus, the database designer will rarely have to deal with more than ten or twenty attributes at a time, and in fact most entities are initially defined in 3NF already. For those tables that are not yet in 3NF, only minor adjustments will be needed in most cases.

In the following we briefly describe the synthesis algorithm for those situations where the ER model is not useful for the decomposition. In order to apply the algorithm, we make use of the well-known Armstrong axioms, which define the basic relationships among FDs.

Inference rules (Armstrong axioms):

Reflexivity	If Y is a subset of the attributes of X, then X–>Y (i.e., if X is ABCD and Y is ABC, then X–>Y. Trivially, X–>X).
Augmentation	If X–>Y and Z is a subset of table R (i.e., Z is any attribute in R), then XZ–>YZ.
Transitivity	If X–>Y and Y–>Z, then X–>Z.
Pseudotransitivity	If X–>Y and YW–>Z, then XW–>Z.
	(Transitivity is a special case of pseudotransitivity when W=null.)
Union	If X–>Y and X–>Z, then X–>YZ (or equivalently, X–>Y,Z).
Decomposition	If X–>YZ, then X–>Y and X–>Z.

These axioms can be used to derive two practical rules of thumb for deriving superkeys of tables, where at least one superkey is already known.

Superkey Rule 1: Any FD involving all attributes of a table defines a superkey as the left side of the FD.

Given: any FD containing all attributes in the table **R** (W,X,Y,Z), that is, XY–>WZ.

Proof:

1. XY–>WZ as given.
2. XY–>XY by applying the reflexivity axiom.
3. XY–>XYWZ by applying the union axiom.
4. XY uniquely determines every attribute in table **R**, as shown in (3).
5. XY uniquely defines table **R**, by the definition of a table as having no duplicate rows.
6. XY is therefore a superkey, by definition.

Superkey Rule 2: Any attribute that functionally determines a superkey of a table is also a superkey for that table.

Given: Attribute A is a superkey for table **R** (A,B,C,D,E), and E–>A.

Proof:

1. Attribute A uniquely defines each row in table **R**, by the definition of a superkey.
2. A–>ABCDE by applying the definition of a superkey and a relational table.
3. E–>A as given.
4. E–>ABCDE by applying the transitivity axiom.
5. E is a superkey for table **R**, by definition.

Before we can describe the synthesis algorithm, we must define some important concepts. Let H be a set of FDs that represents at least part of the known semantics of a database. The closure of H, specified by H^+, is the set of all FDs derivable from H using the Armstrong axioms or inference rules. For example, we can apply the transitivity rule to the following FDs in set H:

A–>B, B–>C, A–>C, and C–>D

to derive the FDs A–>D and B–>D. All six FDs constitute the closure H^+. A cover of H, called H′, is any set of FDs from which H^+ can be derived. Possible covers for this example are:

1. A–>B, B–>C, C–>D, A–>C, A–>D, B–>D (trivial case where H′ and H^+ are equal)
2. A–>B, B–>C, C–>D, A–>C, A–>D
3. A–>B, B–>C, C–>D, A–>C (this is the original set H)
4. A–>B, B–>C, C–>D

A nonredundant cover of H is a cover of H which contains no proper subset of FDs which is also a cover. The synthesis algorithm requires nonredundant covers.

3NF Synthesis Algorithm

Given a set of FDs, H, we determine a minimum set of tables in 3NF.

H:	AB –> C	DM –> NP
	A –> DEFG	D –> M
	E –> G	L –> D
	F –> DJ	PQR –> ST
	G –> DI	PR –> S
	D –> KL	

From this point the process of arriving at the minimum set of 3NF tables consists of five steps:

1. elimination of extraneous attributes in the determinants of the FDs;
2. search for a nonredundant cover, G of H;
3. partitioning of G into groups so that all FDs with the same left side are in one group;
4. merge of equivalent keys; and
5. search for a nonredundant cover again and definition of tables.

Now we will discuss each step in turn, in terms of the preceding set of FDs, H.

5.4.1 Elimination of Extraneous Attributes

The first task is to get rid of extraneous attributes in the determinants of the FDs.

The following two relationships among attributes on the left side (determinant) of an FD provide the means to reduce the left side to fewer attributes.

1. XY –> Z and X –> Z => Y is extraneous on the left side (applying the reflexivity and transitivity axioms).
2. XY –> Z and X –> Y => Y is extraneous; therefore X –> Z (applying the pseudotransitivity axiom).

Applying these relationships to the set of FDs in H, we get:

DM–>NP and D–>M => D–>NP
PQR–>ST and PR–>S => PQR–>T

5.4.2 Search for a Nonredundant Cover

We must eliminate any FD derivable from others in H using the inference rules.

Transitive FDs to be eliminated:

A–>E and E–>G => eliminate A–>G
A–>F and F–>D => eliminate A–>D

5.4.3 Partitioning of the Nonredundant Cover

To partition the nonredundant cover into groups so that all FDs with the same left side are in one group, we must separate the non-fully functional dependencies and transitive dependencies into separate tables. At this point we have a feasible solution for 3NF tables, but it is not necessarily the minimum set.

These non-fully functional dependencies must be put into separate tables:

AB–>C
A–>EF

Groups with the same left side:

G1:	AB–>C	G6:	D–>KLMNP
G2:	A–> EF	G7:	L–>D
G3:	E–>G	G8:	PQR–>T
G4:	G–>DI	G9:	PR–>S
G5:	F–>DJ		

5.4.4 Merge of Equivalent Keys

In this step we merge groups with determinants that are equivalent (e.g., X–>Y and Y–>X imply that X and Y are equivalent). This step produces a minimal set. Groups G6 and G7 have D–>L and L–>D. Therefore, merge these groups into a single group G67: with FDs D–>KLMNP and L–>D. We can also merge groups when the right-hand side of an FD is a prime attribute because this satisfies 3NF.

5.4.5 Definition of Tables

The minimum set has now been computed.

Tables and FDs: **R1**:	AB–>C	**R5**:	F–>DJ
R2:	A–>EF	**R6**:	D–>KLMNP and L–>D
R3:	E–>G	**R7**:	PQR–>T
R4:	G–>DI	**R8**:	PR–>S

Note that this result is not only 3NF, but also BCNF, which is very frequently the case. This fact suggests a practical algorithm for a (near) minimum set of BCNF tables: Use Bernstein's algorithm to attain a minimum set of 3NF tables, then inspect each table for further decomposition (or partial replication, as shown in Section 5.1.5) to BCNF.

5.5 Fourth and Fifth Normal Forms

Normal forms up to BCNF were defined solely on FDs, and for most database practitioners, either 3NF or BCNF is a sufficient level of normalization. However, there are in fact two more normal forms that are needed to eliminate the rest of the currently known anomalies. In this section we will look at different types of constraints on tables: multivalued dependencies and join dependencies. If these constraints do not exist in a table, which is the most common situation, then any table in BCNF is automatically in fourth normal form (4NF) and fifth normal form (5NF) as well. However, when these constraints do exist, there may be further update (especially delete) anomalies that need to be corrected. First, we must define the concept of multivalued dependency.

5.5.1 Multivalued Dependencies

Definition: In a *multivalued dependency (MVD)*, X–>>Y holds on table **R** with table scheme RS if, whenever a valid instance of table **R**(X,Y,Z) contains a pair of rows that contain duplicate values of X, then the instance also contains the pair of rows obtained by interchanging the Y values in the original pair. This includes situations where only pairs of rows exist. Note that X and Y may contain either single or composite attributes.

An MVD X –>> Y is trivial if Y is a subset of X, or if X union Y = RS. Finally, an FD implies an MVD, which implies that a single row with a given value of X is also an MVD, albeit a trivial form.

The following examples show where an MVD does and does not exist in a table. In **R1**, the first four rows satisfy all conditions for the MVDs X–>>Y and X–>>Z. Note that MVDs appear in pairs because of the cross-product type of relationship between Y and Z=RS–Y as the two right sides of the two MVDs. The fifth and sixth rows of **R1** (when the X value is 2) satisfy the row interchange conditions in the above definition. In both rows the Y value is 2, so the interchanging of Y values is trivial. The seventh row (3,3,3) satisfies the definition trivially.

In table **R2**, however, the Y values in the fifth and sixth rows are different (1 and 2), and interchanging the 1 and 2 values for Y results in a row (2,2,2) that does not appear in the table. Thus in **R2** there is no MVD between X and Y or between X and Z, even though the first four rows satisfy the MVD definition. Note that for the MVD to exist, all rows must satisfy the criterion for an MVD.

Table **R3** contains the first three rows that do not satisfy the criterion for an MVD, since changing Y from 1 to 2 in the second row results in a row that does not appear in the table. Similarly, changing Z from 1 to 2 in the third row results in a nonappearing row. Thus **R3** does not have any MVDs between X and Y or between X and Z.

R1:

X	Y	Z
1	1	1
1	1	2
1	2	1
1	2	2
2	2	1
2	2	2
3	3	3

R2:

X	Y	Z
1	1	1
1	1	2
1	2	1
1	2	2
2	2	1
2	1	2

R3:

X	Y	Z
1	1	1
1	1	2
1	2	1
2	2	1
2	2	2

By the same argument, in table **R1** we have the MVDs Y–>> X and Y–>>Z, but none with Z on the left side. Tables **R2** and **R3** have no MVDs at all.

The following inference rules for multivalued dependencies are somewhat analogous to the inference rules for functional dependencies given in Section 5.4 [BFH77]. They are quite useful in the analysis and decomposition of tables into 4NF.

Multivalued dependency inference rules

Reflexivity	X —>> X.
Augmentation	If X —>> Y, then XZ —>> Y.
Transitivity	If X —>>Y and Y —>> Z, then X —>> (Z-Y).
Pseudotransitivity	If X —>> Y and YW —>> Z, then XW —>> (Z-YW). (Transitivity is a special case of pseudotransitivity when W is null.)
Union	If X —>> Y and X —>> Z, then X —>> YZ.
Decomposition	If X —>> Y and X —>> Z, then X —>> Y intersect Z and X —>> (Z–Y).
Complement	If X —>> Y and Z=R–X–Y, then X —>> Z.
FD implies MVD	If X -> Y, then X —>> Y.
FD, MVD mix	If X —>> Y and Z —>> W (where W is contained in Y and Y intersect Z is not empty), then X–>W.

5.5.2 Fourth Normal Form

The goal of fourth normal form is to eliminate nontrivial MVDs from a table by projecting them onto separate smaller tables and thus eliminate the update anomalies associated with the MVDs. This type of normal form is reasonably easy to attain if you know where the MVDs are. In general, MVDs must be defined from the semantics of the database; they cannot be determined from just looking at the data. The current set of data can only verify whether your assumption about an MVD is currently true or not, but this may change each time the data is updated.

> ***Definition.*** A table R is in *fourth normal form (4NF)* if and only if it is in BCNF and, whenever there exists an MVD in R (say X –>> Y), at least one of the following holds: The MVD is trivial or X is a superkey for R.

Applying this definition to the three tables in the example in the previous section, we see that **R1** is not in 4NF because at least one nontrivial MVD exists and no single column is a superkey. In tables **R2** and **R3**, however, there are no MVDs. Thus, these two tables are at least 4NF.

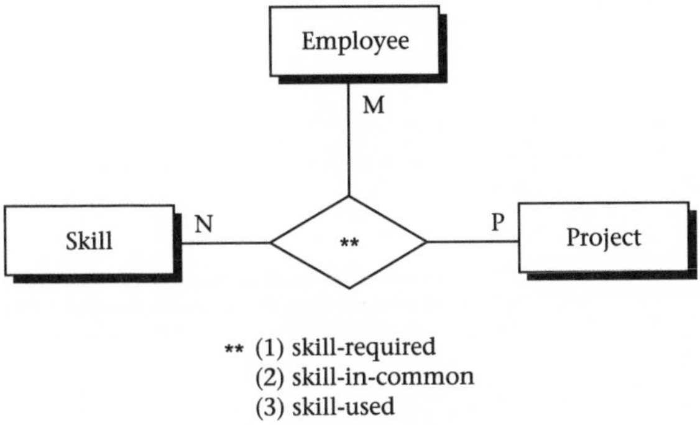

Figure 5.6 Many-to-many-to-many ternary relationship with multiple interpretations

As an example of the transformation of a table that is not in 4NF to two tables that are in 4NF, we observe the ternary relationship skill-required shown in Figure 5.6. The relationship skill-required is defined as "An employee must have all the required skills needed for a project to work on that project." For example, in Table 5.5 the project with proj_no = 3 requires skill types A and B by all employees (see employees 101 and 102). The table **skill_required** has no FDs, but it does have several nontrivial MVDs and is therefore only in BCNF. In such a case it can have a lossless decomposition into two many-to-many binary relationships between the entities Employee and Project, and Project and Skill. Each of these two new relationships represents a table in 4NF. It can also have a lossless decomposition resulting in a binary many-to-many relationship between the entities Employee and Skill, and Project and Skill.

Table 5.5 The table skill_required and its three projections

skill_required	emp_id	proj_no	skill_type	*MVDs (nontrivial)*
	101	3	A	proj_no –>> skill_type
	101	3	B	proj_no –>> emp_id
	101	4	A	
	101	4	C	
	102	3	A	
	102	3	B	
	103	5	D	

(Table 5.5 continues on the following page)

Table 5.5 Continued

skill_req1		*skill_req2*		*skill_req3*	
emp_id	proj_no	emp_id	skill_type	proj_no	skill_type
101	3	101	A	3	A
101	4	101	B	3	B
102	3	101	C	4	A
103	5	102	A	4	C
		102	B	5	D
		103	D		

A two-way lossless decomposition occurs when **skill_required** is projected over {emp_id, proj_no} to form skill_req1 and projected over {proj_no, skill} to form skill_req3. Projection over {emp_id, proj_no} to form skill_req1 and over {emp_id, skill} to form skill_req2, however, is not lossless. A 3-way lossless decomposition occurs when **skill_required** is projected over {emp_id, proj_no}, {emp_id, skill}, and {proj_no, skill}.

Tables in 4NF avoid certain update anomalies (or inefficiences). For instance, a delete anomaly exists when two independent facts get tied together unnaturally so there may be bad side effects of certain deletes. For example, in **skill_required** the last row of a skill_type may be lost if an employee is temporarily not working on any projects. An update inefficiency may occur when adding a new project in **skill_required**, which requires insertions for many rows to include all the required skills for that new project. Likewise, loss of a project requires many deletions. These inefficiencies are avoided when skill_required is decomposed into skill_req1 and skill_req3. In general (but not always), decomposition of a table into 4NF tables results in less data redundancy.

5.5.3 Decomposing Tables to 4NF

Algorithms to decompose tables into 4NF are difficult to develop. We look at some straightforward approaches to 4NF from BCNF and lower normal forms. First, if a table is BCNF, it either has no FDs, or each FD is characterized by its left side being a superkey. Thus, if the only MVDs in this table are derived from its FDs, they have only superkeys as their left sides, and the table is 4NF by definition. If, however, there are other nontrivial MVDs whose left sides are not superkeys, the table is only in BCNF and must be decomposed to achieve higher normalization.

The basic decomposition process from a BCNF table is defined by selecting the most important MVD (or if that is not possible, then by selecting one arbitrarily), defining its complement MVD, and decomposing the table into two tables containing the attributes on the left and right sides of that MVD and its complement. This type of decomposition is lossless because each new table is based on the same attribute which is the left side of both MVDs. The same MVDs in these new tables are now trivial because they contain every attribute in the table. However, other MVDs may still be present, and more decompositions by MVDs and their complements may be necessary. This process of arbitrary selection of MVDs for decomposition is continued until only trivial MVDs exist, leaving the final tables in 4NF.

As an example, let **R**(A,B,C,D,E,F) with no FDs, and with MVDs A –>> B and CD –>> EF. The first decomposition of **R** is into two tables **R1**(A,B) and **R2**(A,C,D,E,F) by applying the MVD A –>> B and its complement A –>> CDEF. Table **R1** is now 4NF because A –>> B is trivial and is the only MVD in the table. Table **R2**, however, is still only BCNF because of the nontrivial MVD CD –>> EF. We then decompose **R2** into **R21**(C,D,E,F) and **R2**(C,D,A) by applying the MVD CD –>> EF and its complement CD –>> A. Both **R21** and **R22** are now 4NF. If we had applied the MVD complement rule in the opposite order, using CD –>> EF and its complement CD –>> AB first, the same three 4NF tables would result from this method. However, this does not occur in all cases, but only those tables where the MVDs have no intersecting attributes.

This method, in general, has the unfortunate side effect of potentially losing some or all the FDs and MVDs. Therefore, any decision to transform tables from BCNF to 4NF must take into account the trade-off between normalization and the elimination of delete anomalies, and the preservation of FDs and possibly MVDs. It should also be noted that this approach derives a feasible, but not necessarily a minimum, set of 4NF tables.

A second approach to decomposing BCNF tables is to ignore the MVDs completely and split each BCNF table into a set of smaller tables with the candidate key of each BCNF table being the candidate key of a new table, with the nonkey attributes distributed among the new tables in some semantically meaningful way. This form of decomposing by candidate key (that is, superkey) is lossless because the candidate keys uniquely join; and it usually results in the simplest form of 5NF tables, those with a candidate key and one nonkey attribute, and no MVDs. However, if a table thus constructed has a composite key and there exists one or more MVDs still, further decomposition must be done with the MVD/MVD-complement approach given above. The decomposition by candidate keys preserves FDs, but the MVD/MVD-complement approach does not preserve either FDs or MVDs.

Tables that are not yet in BCNF can also be directly decomposed into 4NF using the MVD/MVD-complement approach. Such tables can often be decomposed into smaller minimum sets than those derived from transforming into BCNF first and then 4NF, but with a greater cost of lost FDs. In most database design situations, it is preferable to develop BCNF tables first, then evaluate the need to normalize further while preserving the FDs.

5.5.4 Fifth Normal Form

> ***Definition:*** A table is in *fifth normal form (5NF)* if it cannot have a lossless decomposition by the projection operation into any number of smaller tables.

As we recall, a lossless decomposition of a table implies that it can be decomposed by two or more projections, followed by a natural join of those projections (in any order) that results in the original table, without any spurious or missing rows. The general lossless decomposition constraint, involving any number of projections, is also known as a *join dependency (JD)*. In other words, a table is not in 5NF if it can be lossless decomposed/joined via some n1 projections.

A lossless decomposition of two projections is equivalent to an MVD, and the table may be in BCNF (if the MVD is trivial) or 4NF (if the MVD is trivial or the left side is a superkey). A lossless decomposition of three or more projections is equivalent to a JD, and the table is only in 4NF. Thus, an MVD is a special case of a JD where the number of projections is two. It is difficult to determine if a table is in 5NF, but for ternary relationship tables, the number of possible decompositions is small and tractable (several examples follow).

If a table is already 4NF, with at least some of the FDs preserved, then the most appropriate decomposition to 5NF is by candidate key, with each smaller table having the candidate key replicated and one nonkey associated with the candidate key. If there is only one candidate key—the composite of all attributes—further decomposition is accomplished by trial and error using various (more than two) subsets of the table's attributes.

The following example demonstrates a situation with two seemingly similar tables, one that is 5NF and another that is not. A table representing a ternary relationship may not have any two-way lossless decompositions; however, it may have a three-way lossless decomposition, which is equivalent to three binary relationships based on the three possible projections of this table. This situation occurs in the relationship skill-in-common (Figure 5.6), which is defined as "The employee must apply the intersection of his or her available skills with the skills needed to work on certain projects." In this example skill-in-common is less restrictive than skill-required because it allows an employee to work on a project even if he or she does not have all the skills required for that project. The associated table, **skill_in_common**, is in 4NF because it has no MVDs, but it is not 5NF because it can have a lossless decomposition into three binary tables. In general, if the relationship can be represented as a 5NF table, then it is truly ternary; otherwise, it can be decomposed into equivalent binary relationships.

As Table 5.6 shows, the three projections of **skill_in_common** result in a three-way lossless decomposition. There are no two-way lossless decompositions and no MVDs; thus, the table **skill_in_common** is in 4NF.

Table 5.6 The table skill_in_common and its three projections

skill_in_common	emp_id	proj_no	skill_type
	101	3	A
	101	3	B
	101	4	A
	101	4	B
	102	3	A
	102	3	B
	103	3	A
	103	4	A
	103	5	A
	103	5	C

skill_in_com1		*skill_in_com2*		*skill_in_com3*	
emp_id	proj_no	emp_id	skill_type	emp_id	skill_type
101	3	101	A	3	A
101	4	101	B	3	B
102	3	102	A	4	A
103	3	102	B	4	B
103	4	103	A	5	A
103	5	103	C	5	C

The ternary relationship in Figure 5.6 can be interpreted yet another way. The meaning of the relationship skill-used is We can selectively record different skills that each employee applies to working on individual projects. It is equivalent to a table in 5NF that cannot be decomposed into either two or three binary tables. Note by studying Table 5.7 that the associated table, **skill_used**, has no MVDs or JDs.

Table 5.7 The table skill_used, its three projections, and natural joins of its projections

skill_used

emp_id	proj_no	skill_type
101	3	A
101	3	B
101	4	A
101	4	C
102	3	A
102	3	B
102	4	A
102	4	B

Three projections on **skill_used** result in:

skill_used1

emp_id	proj_no
101	3
101	4
102	3
102	4

skill_used2

proj_no	skill_type
3	A
3	B
4	A
4	B
4	C

skill_used3

emp_id	skill_type
101	A
101	B
101	C
102	A
102	B

join **skill_used1** with **skill_used2** to form:

skill_used_12

emp_id	proj_no	skill_type
101	3	A
101	3	B
101	4	A
101	4	B
101	4	C
102	3	A
102	3	B
102	4	A
102	4	B
102	4	C

join **skill_used12** with **skill_used3** to form:

skill_used_123

emp_id	proj_no	skill_type
101	3	A
101	3	B
101	4	A
101	**4**	**B (spurious tuple)**
101	4	C
102	3	A
102	3	B
102	4	A
102	4	B

A table may have constraints that are FDs, MVDs, and JDs. An MVD is a special case of a JD. In order to determine the level of normalization of the table, analyze the FDs first to determine normalization through BCNF; then analyze the MVDs to determine which BCNF tables are also 4NF; and, finally, analyze the JDs to determine which 4NF tables are also 5NF.

A many-to-many-to-many ternary relationship is:

1. BCNF if it can be replaced by two binary relationships,
2. 4NF if it can only be replaced by three binary relationships, and
3. 5NF if it cannot be replaced in any way (and thus is a true ternary relationship).

We observe the equivalence between certain ternary relationships and the higher normal form tables transformed from those relationships. Ternary relationships that have at least one "one" entity cannot be decomposed (or broken down) into binary relationships because that would destroy the one or more functional dependencies required in the definition, as shown above. A ternary relationship with all "many" entities, however, has no FDs, but in some cases may have MVDs, and thus have a lossless decomposition into equivalent binary relationships.

In summary, the three common cases that illustrate the correspondence between a lossless decomposition in a many-to-many-to-many ternary relationship table and higher normal forms in the relational model are shown Table 5.8 below:

Table 5.8 Summary of higher normal forms

Table name	*Normal form*	*2-way lossless decomp/ join?*	*3-way lossless decomp/ join?*	*Nontrivial MVDs*
skill_required	BCNF	yes	yes	2
skill_in_common	4NF	no	yes	0
skill_used	5NF	no	no	0

5.6 Summary

In this chapter we defined the constraints imposed on tables: FDs, MVDs, and JDs. Based on these constraints, normal forms for database tables were defined: 1NF, 2NF, 3NF, and BCNF. All are based on the types of FDs present. The 4NFs and 5NFs are dependent on the type of MVDs and JDs present. In this chapter, a practical algorithm for finding the minimum set of 3NF tables was given.

The following statements summarize the functional equivalence between the ER model and normalized tables:

1. *within an entity*—the level of normalization is totally dependent upon the interrelationships among the key and nonkey attributes. It could be any form from unnormalized to BCNF or higher.
2. *binary (or binary recursive) one-to-one or one-to-many relationship*—within the "child" entity, the foreign key (a replication of the primary key of the "parent") is functionally dependent upon the childs primary key. This is at least BCNF, assuming the entity by itself, without the foreign key, is already BCNF.
3. *binary (or binary recursive) many-to-many relationship*—the intersection table has a composite key and possibly some nonkey attributes functionally dependent upon it. This is at least BCNF.
4. *ternary relationship:*
   a. one-to-one-to-one = three overlapping composite keys, at least BCNF;
   b. one-to-one-to-many = two overlapping composite keys, at least BCNF;
   c. one-to-many-to-many = one composite key, at least BCNF;
   d. many-to-many-to-many = one composite key with three attributes, at least BCNF. In some cases it can also be 4NF, or even 5NF.

In the next chapter we will look at ways to refine the relational database for use by various applications. In order to make these refinements, the fundamentals of physical database design by using access methods will be presented.

Literature Summary

Good summaries of normal forms can be found in [Date86, Kent83, DuHa89, Smit85]. Algorithms for normal form decomposition and synthesis techniques are given in [Bern76, Fagi77, Ullm88, Lien81, ZaMe81, Mart83, Maie83, Yao85]. Earlier work in normal forms was done by [Codd70, Codd74].

[Bern76] Bernstein, P. "Synthesizing 3NF Tables from Functional Dependencies," *ACM Trans. Database Systems* 1,4 (1976), pp. 272–298.

[Codd70] Codd, E. "A Relational Model for Large Shared Data Banks," *Comm. ACM* 13,6 (June 1970), pp. 377–387.

[Codd74] Codd, E. "Recent Investigations into Relational Data Base Systems," *Proc. IFIP Congress,* North-Holland, Amsterdam, 1974.

[Date90] Date, C.J. *An Introduction to Database Systems, Vol. 1* (5th Ed.), Addison-Wesley, Reading, MA, 1990.

[DuHa89] Dutka, A.F. and Hanson, H.H. *Fundamentals of Data Normalization,* Addison-Wesley, Reading, MA, 1989.

[Fagi77] Fagin, R. "Multivalued Dependencies and a New Normal Form for Relational Databases," *ACM Trans. Database Systems* 2,3 (1977), pp. 262–278.

[Kent83] Kent, W. "A Simple Guide to Five Normal Forms in Relational Database Theory," *Comm. ACM* 26,2 (Feb. 1983), pp. 120–125.

[Lien81] Lien, Y. "Hierarchical Schemata for Relational Databases," *ACM Trans. Database Systems* 6,1 (1981), pp. 48–69.

[Maie83] Maier, D. *Theory of Relational Databases,* Computer Science Press, Rockville, MD, 1983.

[Mart83] Martin, J. *Managing the Data-Base Environment,* Prentice-Hall, Englewood Cliffs, NJ, 1983.

[Smit85] Smith, H. "Database Design: Composing Fully Normalized Tables from a Rigorous Dependency Diagram," *Comm. ACM* 28,8 (1985), pp. 826–838.

[Ullm88] Ullman, J. *Principles of Database and Knowledge-Base Systems, Vols. 1 and 2,* Computer Science Press, Rockville, MD, 1988.

[Yao 85] Yao, S.B. (editor). *Principles of Database Design,* Prentice-Hall, Englewood Cliffs, NJ, 1985.

[ZaMe81] Zaniolo, C. and Melkanoff, M. "On the Design of Relational Database Schemas," *ACM Trans. Database Systems* 6,1 (1981), pp. 1–47.

EXERCISES

Problem 5-1

Answer each question "yes" or "no." Justify each answer. In each case you will be given a relation R with a list of attributes without the candidate keys shown.

Given: R(A,B,C,D) and the functional dependencies A–>B, A–>C, and A–>D:

1. Is A a candidate key?
2. Is this relation, R, in 3NF?

Given: R(A,B,C,D) and the functional dependencies A–>B, B–>C, and C–>D:

3. Does A–>D?
4. Is A a candidate key?

Given: R(A,B) and the functional dependencies A–>B and B–>A:

5. Are both A and B candidate keys?
6. Is R in BCNF?

Given: R(A,B,C) and the functional dependencies A–>B, B–>C, and C–>A:

7. Is A the only candidate key?
8. Is R only in 2NF?

Given: R(A,B,C) and the functional dependencies AB–>C and C–>A:

9. Is AB a candidate key?
10. Is C a candidate key?
11. Is R in 3NF?
12. Is R in BCNF?

Given: R(A,B,C) and the functional dependency C–>A:

13. Is R in 3NF?
14. Is R in BCNF?

Given: R(A,B,C,D) and the functional dependencies A–>B and C–>D:

15. Is A a candidate key?
16. Is C a candidate key?
17. Is R in 3NF?

Given: R(A,B,C) and the functional dependencies AB–>C, AC–>B, and BC–>A:

18. Is A a candidate key?
19. Is BC a candidate key?
20. Is R in 3NF?

Given: R(A,B,C) and the functional dependencies AB–>C and AC–>B:

21. Is ABC a superkey?
22. Is AC a candidate key?
23. Is R in 3NF?
24. Is R in BCNF?

Given: R(A,B,C) with no functional dependencies:

25. Is AB a candidate key?
26. Is ABC a superkey?
27. Is R in BCNF?

Given: R(A,B,C,D) with the functional dependency A–>B:

28. Is A a candidate key?
29. Is ACD a superkey?
30. Is R in 3NF?

Problem 5-2

Answer each question "yes" or "no." Justify each answer. In each case you will be given a relation R with a list of attributes, with one explicit candidate key (the candidate key may be either a single attribute or composite attribute key, shown underlined). Other candidate keys may be possible.

Given: R(A,B,C) and the functional dependencies A–>B and B–>C:

1. Is R in 3NF?

Given: R(A,B,C) and the functional dependency BC–>A:

2. Is R in 3NF?
3. Is R in BCNF?
4. Is BC a candidate key?

Given: R(A,B,C) and the functional dependency A–>C:

5. Is R in 3NF?
6. Does AB–>C?

Given: R(A,B,C,D) and the functional dependency C–>B:

7. Is R in 3NF?

Problem 5-3

Given the assertions below for the current-term enrollment at a large university, do the following:

1. List the obvious functional dependencies (FDs) from the given description.
2. At what level of normalization is the database implemented as a single table with no repeating columns? Justify your answer.
3. If not in BCNF already, convert the database to BCNF.

Assertions:

a. An instructor may teach none, one, or more courses in a given term (average is 2.0 courses).

b. An instructor must direct the research of at least one student (average = 2.5 students).

c. A course may have none, one, or two prerequisites (average = 1.5 prerequisites).

d. A course may exist even if no students are currently enrolled.

e. All courses are taught by only one instructor.

f. The average enrollment in a course is 30 students.

g. A student must select at least one course per term (average = 4.0 course selections).

Problem 5-4

Answer each question as true or false.

When a relation R in 2NF with functional dependencies (FDs) A –> B and B –> CDEF (where A is the only candidate key), is decomposed into two relations R1 (with A –> B) and R2 (with B –> CDEF), the relations R1 and R2:

1. Are always a lossless decomposition of R.
2. Usually have total combined storage space less than R.
3. Have no delete anomalies.
4. Will always be faster to execute a query than R.

When a relation S in 3NF with FDs GH –> I and I –> H is decomposed into two relations S1 (with GH –> null, i.e., all key) and S2 (with I –> H), the relations S1 and S2:

5. Are always a lossless decomposition of S.
6. Are both dependency preserving.
7. Are both in BCNF.

When a relation T in BCNF with FDs W –> XYZ (where W is the primary key) is decomposed into two relations T1 (with W –> X) and T2 (with W –> YZ), the resulting two relations T1 and T2:

8. Are always dependency preserving.
9. Usually have total combined storage space less than T.
10. Have no delete anomalies.

Note: A –> BC implies that A –> B and A –> C (an Armstrong axiom).

Problem 5-5

The following functional dependencies (FDs) represent a set of airline reservation system database constraints. Design a minimum set of 3NF relations, preserving all FDs, and express your solution in terms of the code letters given below (a timesaving device for your analysis).

reservation_no –> agent_no, agent_name, airline_name, flight_no, passenger_name

reservation_no –> aircraft_type, departure_date, arrival_date, departure_time, arrival_time

reservation_no –> departure_city, arrival_city, type_of_payment, seating_class, seat_no

airline_name, flight_no –> aircraft_type, departure_time, arrival_time

airline_name, flight_no –> departure_city, arrival_city, meal_type

airline_name, flight_no, aircraft_type –> meal_type

passenger_name –> home_address, home_phone, company_name

aircraft_type, seat_no –> seating_class

company_name –> company_address, company_phone

company_phone –> company_name

A:	reservation_no	L:	departure_city
B:	agent_no	M:	arrival_city
C:	agent_name	N:	type_of_payment
D:	airline_name	P:	seating_class
E:	flight_no	Q:	seat_no
F:	passenger_name	R:	meal_type
G:	aircraft_type	S:	home_address
H:	departure_date	T:	home_phone
I:	arrival_date	U:	company_name
J:	departure_time	V:	company_address
K:	arrival_time	W:	company_phone

Problem 5-6

Given the following set of FDs, find the minimum set of 3NF relations. Designate the candidate key attributes of these relations. Is the set of relations you derived also BCNF?

1. A –> B
2. A –> C
3. B –> C
4. B –> D
5. D –> B
6. ABE –> F
7. E –> J
8. EG –> H
9. H –> G

Problem 5-7

Given the following set of FDs, find the minimum set of 3NF relations. Designate the candidate key attributes of these relations. Is the set of relations you derived also BCNF?

1. J –> KLMNP
2. JKL –> MNP
3. K –> MQ
4. KL –> MNP

5. KM –> NP
6. N –> KP

Problem 5-8

Given the following set of FDs, find the minimum set of 3NF relations. Designate the candidate key attributes of these relations. Is the set of relations you derived also BCNF?

1. A –> BCDEF
2. AB –> CDEF
3. ABC –> DEF
4. ABCD –> EF
5. ABCDE –> F
6. B –> DG
7. BC –> DEF
8. BD –> EF
9. E –> BF

Problem 5-9

Given the following functional dependencies, determine the minimum set of 3NF relations. Make sure that all functional dependencies are preserved. Specify the candidate keys of each relation. Note that each letter represents a separate data element (attribute). Is the set of relations you derived also BCNF?

1. A –> BGHJ
2. AG –> HK
3. B –> K
4. EA –> F
5. EB –> AF
6. EF –> A
7. H –> J
8. J –> AB

Problem 5-10

Given the following functional dependencies, determine the minimum set of 3NF relations. Make sure that all functional dependencies are preserved. Specify the candidate keys of each relation. Note that each letter represents a separate data element (attribute). Is the set of relations you derived also BCNF?

1. ABCD –> EFGHIJK
2. ACD –> JKLMN
3. A –> BH
4. B –> JKL
5. BH –> PQR
6. BL –> PS
7. EF –> ABCDH
8. JK –> B
9. MN –> ACD
10. L –> JK
11. PQ –> S
12. PS –> JKQ
13. PSR –> QT

Problem 5-11

Given the following functional dependencies, determine the minimum set of 3NF relations. Make sure that all functional dependencies are preserved. Specify the candidate keys of each relation. Note that each letter represents a separate data element (attribute).

1. A –> B
2. AB –> DE
3. ABCDET –> GHIJKW
4. ABDET –> CGHIJKW
5. CG –> KW
6. DT –> K
7. E –> ABCMNPQRT
8. GH –> AIJKT
9. HJR –> S

10. HJS -> R
11. HRS -> J
12. J -> BCKT
13. JRS -> H
14. KW -> M
15. KM -> W
16. M -> PQR
17. MN -> P
18. N -> T
19. T -> MN

If we add the functional dependency J-> A in the above list, what effect does this have on the solution?

Problem 5-12 (FDs and MVDs)

Answer each question "yes" or "no." Justify each answer. In most cases you will be given a relation R with a list of attributes, with at most one candidate key (the candidate key may be either a single attribute or composite attribute key, shown underlined).

Given: R(A,B,C,D) and the functional dependency AB->C:

1. Is R in 3NF?
2. Is R in BCNF?
3. Does the multivalued dependency AB ->>C hold?
4. Does the set {R1(A,B,C), R2(A,B,D)} satisfy the lossless join property?

Given: R(A,B,C) and the set {R1(A,B), R2(B,C)} satisfies the lossless decomposition property:

5. Does the multivalued dependency B->>C hold?
6. Is B a candidate key?
7. Is R in 4NF?

Given: a relation "skills_available" with attributes empno, project, and skill. The semantics of "skills_available" state that every skill an employee has must be used on every project that employee works on.

8. Is the level of normalization of "skills_available" at least 4NF?

Given: relation R(A,B,C) with actual data shown below:

9. Does the multivalued dependency B–>>C hold?
10. Is R in 5NF?

R:

A	B	C
w	x	p
w	x	q
z	x	p
z	x	q
w	y	q
z	y	p

Problem 5-13 (MVDs and 4NF)

Given the minimum set of BCNF tables constructed from Problem 5-10, determine which tables are also 4NF from the explicit MVDs given below:

1. B –>> H
2. K –>> B
3. LP –>> S
4. T –>> PSR

CHAPTER 6

ACCESS METHODS

Physical database design normally commences after the logical design of the schema (SQL tables) has been completed. Generally, the physical database designer has the option to pick one normalized schema from the many schemas available; cluster two or more record types together (using the SQL "create cluster" command); specify primary keys for fast random access to individual records; define indices on primary keys and secondary indices to allow fast access by nonkey attributes (using the SQL "create index" command); and specify physical parameters such as block size, buffer pool size, lock granularity, and recovery protocol.

This chapter focuses on the various access methods available and the system parameters associated with them. In order to classify access methods, we define three broad categories of database applications in terms of generic data manipulation commands:

1. *sequential access*: select all records of a given type (or a large subset of those records);
2. *random access*: select one record of a given type; and
3. *Boolean query access*: select a group of records based on some Boolean search criterion.

Each type of application, which includes both query and update requirements, implies a class of efficient access methods. The algebra used to describe the performance of each access method is typical of what a query optimizer might calculate to determine good query plans.

The logical design of a database results in the schema definition of logical records. A *logical record* (or record) is a named collection of data items or attributes treated as a unit by an application program. In storage, a record includes the pointers and record overhead needed for identification and processing by the database management system. A *file* is a set of similarly constructed records of one or more types. For simplicity, in this chapter we will assume that a file consists of records of a single type. A *physical database* (or database) is a collection of interrelated records of different types, possibly

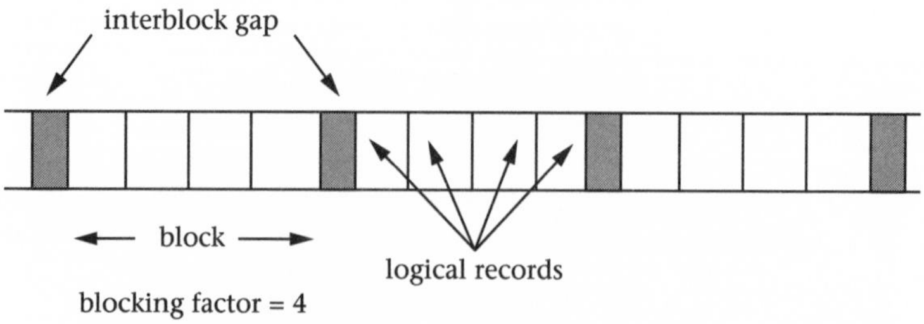

Figure 6.1 Sequential file parameters

including a collection of interrelated files. Query and update transactions (or applications) to a database are made efficient by the implementation of certain access methods as part of the database management system.

An *access method* consists of two integrated components: data structure and search mechanism. The data structure defines the framework for storing index and data blocks in memory. The search mechanism defines the access path—that is, how the tables are searched. As an example, consider a sequential file. The data structure is simply a collection of contiguously stored records of a single type. The search mechanism, however, could be either a sequential search of all the records in storage order, a binary search, or some other type of random search mechanism; each combination of the one data structure with one of the several search mechanisms would be considered a different access method.

Let us now look at some simple models of database access methods. We shall see that we can capture the essence of database performance by defining and analyzing just a few important parameters.

6.1 Sequential Files

A sequential file is a set of contiguously stored records on a physical device such as a disk, tape, or CD-ROM. Let us consider a sequential file of n records. To be stored on disk, these n records must be grouped into physical blocks as shown in Figure 6.1. A block is the basic unit of input/output from disk to main memory. It can range in size from a fraction of a record to hundreds or thousands of records. Typically a block size ranges from 1 to 100 records. If a database has normalized records—that is, records of constant size—the number of records in a block is called the *blocking factor (bf)*. For consistency and ease of programming, block sizes are usually constant for a whole system. On the other hand, almost all relational systems allow variable size records; thus, we will use average record size for simplicity in our performance analysis.

6.1.1 Sequential Processing for an Entire File

If we have a file of n records and a blocking factor bf, the basic performance measures for a sequential search of the entire file are as follows.

lra = n	logical record accesses	(6.1)
sba = ceil(n/bf)	sequential block accesses	(6.2)
rba = 0	random block accesses	(6.3)
iotime = sba*Tsba + rba*Trba		
= ceil(n/bf)*Tsba	seconds	(6.4)

where Tsba is the average disk I/O service time for a sequential block access, and Trba is the average disk I/O service time for a random block access. Note that the ceiling function, ceil, in Equation 6.2 is the next higher whole number (or integer) when the number of block accesses is a fraction instead of a whole number. Note that the second term in iotime drops out because rba = 0.

Obviously, sequential block accesses can be minimized when the blocking factor is maximized. However, block size is usually a function of some portion of a disk track. It is also limited by the size of buffers allowed in main memory, since block size and buffer size must be the same for efficient data transfer from disk to main memory.

If we were to access the sequential file of n records in a completely random sequence, the performance measures would be

lra = n	logical record accesses	(6.5)
sba = 0	sequential block accesses	(6.6)
rba = n	random block accesses	(6.7)
iotime = sba*Tsba + rba*Trba		
= n*Trba	seconds	(6.8)

Note that the first term in iotime drops out because sba = 0.

These two situations, sequential and random access to a sequential file, show that a sequential search mechanism makes efficient use of the blocking factor, but a random search mechanism does not. Thus, when random searches are required of a sequential file, a blocking factor of 1 minimizes the search time (I/O service time), assuming that 1 is the lowest value we can use in a typical system.

Because time is a common unit for all databases, I/O service time is the most important performance measure. Response time as a performance measure is too difficult to control from the database designer perspective; that is, response time includes disk and CPU wait times which are often dependent on the rest of the computing environment workload. Response time also includes CPU service time, which unfortunately is dependent on the amount of processing a database user does with the records retrieved, and it is not a function of the access method or database implementation.

The disk service time can be estimated from this simple model:

$$\text{Tsba} = \text{rot}/2 + \text{bks}/\text{tr} \qquad (6.9)$$

where rot is the disk rotation time (for a full rotation), bks is the block size in bytes (bf*record size), and tr is the disk transfer rate in bytes per second.

In other words, the average sequential block I/O service time is the average time to access the next block on disk, which is a half rotation as the average rotational delay, plus the block transfer time. The average random block I/O service time is similarly computed:

$$\text{Trba} = \text{seek(file)} + \text{rot}/2 + \text{bks}/\text{tr} \qquad (6.10)$$

where seek(file) is the average seek time over the extent of the file on disk.

The average random block I/O service time is the average seek time over the extent of the file plus the average rotational delay plus the block transfer time. The average seek time assumption depends on the type of disk and the workload environment, dedicated or shared. In a dedicated disk environment, the disk arm is confined to the extent of the file, which we assume is in contiguous storage. In a shared-disk environment, the disk arm is moved an average seek distance for each block access to your file; this assumes that other users of this disk move the disk arm away from your file some random distance.

Consequently, in a shared-disk environment, we have

$$\text{Tsba} = \text{Trba} = \text{seek(disk)} + \text{rot}/2 + \text{bks}/\text{tr} \qquad (6.11)$$

where seek(disk) is the average seek time over the extent of the entire disk.

Equation 6.11 is the same as Equation 6.10 except that the seek component is potentially greater in size. In this chapter we will assume that the disk environment is dedicated unless stated otherwise. Also, in the following analyses we will compute only lra, sba, and rba and assume that the disk characteristics are known to compute the disk I/O service time, iotime.

The disk time analysis can sometimes be further simplified by noting that many systems do some sort of prefetching of multiple blocks (typically 64 KB per disk I/O, such as in DB2) to speed up the sequential processing activity. Under these conditions, dedicated disks have negligible seek times and rotational delay, while shared disks are dominated by seek times and data transfers.

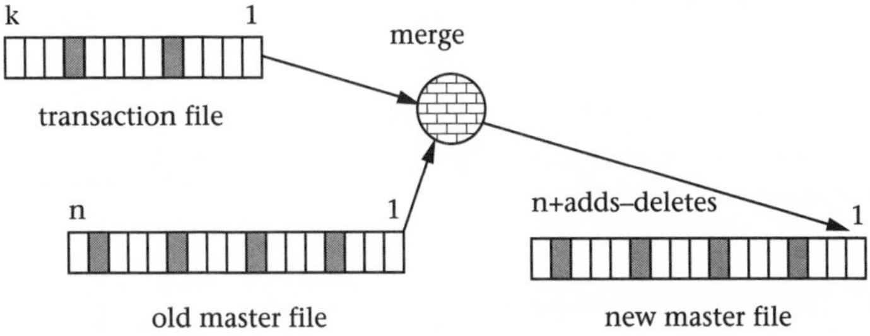

Figure 6.2 Batch processing of sequential files

6.1.2 Sequential Processing for a Single Record

If there are n records in a sequential file that is sorted by primary key, a sequential search for a single record, whether that record exists or not, requires approximately

lra = n/2	logical record accesses	(6.12)
sba = ceiling(lra/bf)	sequential block accesses	(6.13)

If the file is unsorted, a sequential search for the record is lra=n/2 if the record exists and lra=n when the record does not exist.

6.1.3 Batch Processing of k Records

One of the advantages of a sequential database or file is the efficiency of batch processing. Let us assume a batch system with a master file and a transaction file (Figure 6.2). Both files are sorted by primary key. The transaction file is assumed to have records of fixed size that specify what update action is to be taken on a record in the master file. Thus, each transaction record includes the primary key of a master file record, but the record size of the transaction file may be quite different from the record size in the master file. The I/O service time to execute the batch of update transactions is the sum of the time to read the entire transaction file, read the entire master file, and create a new master file. In other words:

read the transaction file

lra = k where k=number of transaction records (6.14)

sba = ceil(k/tfbf) where tfbf is the transaction file blocking factor (6.15)

read the master file

lra = n (6.16)

sba = ceil(n/bf) where bf is the master file blocking factor (6.17)

write a new master file

lra = n+adds–deletes (6.18)

sba = ceil((n+adds–deletes)/bf) (6.19)

where adds is the number of records added or inserted, and deletes is the number of records deleted.

6.2 Random Files

Random files differ from sequential files in that the access to individual records is done much more directly, either through a hashing mechanism or an index, instead of an exhaustive search. Physically, the data structure of random files may be either similar or quite different from sequential files, depending on the access method used.

6.2.1 Hashing

Hashing is the most common form of purely random access to a file or database. It is also used to access columns that do not have an index as an optimization technique. The most popular form of hashing is division hashing with chained overflow, which is illustrated in Figure 6.3. The basic mechanism is the transformation of a primary key identifier directly to a physical address, called a *bucket*, or indirectly to a bucket by first transforming it to a logical address (an integer) and letting the database management system transform it again to a physical address.

Address transformation is done by the central processing unit. The actual access to the target database is done using the disk. The address transformation for division hashing is typically done by dividing the primary key into partitions and applying a simple arithmetic function (such as adding) to those partitions to get a single address value. For instance, given a primary key of a person's social security number, 527-45-6783, we can add the subset numbers: 527+45+6783=7355. Then we can transform this number into a physical disk address for a disk with 32 devices, 404 cylinders per disk, 20 tracks per cylinder, and 5 blocks per track:

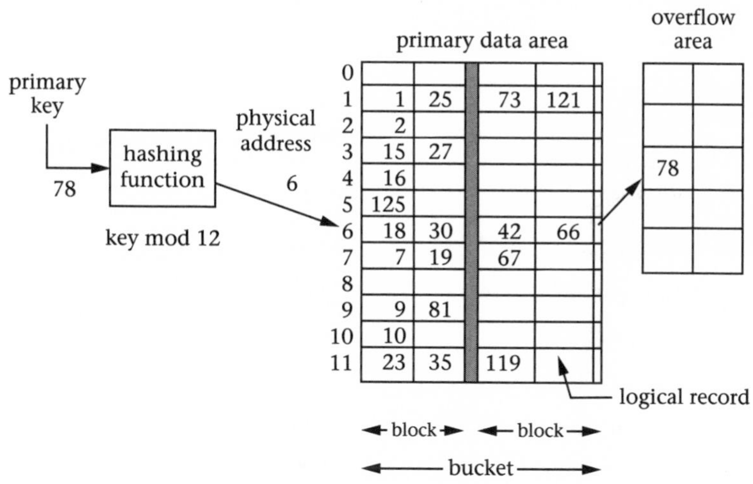

Figure 6.3 Hashing access method with separate chaining for overflow

device address = 7355 mod 32 = 27

cylinder address = 7355 mod 404 = 83

track address = 7355 mod 20 = 15 (6.20)

Access to this physical address allows us to either retrieve an existing record or store a new record in a block on that track.

Collisions occur when the database user attempts to insert a record into the target (bucket) address and the bucket is filled, causing overflow. *Collision resolution* is the process of deciding where to store (and later to find) the next record when a collision occurs. The *open addressing* approach involves a sequential search of the records until an open position is found [ElNa94].

Another approach, *chained overflow*, is typically handled by establishing a series of overflow blocks (on each track), tracks (on each cylinder), and cylinders (on each disk). Overflow records are chained in some order, usually either FIFO (first in, first out) or LIFO (last in, first out), and the length of overflow chains is a function of the density of the database and the type of overflow data structure and search mechanism [TeFr82].

A third approach, *multiple hashing* or *rehashing*, involves calculating a second hashing function when the first one results in a collision. If the second hashing function also results in a collision, then either open addressing or further rehashing is attempted until an open record position is reached.

For our simple model, we compute the performance for chained overflow as follows.

random access to a hashed file

lra = 1 + overflow(avg) (6.21)

rba = 1 + overflow(avg) (6.22)

insertion into a hashed file

lra = 1 + overflow(avg) + rewrite (6.23)

rba = 1 + overflow(avg) (6.24)

rba = 1 for the rewrite (6.25)

Note that a rewrite of a block accessed requires a single random block access (rba), assuming a dedicated disk. That is, a rewrite occurs after we have retrieved the block and processed the information in that block (e.g., searched for the record position needed for a rewrite and then rewritten into the block in main memory). When we are ready to do the rewrite on disk, the disk physical position is at a random distance from the beginning of the block position where we want to write, so the average delay to get to that point is Trba. Thus, a rewrite is simply a single rba. In a shared-disk environment, a rewrite is also a single random block access (rba).

Techniques that combine basic hashing with dynamic file expansion are also very popular today [ElNa94]. In dynamic hashing, for example, the number of buckets grows or contracts, depending on the need. When a bucket becomes full, it splits into two buckets and records in the bucket are reallocated to the two new buckets based on whether the first bit of their hash value is 0 or 1. Thus, collisions are resolved immediately and dynamically, and long sequential searches, long overflow chains, and multiple hashing computations are avoided.

6.2.2 B-trees and B^+-trees

The *B-tree* is the access method supported by DB2, SQL/DS, Oracle, and NonStop/SQL and is the dominant access method used by other relational database management systems such as Ingres and Sybase. It features not only fast random and sequential access, but also the dynamic maintenance that virtually eliminates the overflow problems that occur in the older hashing and indexed sequential methods (although we noted above that the more recent dynamic hashing methods make use of the dynamic maintenance capability as well).

(a) B-tree with embedded records at each node

(b) B-tree with key-data pointer pairs in each node

● tree pointer ■ data pointer

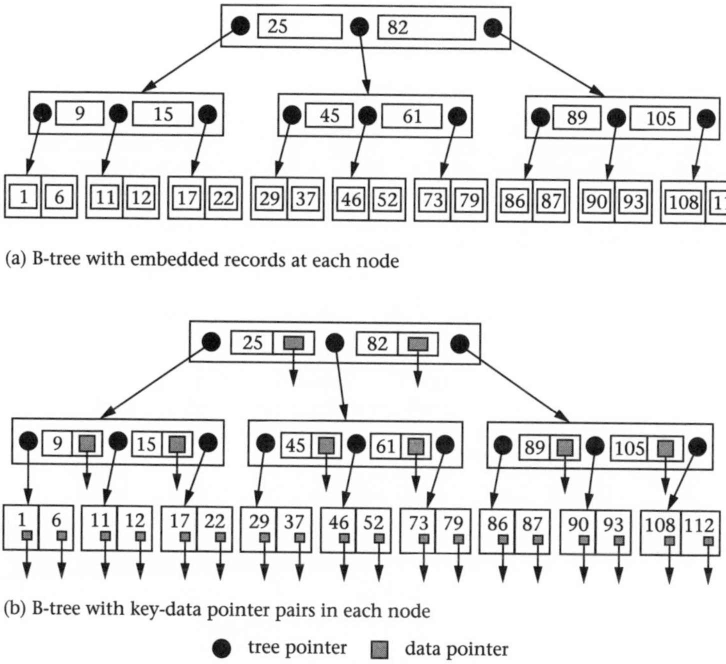

Figure 6.4 B-tree configurations with order 3 (p = 3)

The data structure of a B-tree has evolved considerably since its inception in 1972 [BaMc72, ElNa94]. Originally, each node in the tree consisted of p–1 records and p tree pointers to the next level in the tree, consisting of p nodes (see Figure 6.4a). The value p is known as the order of the B-tree. More recently, the structure of each node has been modified to become p pointers and p–1 sets of pairs: a search key value for a data record and a pointer to that data record, called a data pointer (Figure 6.4b). The actual record is stored elsewhere, not in the path of the B-tree search. Because the search key value and data-pointer pair is usually much smaller than the entire logical record, the order of a B-tree is potentially much larger than originally defined, given a physical limit on node size (similar to the limit on block size). Thus, the search time to a random record in the file or database can be greatly decreased.

The most often used implementation of the B-tree is the B^+-tree (or B*-tree). This variation eliminates the data pointers from all nodes but the leaf nodes in the B^+-tree index (see Figure 6.5). Therefore, the tree index search is very efficient. Each nonleaf index node consists of p tree pointers and p–1 key values. The key values denote where to search to find records that have either

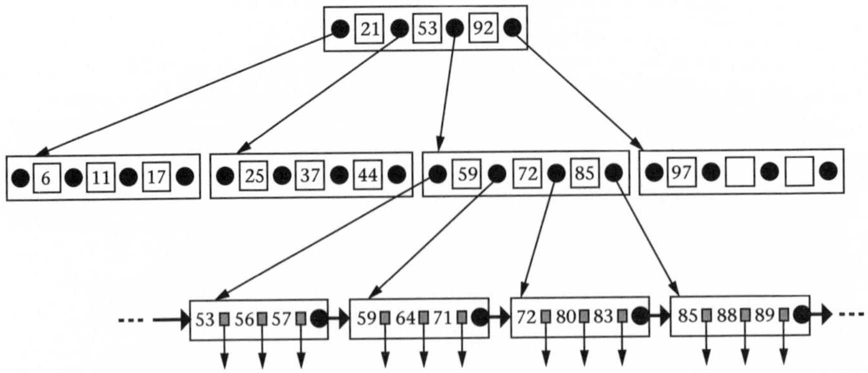

Figure 6.5 B^+-tree configuration with order 4 and height 3

smaller key values (by taking the tree pointer to the left of the key) or greater or equal key values (by taking the tree pointer to the right of the key). Each leaf index node consists of a series of key and data-pointer combinations that point to each record. The leaf index nodes (and the associated data blocks) are connected logically by block pointers so that an ordered sequence of records can be found quickly.

Example: B^+-tree

To determine the order of a B^+-tree, let us assume that the database has 500,000 records of 200 bytes each, the search key is 15 bytes, the tree and data pointers are 5 bytes, and the index node (and data block size) is 1024 bytes. For this configuration we have

$$\text{nonleaf index node size} = 1024 \text{ bytes} = p*5 + (p-1)*15 \text{ bytes}$$
$$p = \text{floor}((1024+15)/20) = \text{floor}(51.95) = 51 \quad (6.26)$$

where the floor function is the next lower whole number, found by truncating the actual value to the next lower integer. Therefore, we can have up to p–1 or 50 search key values in each nonleaf index node. In the leaf index nodes there are 15 bytes for the search key value and 5 bytes for the data pointer. Each leaf index node typically has a single pointer to the next leaf index node to make a sequential search of the data records possible without going through the index-level nodes. In this example the number of entries in the leaf nodes is floor ((1024–5)/(15+5))=50.

The height h of the B^+-tree is the number of index levels, including the leaf nodes. It is computed by noting that the root index node (ith level) has p pointers, the i-1st level has p2 tree pointers, i-2nd level has p3 tree pointers, and so on. At the leaf level the number of key entries and pointers are p–1 per index node; the total number of pointers over all nodes at that level must be greater than or equal to the number of records in the database, n. Therefore,

$$p^{h-1}(p-1) > n$$
$$(h-1)\log p + \log(p-1) > \log n$$
$$(h-1)\log p > \log n - \log(p-1)$$
$$h > 1 + (\log n - \log(p-1))/\log p \qquad (6.27)$$

In this example, therefore,

$$h > 1 + (\log 500{,}000 - \log 49)/\log 50 = 3.34$$
$$h = 4$$

A good approximation can be made by assuming that the leaf index nodes are implemented with p pointers and p key values:

$$p^h > n$$
$$h \log p > \log n$$
$$h > \log n/\log p \qquad (6.28)$$

In this case, the result above becomes $h > 3.35$ or $h = 4$.

Query of a single record in a B^+-tree is simply the time required to access all h levels of the tree index plus the access to the data record. All accesses to different levels of index and data are assumed to be random, while a rewrite of a record just read is sequential in a dedicated-disk environment and random in a shared-disk environment.

$$\text{read a single record } (B^+\text{-tree}) = (h+1) \text{ rba} \qquad (6.29)$$

Updates of records in a B^+-tree can be accomplished with a simple query and rewrite unless the update involves an insertion that overflows a data or index node or a deletion that empties a data or index node. For the simple case of updating data values in a record, assuming that each index node is implemented as a block:

$$\text{update a single record } (B^+\text{-tree}) = \text{search cost} + \text{rewrite data block}$$
$$= (h+1) \text{ rba} + 1 \text{ rba} \qquad (6.30)$$

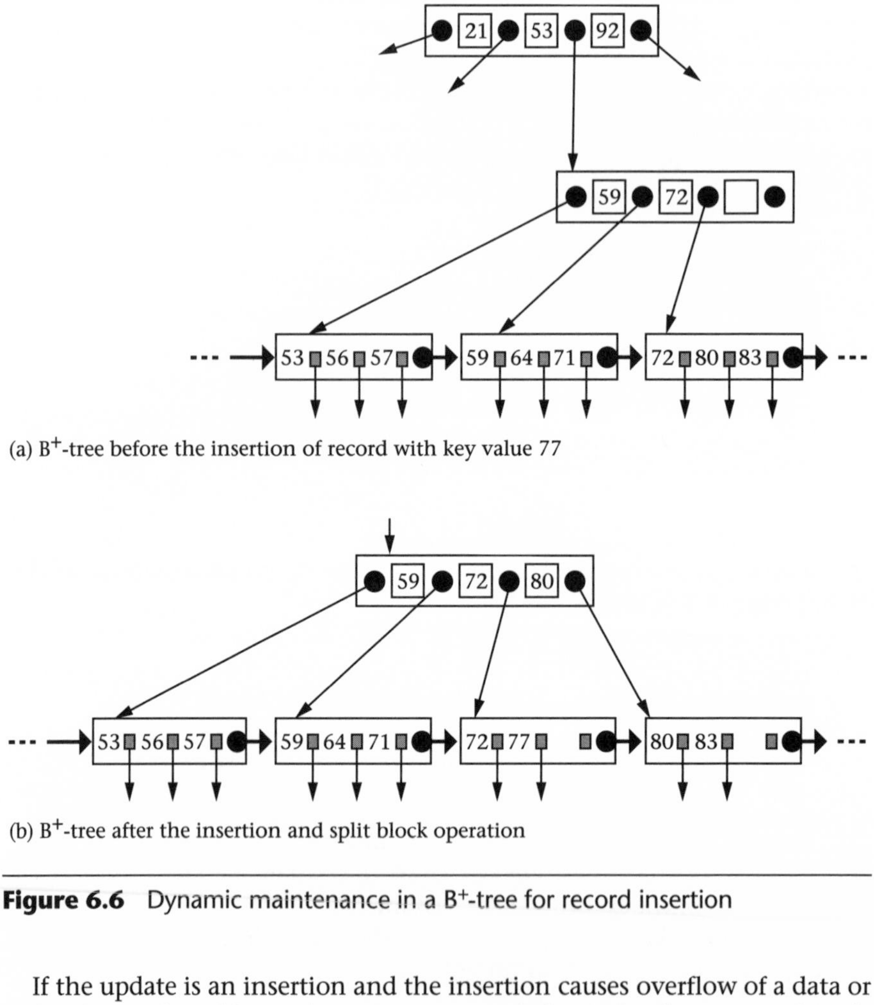

(a) B^+-tree before the insertion of record with key value 77

(b) B^+-tree after the insertion and split block operation

Figure 6.6 Dynamic maintenance in a B^+-tree for record insertion

If the update is an insertion and the insertion causes overflow of a data or leaf index node, additional accesses are needed to split the saturated node into two nodes that are half-filled (using the basic splitting algorithm) and to rewrite the next higher index node with a new pointer to the new index node (see Figure 6.6). The need for a split is recognized after the initial search for the record has been done. A split of an leaf index node requires a rewrite of the saturated leaf index node, half-filled with data, plus a random write of a new leaf index node also half-filled, plus a rewrite of the nonleaf index node with a new pointer value to the new leaf index node. When multiple rewrites are required, only the rewrite of the data block is typically sequential, since it can be done immediately after it has been read; and all other rewrites are random.

Occasionally, the split operation of a leaf index node necessitates a split of the next higher index node as well, and in the worst case the split operations may cascade all the way up to the index root node. The probability of additional splits depends on the type of splitting algorithm and the dynamics of insertions and deletions in the workload, and is beyond the scope of this text. However, we can estimate the cost of each additional split in terms of block accesses required, as follows.

general update cost for insertion (B^+-tree)
= search cost (i.e., h+1 reads)
+ simple rewrite of data block and leaf index node pointing to the data block (i.e., 2 rewrites)
+ nos*(write of new split index node
+ rewrite of the index node pointer to the new index node)
+ nosb*(write of new split data block)
= (h+1) rba + 2 rba + nos*(2 rba) + nosb*(1 rba) (6.31)

where nos is the number of index split node operations required and nosb is the number of data split block operations required. Note that nosb is either 0 or 1. A more detailed treatment of B^+-tree splitting can be found in [ElNa94].

Deletions may result in emptying a data block or index node, which necessitates the consolidation of two nodes into one. This may require a rewrite of the leaf index node to reset its pointers. The empty data node can be either left alone or rewritten with nulls, depending on the implementation. We will assume that the node where data is deleted need not be rewritten. Occasionally, the leaf or nonleaf nodes become empty and need consolidation as well. Thus, we obtain the cost of deletion:

general update cost for deletion (B^+-tree)
= search cost (i.e., h+1 reads)
+ simple rewrite of data block and leaf index node pointing to the data block (i.e., 2 rewrites)
+ noc*(rewrite of the node pointer to the remaining node)
= (h+1) rba + 2 rba + noc*(1 rba) (6.32)

where noc is the number of consolidations of index nodes required.

As an example, consider the insertion of a node (with key value 77) to the B^+-tree shown in Figure 6.6. This insertion requires a search (query) phase and an insertion phase with one split node. The total insertion cost for height 3 is

insertion cost = (3 + 1) rba search cost + 2 rba rewrite cost
+ 1 split *(2 rba rewrite cost)
= 8 rba (6.33)

6.3 Secondary Indices

A secondary index is an access method that efficiently searches a base (database) table, given a Boolean search criterion. Secondary indices are tables that replicate secondary key data from the base table to allow quick lookup of the primary key, given secondary key values. Boolean search criteria such as "find all employee records where the job title is 'database administrator' and location is 'chicago'" result in the access to a set of target records that is typically a small subset of the entire population of records, but usually significantly more than a single record. Using access methods based on the primary key will not work here, and frequent exhaustive scans of the entire base table is usually prohibitively expensive.

Conceptually, the basic components of a secondary index (Figure 6.7) are the attribute type index, attribute value index, an accession list, and the data blocks which house the base table. The attribute type index is a simple index that lists all the attributes you wish to build secondary indices on; each entry consists of the attribute name and a pointer to the appropriate attribute value index for that name. The attribute value index, in turn, has entries for each possible attribute value for each attribute type, and a pointer to an accession list for that value. Attribute type and value indices are usually quite small and are usually permanently stored in main memory while the database is active.

An accession list is an ordered list of pointers to records that contain the appropriate attribute value specified in the attribute value index that points to the accession list. Each pointer consists of a block address plus a record offset that ensures that each pointer is unique in the file or database.

Each attribute value has its own individual accession list. The pointers are ordered by record address (block address and record offset) so that multiple accession lists representing a complex AND condition in a query can be merged in a single pass. For example, in our query "Find all employee records where the job title is 'database administrator' and location is 'chicago'," an accession list for job_title='database administrator' and an accession list for location='chicago' must be searched to find the intersection of records that satisfy both conditions. The result of this merge is a new target accession list, held in a buffer in main memory unless larger than the block size. This list points to the target records that satisfy the conjunctive AND (condition AND condition AND condition AND . . . .) query. A query that contains disjunctive OR conditions involves searching target records for each condition separately and appending the results to each other at the completion of each search. Queries that combine AND and OR conditions use a combination of the individual approaches, with the AND conditions within each OR condition executed first.

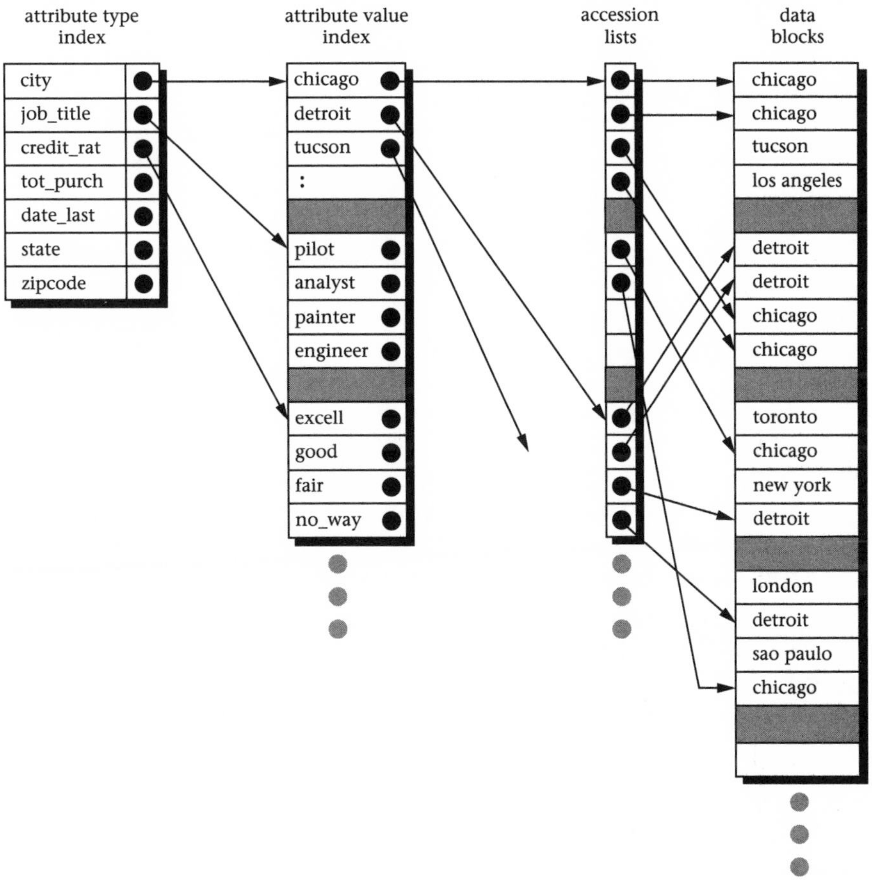

Figure 6.7 Secondary index structure

Assuming that the attribute type and attribute value indexes are stored in main memory, no disk access analysis is needed. However, we do need to analyze the access cost to the accession list and the target data blocks. The accession lists can be assumed to be linked sequential files, and the merge operation is similar to the merge required for a sequential file batch processing operation. Access to the data blocks is assumed to be strictly random via hashing or B-tree search. Each record pointer is treated as a random access, since the data is rarely ordered by secondary key value.

Boolean query cost (secondary index)
 = search attribute type index + search attribute value index
 + search and merge m accession lists + access t target records
 = (0 + 0 + sum of m accession list accesses) rba + t rba (6.34)

where m is the number of accession lists to be merged and t is the number of target records to be accessed after the merge operation.

accession list cost (for accession list j) = ceil(pj/bfac) rba (6.35)

where pj is the number of pointer entries in the jth accession list and bfac is the blocking factor for all accession lists

bfac = block_size/pointer_size (6.36)

We assume that all block accesses to the accession list are random because physical sequentiality usually cannot be guaranteed. In practice it is usually random. Generally we ignore errors of 1% or less in this type of analysis, because of the simplifying assumptions we often make.

Example: Mail-Order Business

Assume we have a file of 10,000,000 records of mail-order customers for a large commercial business. Customer records have attributes for customer name, customer number, street address, city, state, zip code, phone number, employer, job title, credit rating, date of last purchase, and total amount of purchases. Assume that the record size is 250 bytes; block size is 5000 bytes (bf=20); and pointer size, including record offset, is 5 bytes (bfac=1000). The query to be analyzed is "Find all customers whose job title is 'engineer', city is 'chicago', and total amount of purchases is greater than $1000." For each AND condition we have the following hit rates—that is, records that satisfy each condition:

job title is 'engineer': 84,000 records
city is 'chicago': 210,000 records
total amount of purchases > $1000: 350,000 records
total number of target records that satisfy all three conditions = 750

Applying Equations 6.34 through 6.36, we estimate the query access cost to be

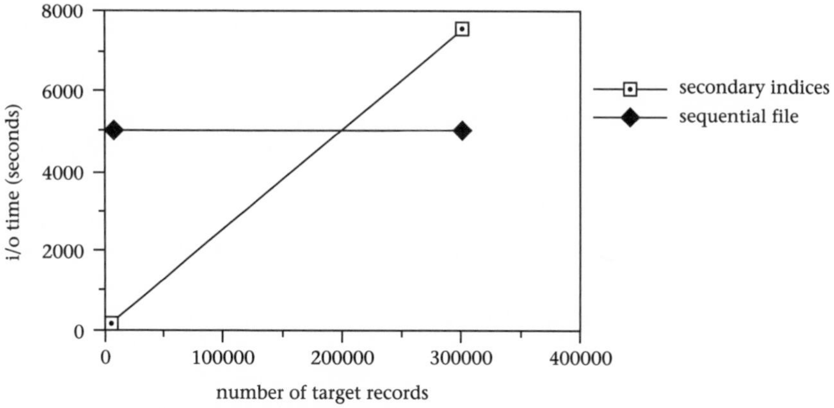

Figure 6.8 Secondary indices versus sequential

query cost (inverted file)
= merge of 3 accession lists + access 750 target records
= [ceil(n1/bfac) + ceil(n2/bfac) + ceil(n3/bfac)] rba + 750 rba
= [ceil(84,000/1000) + ceil(210,000/1000) + ceil(350,000/1000] rba + 750 rba
= (84+210+350) rba + 750 rba
= 1394 rba (6.37)

If we assume Tsba is 10 milliseconds and Trba is 25 milliseconds, we obtain

query iotime (secondary index)
= 1394 rba*25 ms
= 34850 ms
= 34.85 sec (6.38)

query iotime (sequential scan)
= ceil(n/bf) sba *Tsba
= ceil(10,000,000/20)*10 ms
= 5,000,000 ms
= 5000 sec (6.39)

Thus, we see that the secondary index time reduces the exhaustive scan time by a factor of almost 150. In Figure 6.8 we see that at approximately 200,000 target records, sequential becomes the more efficient method.

There is an inherent inefficiency in secondary indices with large numbers of target records in that each target record in a given data block has a separate (redundant) pointer to it from each accession list, and from the target accession list. Variants of secondary indices exist in which these redundant pointers are eliminated so that each accession list pointer references a data block that contains at least one target record for that Boolean condition, and it has a target accession list pointer that references a data block that contains at least one target record for all the Boolean conditions in the query. This reduces the lengths of the accession lists as well as the number of accesses to the target records, since an access to a data block containing at least one target record will result in accesses to all target records in that block.

6.4 Usage Refinement or Denormalization of Logical Databases

Database designers for network systems (CODASYL, for example) and hierarchical systems often used processing requirements to refine the DBMS schema before or during the physical design phase, if there were obvious efficiency gains to be made. If it produced more efficient database schemas without loss of data integrity, a similar technique could be applied to relational databases, and it would be relatively easy to implement. Let us look at a relational schema refinement algorithm based on a process-oriented, or usage view, that increases database efficiency for current processing requirements and yet retains all the information content of the natural view of data.

The application of a usage refinement algorithm is the logical next step in practical database design methodologies. Usage refinement is often used to analyze alternative logical structures during physical design and thus provide the designers with other feasible solutions to choose from. More efficient databases are the likely outcome of evaluating alternative structures.

The process of usage refinement is referred to as denormalization in real-world databases [Rodg89] because the transformation can cause the degree of normalization in the resulting table to be less than the degree of at least one of the original tables. Five basic types of denormalization are defined as:

1. ***Two entities in a many-to-many relationship***. The relationship table resulting from this construct is composed of the primary keys of each of the associated entities. If we implement the join of this table with one of the entity tables as a single table instead of the original tables, we can avoid certain frequent joins that are based on both keys, but only the nonkey data from one of the original entities. This is similar to the so-called semi-join operation [CePe84]. This type is illustrated in the examples to follow.

2. ***Two entities in a one-to-one relationship***. The tables for these entities could be implemented as a single table, thus avoiding frequent joins required by certain applications.

3. ***Reference data in a one-to-many relationship***. When artificial primary keys are introduced to tables that either have no primary keys or have keys that are very large composites, they can be added to the child entity in a one-to-many relationship as a foreign key and avoid certain joins in current applications.

4. ***Entities with the most detailed data***. Multivalued attributes (such as dependents or months in a year) are usually implemented as entities, and are thus represented as separate records in a table. Sometimes it is more efficient to implement them as individually named columns as an extension of the parent entity (table) when the number of replications is a small fixed number for all instances of the parent entity.

5. ***Derived attributes***. If one attribute is derived from another at execution time, then in some cases it is more efficient to store both the original value and the derived value directly in the database. This adds at least one extra column to the original table and avoids repetitive computation.

Let us look at the first type of denormalization described above. We assume that all attributes are initially assigned to tables based on FDs, and that the tables are at least 3NF. This establishes the requirement of an accurate representation of reality and of the flexibility of the design for future processing requirements. Efficiency of the current query requirements can be increased by redundantly adding attributes, used together in a query, to an existing table so that all attributes needed for that query reside in a new table, called a join table. Access time will now be greatly reduced because fewer joins will be needed. However, the side effects of this redundant extension include an increase in required storage space, an increase in the update cost, potential denormalization and loss of integrity, and the necessity for program transformations for all relevant queries. These effects require careful consideration.

To illustrate some of these effects, let us assume that the table **review** is associated with the tables **employee** and **manager** as the table that follows shows. The extension of the **review** table, **review-ext**, is shown as a means of reducing the number of joins required in the query shown below. This extension results in a real denormalization, that is,

review_no –> emp_id –> emp_name, emp_address

with the side effects of add and update anomalies. However, the delete anomaly cannot occur because the original data is redundant in the extended schema.

Original tables and process (query)

Table	*Primary key*	*Nonkeys*
employee	emp_id	emp_name, emp_address, mgr_id
manager	mgr_id	emp_name, emp_address
review	review_no	emp_id, mgr_id

Query: For a given review number, display the employee name and address.

select e.emp_name, e.emp_addr
from **employee** as e, **review** as r
where r.review_no = 'xxxx'
and e.emp_id = r.emp_id;

Extended table **review_ext** in 2NF (using an SQL construct that produces a permanent table as the result of a query, not a standard SQL-92 construct, but available in other versions of SQL):

create table **review_ext** as
select r.review_no, e.emp_id, e.emp_name, e.emp_addr, e.mgr_id
from **employee** as e, **review** as r
where e.emp_id = r.emp_id;

The storage and processing cost of a logical relational database is to be computed for both the existing and new join tables. The formula for the computation follows.

$$\text{total cost} = [\text{iotime(q)} + \text{iotime(u)}]*\text{cost(q)} + \text{volume(s)}*\text{cost(s)} \quad (6.40)$$

where

cost(q) = unit cost per I/O second for query or update processes

cost(s) = unit cost per byte for stored data

iotime(q) = I/O service time (sec) for query processes

iotime(u) = I/O service time (sec) for update processes

volume(s) = total volume in bytes for stored data

Unit costs are selected based on the computing environment defined in the requirements specification. The I/O service time for query and update can be determined from the processing operations, their frequencies, and the hardware device characteristics; stored data volume can be obtained from the size of the tables defined. Each query process must be expressed in terms of basic relational algebra—operations such as selection, projection, and join. At this point some initial assumptions must be made about sequential and random accesses needed to efficiently accomplish the query or update, but the actual use of indexes, sorting, and the like is deferred to physical design, when the final configuration decisions are made.

6.5 Table Usage Refinement Algorithm

A practical strategy for table usage refinement is to select only the most dominant processes to determine those modifications that will most likely improve performance. The basic modification is to add attributes to existing tables to reduce join operations. The steps of the strategy follow.

1. Select the dominant processes based on such criteria as high frequency of execution, high volume of data accessed, response time constraints, or explicit high priority. Remember this rule of thumb: Any process whose frequency of execution or data volume accessed is 10 times that of another process is considered to be dominant.
2. Define join tables, when appropriate, for the dominant processes.
3. Evaluate total cost for storage, query, and update for the database schema, with and without the extended table, and determine which configuration minimizes total cost.
4. Consider also the possibility of denormalization due to a join table and its side effects. If a join table schema appears to have lower storage and processing cost and insignificant side effects, then consider using that schema for physical design in addition to the original candidate table schema. Otherwise use only the original schema.

In general, avoid joins based on nonkeys. They are likely to produce very large tables, thus greatly increasing storage and update costs. For example, if two tables have 100 and 200 records, respectively, then a join based on the key of either one results in a maximum of 200 records, but a join based on a nonkey of either one can result in a maximum of 100*200, or 20,000 records. Null values are also restricted to nonkey attributes so that they will not be used inadvertently in join operations.

6.6 Join Strategies

We now apply our knowledge of access methods to a comparison of join processing strategies. Our basic parameters are the number of rows, m and n, in the two tables to be joined; the blocking factor for each table, bfm and bfn; and the physical order of rows in each table. The basic join strategies we will consider are

- nested loop: complexity O(mn)
- merge-join: complexity O(n $\log_2$ n)
- indexed join: complexity O(2m)
- hash-join: complexity O(m+n)

where the complexities are based on the assumption that if the join is between a table whose foreign key matches another table's primary key, then m represents the number of rows in the table with the primary key and n represents the number of rows in the table with the foreign key. If the join is not between two such tables, then the designations of which table has m rows and which one has n rows is arbitrary.

The nested loop strategy is the basic method of join. The outer loop is a sequential scan of the first table, and for each row in the first table scanned, the inner loop is executed, a sequential scan of the second table. The complexity is O(mn) because of the double loop. We assume that each table is stored in physically contiguous disk space; otherwise, each disk access becomes a random access (rba) instead of a sequential access (sba). The time cost of executing this strategy also depends on which table we select for the outer and inner loops. Continuing the example we defined in Chapters 2 through 4, let us assume that the **assigned_to** table has 50,000 rows and the **project** table has 250 rows. Let the blocking factors for the **assigned_to** and **project** tables be 100 and 50, respectively, and the block size be equal for the two tables. The common join column is project_name. We omit the time required to display the results of the join since it is constant for all the strategies and depends heavily on the display medium.

```
select project_name, emp_id
    from project as p, assigned_to as a
    where p.project_name = a.project_name;
```

Nested Loop Case 1: **assigned_to** is the outer loop table.

join cost = scan **assigned_to** once, scan **project** n times
= 50,000/100 + 50,000*250/50
= 500 + 250,000
= 250,500 sequential block accesses (sba)

If a sequential block access requires an average of 10 ms, the total time required is 2505 seconds.

Nested Loop Case 2: **project** is the outer loop table.

join cost = 250/50 + 250*50,000/100
= 5 + 125,000
= 125,005 sequential block accesses (or 1250 seconds)

The nested loop strategy can obviously improve its performance by a proper selection of outer and inner loop tables, but for this example both cases result in a prohibitively long query (approximately 20 to 40 minutes). Note that this strategy does not take advantage of row order for these tables.

The merge-join strategy, unlike the nested loop strategy, takes advantage of row order in the same way that batch processing does (see Section 6.1). If the tables are both sorted on the join columns, then only a single sequential scan of each table is required to complete the join. If one or both tables are not sorted on the join column, then each unsorted table is sorted before the merge is executed. Even with the overhead of a sort operation, this algorithm is faster than nested loop. We assume the complexity of the sort of n rows is $O(n*\log_2*n)$.

Merge-Join Case 1: Both **project** and **assigned_to** are already ordered by project_name.

join cost = merge time (to scan both tables)
= 50,000/100 + 250/50
= 505 sequential block accesses (or 5 seconds)

Merge-Join Case 2: Only **project** is ordered by project_name.

join cost = sort time for **assigned_to** + merge time (to scan both sorted tables)
= $(50{,}000*\log_2 50{,}000)/100 + 50{,}000/100 + 250/50$
= (50,000*16)/100 + 500 + 5
= 8505 sequential block accesses (or 85 seconds)

Merge-Join Case 3: Neither **project** nor **assigned_to** are ordered by project_name.

join cost = sort time for both tables + merge time for both tables
= $(50{,}000*\log_2 50{,}000)/100 + (250*\log_2 250)/50 + 50{,}000/100 + 250/50$
= 8000 + 40 + 500 + 5
= 8545 sequential block accesses (or 85 seconds)

We see that the sort phase of the merge-join strategy is the costliest component, but it still significantly improves performance compared to the nested loop strategy.

The indexed join is most useful when one of the common join columns is a primary key and has an index already available, and the join selectivity (percentage of rows actually participating in the join) is very low. It can also be effectively used with nonunique (secondary) indexes as long as the join selectivity is low. The stategy is to do a full scan of first table and, for each qualifying join attribute value, locate the corresponding row in the second table via the index. If there are mt qualifying rows in the first table, and nt qualifying rows in the second table, there will be m/bfm sequential block accesses for the first table and mt random block accesses to the second table, one rba for each qualifying row found in the first table. Let mt=100 qualifying rows for the first table (**assigned_to**) and let nt=5 qualifying rows for the second table (**project**) in the example below.

> select project_name, emp_id
> from **project** as p, **assigned_to** as a
> where p.project_name = a.project_name
> and p.project_type = 'financial analysis';

Indexed join basic algorithm:

join cost = scan entire first table (**assigned_to**)
+ access second table (**project**) qualifying rows
= 50,000/100 sba + 100 rba
= 500 sba + 100 rba

If Tsba=10 ms and Trba=40 ms, then the total iotime is 9 seconds.

The hash join strategy is also effective for low selectivity joins. The basic strategy is to scan each table once, and hash the qualifying join column attribute value to a hash file in main memory. Each entry in the hash file contains the attribute value and a pointer to the table row containing that value. The second phase of the algorithm is to access the actual qualifying rows from each of the two tables, that is, those rows from the tables with matching attribute values in the hash file. As in the indexed join example above, let mt=100 and nt=5 qualifying rows for the first and second tables, respectively.

Hash join basic algorithm:

join cost = scan first table (**assigned_to**) + scan second table
(**project**) + access qualifying rows in the two tables
= 50,000/100 sba + 250/50 sba + 100 rba + 5 rba
= 505 sba + 105 rba

Thus we get iotime of 9.25 seconds for this case when Tsba=10 ms and Trba=40 ms.

6.7 Summary

This chapter discussed the basic principles of physical database design in terms of the types of processing of data typically done in database applications and the access methods needed to do each type of processing efficiently. Database performance is defined at three levels of detail: logical record access, sequential and random block access, and disk I/O service time. The I/O time computation applies to a dedicated or shared disk environment.

Sequential processing uses sequential data structures and search mechanisms that range from sequential scans to binary searches. Random processing of individual records is best done by hashing. The B-tree, and in particular the B^+-tree, is the dominant sequential and random-access method used today, and it has the added advantage of dynamically maintaining the database and avoiding the severe performance degradation that results from long overflow chains, such as in indexed sequential files. Hashing methods that use the dynamic maintenance facilities found in B-trees are rapidly replacing the older implementations.

Database applications involving complex Boolean queries are used effectively only with systems that have some form of secondary index capability. Secondary indices are implemented using accession lists of pointers to target records and can be merged easily for complex query conditions. Cellular secondary indices are variants of secondary indices that enhance performance, particularly when target records are clustered in data blocks.

Usage refinement of relational databases is seen as a method to decrease query time for certain queries requiring multiple table joins. Analysis of the effectiveness of a pre-join strategy is done using the block access and I/O time approach defined earlier in this chapter and illustrated in the example in Chapter 7.

Literature Summary

The idea for extending a table for usage efficiency came from [ScSo80], and practical advice on denormalization is given in [Rodg89]. Comprehensive surveys of access methods can be found in [Harb88, Gros86, Loom83, TeFr82, Wied87], and brief surveys are given in [Card85, ElNa94].

[BaMc72] Bayer, R. and McCreight, E. "Organization and Maintenance of Large Ordered Indexes," *Acta. Inf.* 1,3 (1972), pp. 173–189.

[Card85] Cardenas, A.F. *Data Base Management Systems* (2nd ed.), Allyn and Bacon, Boston, 1985.

[ElNa94] Elmasri, R. and Navathe, S.B. *Fundamentals of Database Systems* (2nd Ed.), Addison-Wesley, Benjamin/Cummings, Redwood City, CA, 1994.

[GrRe93] Gray, J. and Reuter, A. *Transaction Processing: Concepts and Techniques*, Morgan Kaufmann, San Mateo, CA, 1993.

[Gros86] Grosshans, D. *File Systems Design and Implementation,* Prentice-Hall, Englewood Cliffs, NJ, 1986.

[Harb88] Harbron, T.R. *File Systems Structures and Algorithms,* Prentice-Hall, Englewood Cliffs, NJ, 1988.

[Loom83] Loomis, M.E.S. *Data Management and File Processing,* Prentice-Hall, Englewood Cliffs, NJ, 1983.

[Rodg89] Rodgers, U. "Denormalization: Why, What, and How?" *Database Programming and Design* 2,12 (Dec. 1989), pp. 46–53.

[ScSo80] Schkolnick, M. and Sorenson, P. "Denormalization: A Performance Oriented Database Design Technique," *Proc. AICA 1980 Congress,* Bologna, Italy, AICA, Brussels, 1980, pp. 363–377.

[TeFr82] Teorey, T. and Fry, J. *Design of Database Structures,* Prentice-Hall, Englewood Cliffs, NJ, 1982.

[Wied87] Wiederhold, G. *File Organization for Database Design,* McGraw-Hill, New York, 1987.

EXERCISES

Problem 6-1

In this problem set you are given disk and data volume statistics for a simple customer database. Answer each question with the appropriate numerical value. Assume KB => 1000 bytes and MB => 1,000,000 bytes. Assume a *dedicated disk* unless specified otherwise. Also assume the 1% error rule, that is, ignore parameters that affect the performance by <1%.

Disk minimum seek time (to the next adjacent cylinder) = 10 milliseconds (ms)

Disk average seek time (over all cylinders) = 20 ms

Disk (full) rotational time = 20 ms

Disk data transfer rate = 3 MB/second

Data block size = 15 KB

CUSTOMER record size = 650 Bytes

Pointer size = 4 Bytes

Primary key size = 12 Bytes

Block size for the transaction file = 15 KB (avg. of 20 transactions per block)

1. What is the average elapsed I/O service time for a sequential block access (Tsba)?
2. What is the average elapsed I/O service time for a random block access (Trba) over the whole disk?
3. What is the average elapsed I/O service time for a random block access (Trba) for a table (file) that fills up exactly two contiguous (adjacent) dedicated-disk cylinders?
4. What is the cost (in sba's) to sequentially search 2,000,000 CUSTOMER records?
5. How much elapsed I/O service time does this represent, in *seconds*?
6. If the blocking factor is doubled, what is the elapsed time, in *seconds*?
7. Design a B^+-tree for 2,000,000 CUSTOMER records that has minimum "order" and no more than 4 index levels (plus a data level). Assume that each data node is a block of 15 KB. Note that "order" is the number of tree pointer values in each index node. In summary, find the minimum order p, assuming the approximation $p^h >>= n$, where h is the height and n is the total number of records.

   Given a database with the following characteristics:

   a. One record type
   b. 2,000,000 records with record size of 200 Bytes each
   c. 11 attributes (primary key and ten nonkeys)
   d. Nonkey attributes can have anywhere from 2 values to 50,000 values
   e. 40,000 blocks (i.e., bf=50) for data, with blocksize of 10 KB
   f. Blocking factor for accession lists = 2,000 (each pointer is assumed to be 5 Bytes)
   g. Attribute name and attribute value indexes are always in main memory

   A particular query for this *inverted file* requires the merge of accession lists of 10,000, 20,000, and 50,000 entries, respectively, and 300 target records that satisfy all three query conditions.

8. What is the total cost in rba's, sba's, and elapsed I/O service time for this query (assuming that access to the first block in the accession list is a sequential access, and assuming a dedicated-disk environment)?
9. What is the total cost in rba's, sba's, and elapsed I/O service time for this query (assuming that access to the first block in the accession list is a sequential access, and assuming a dedicated-disk environment), if we use a *cellular inverted file* instead of just an inverted file?

Problem 6-2

A single record-type database (i.e., a file) stored on disk and typical queries on that database are described below. Attribute sizes are given in Bytes (B):

Database:

Number of employees = 150,000 (*id-no=10 B (key)*, name=25 B, addr=30 B)

Number of departments = 80 (dept-no=2 B, dept-name=12 B)

Number of degree types = 6 (degree=3 B)

Number of job titles = 150 (job-title=18 B)

Other attributes total 300 B (*Note:* total of 20 attributes)

Total logical records (tuples) = 150,000 (size of each record is 400 B)

Block size (data and index blocks) is 6000 B

Pointer size is 5 B

Average I/O time for a sequential block access = 15 ms

Average I/O time for a random block access = 30 ms over the file or disk

We also assume the following:

a. The database is new and has no overflow or other degradation.
b. Dedicated-disk environment.
c. The pointers in B^+-tree data blocks can be ignored.
d. Any level of an index that fits into a single index block can be considered to reside in main memory and does not need a disk access.

Queries:

Q1. List all employee information in id-no order.

Q2. Display all employee data for id-no = zzzzzzzzzz.

Q3. Display the name and department name of employees with job title x and holding degree y. Average number of target records = 600.

1. Given that B^+-tree is to be used for some of these queries, how many levels of indexing would be required for an order-14 B^+-tree index? How many index nodes could fit into a single index block?
2. Compute the time for sequential access for Query Q1.
3. Compute the I/O service time for sequential and B^+-tree access for Query Q2.
4. Analyze the trade-offs between sequential access and secondary index for Query Q3, given that the number of target records is 600.

Problem 6-3

Given the relational schema and physical characteristics shown below, evaluate the total I/O time for the following access methods to obtain "all students whose research is directed by John Smith." State all the assumptions that you must make.

1. Sequential search of the student records (rows), testing for the foreign key for the research instructor.
2. Secondary index access to student records (rows).

Each instructor directs the research of an average of 10 students. Not all students conduct research, only seniors and graduate students.

Each instructor teaches an average of three course sections per term.

Each student takes an average of five courses per term.

Courses contain an average of 25 students.

Relational schema (SQL):

create table **instructor** (instr_id char(9),
instr_name char(20),
instr_room_no char(6),
primary key (instr_id));

create table **course** (course_no char(6),
course_name char(15),
course_instr_name char(20),
day char(5),
hour char(2),
primary key (course_no),
foreign key (course_instr_name) references **instructor**);

```
create table student      (student_id char(10),
                           student_name char(20),
                           student_addr char(25),
                           research_instr_id char(9),
                           primary key (student_id),
                           foreign key (research_instr_id) references
                                 instructor);
create table enrollment   (student_id char(10),
                           course_no char(6)
                           primary key (student_id, course_no),
                           foreign key (student_id) references student,
                           foreign key (course_no) references course);
```

Number of instructor records = 2500

Number of course records = 4000

Number of student records = 20,000

Number of enrollment records = 100,000

Blocksize = 1000 B

Disk seek time = 40 ms (avg.)

Disk full rotation time = 20 ms

Disk transfer rate = 200 KB/second

Problem 6-4

Given the tables and applications (queries with equal frequency) specified below, state one argument in favor of and one argument against each of the two proposed schema refinements, taking into consideration usage and integrity:

Table	*Primary key*	*Foreign key(s)*	*Other attributes*
employee	emp_no	dept_no; proj_no; office_no	emp_name, address, phone_no
emp_job	emp_no, start_date	emp_no	job_title, salary_level
department	dept_no	–	dept_name, manager_no
office	office_no	–	office_size, office_type
project	proj_no	–	proj_name, proj_manager_no

Proposal 1: Split relation **employee** into two tables with only the employee's name and address in one table, and the other table containing everything except the address.

Proposal 2: Add the foreign key dept_no to table **office**.

Queries:

Q1. Which office numbers are associated with each department?

Q2. List all employee names and their addresses.

Q3. Which employees currently work on the "clean air" project?

CHAPTER 7

AN EXAMPLE OF RELATIONAL DATABASE DESIGN

The following example illustrates how to proceed through the database life cycle, in a practical way, for a centralized relational database. We will see how physical design for usage refinement and index selection extends a logical design methodology to attain significant improvements in performance, given that the available access methods are known.

7.1 Requirement Specification

The management of a large retail store would like a database to keep track of sales activities. The requirements for this database leads to the following six entities and their unique identifiers:

Entity	*Entity id*	*Id length(avg) in characters*	*Cardinality*
Customer	cust-no	6	80,000
Job	job-title	24	80
Order	order-no	9	200,000
Salesperson	sales-name	20	150
Department	dept-no	2	10
Item	item-no	6	5,000

The following assertions describe the data relationships:

- Each customer has one job-title, but different customers may have the same job-title.
- Each customer may place many orders, but only one customer may place a particular order.
- Each department has many salespeople, but each salesperson must work in only one department.
- Each department has many items for sale, but each item is sold in only one department. (Item means item type, like IBM PC.)
- For each order, items ordered in different departments must involve different salespeople, but all items ordered within one department must be handled by exactly one salesperson. In other words, for each order, each item has exactly one salesperson; and for each order, each department has exactly one salesperson.

Design Problems

1. Using the information given and, in particular, the six assertions, derive an ER diagram and a set of FDs that represent all the data relationships.
2. Transform the ER diagram into a set of candidate tables. List the tables, their primary keys, and other attributes.
3. Find the minimum set of 3NF tables that are functionally equivalent to the candidate tables. Analyze performance and integrity trade-offs resulting from the definition of this minimum set.
4. Given the transactions "Select all order numbers assigned to customers who are computer engineers" and "Add a new customer and the customers order to the database," analyze the performance and data integrity trade-offs for strategies to execute these transactions by using both the minimum set 3NF schema and a refined schema designed to reduce the number of joins needed for data retrieval.

7.2 Logical Design

Our first step is to develop an ER diagram and a set of FDs to correspond to each of the assertions given. Figure 7.1 presents the diagram. Normally the ER diagram is developed without knowing all the FDs, but in this example the nonkey attributes are omitted so that the entire database can be represented with only a few statements and FDs. The result of this analysis, relative to each of the assertions given, follows.

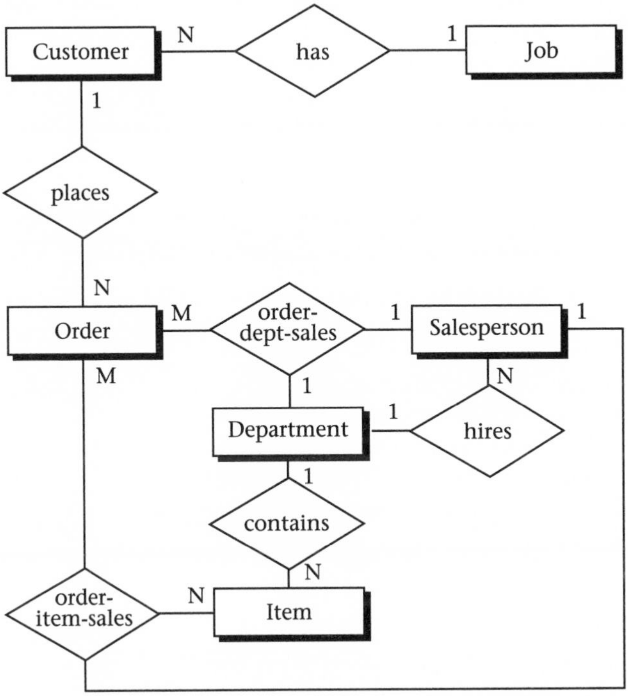

Figure 7.1 ER diagram for the retail store database example

ER construct	*FDs*
Customer(many):Job(one)	cust-no –> job-title
Order(many): Customer(one)	order-no –> cust-no
Salesperson(many): Department(one)	sales-name –> dept-no
Item(many): Department(one)	item-no –> dept-no
Order(many): Item(many): Salesperson(one)	order-no,item-no–>sales-name
Order(many): Department(many): Salesperson(one)	order-no,dept-no–> sales-name

The candidate tables needed to represent the semantics of this problem can be easily derived from the constructs for entities and relationships. Primary keys and foreign keys are explicitly defined.

```
create table customer (cust_no char(6),
        job_title varchar(256),
        primary key (cust_no),
        foreign key (job_title) references job
                on delete set null on update cascade);

create table job (job_title varchar(256),
        primary key (job_title));

create table order (order_no char(9),
        cust_no char(6) not null,
        primary key (order_no),
        foreign key (cust_no) references customer
                on delete cascade on update cascade);

create table salesperson (sales_name varchar(256),
        dept_no char(2),
        primary key (sales_name),
        foreign key (dept_no) references department
                on delete set null on update cascade);

create table department (dept_no char(2),
        primary key (dept_no));

create table item (item_no char(6),
        dept_no char(2),
        primary key (item_no),
        foreign key (dept_no) references department
                on delete set null on update cascade);

create table order_item_sales (order_no char(9),
        item_no char(6),
        sales_name varchar(256) not null,
        primary key (order_no, item_no),
        foreign key (order_no) references order
                on delete cascade on update cascade,
        foreign key (item_no) references item
                on delete cascade on update cascade,
        foreign key (sales_name) references salesperson
                on delete cascade on update cascade);
```

```
create table order_dept_sales (order_no char(9),
    dept_no char(2),
    sales_name varchar(256) not null,
    primary key (order_no, dept_no),
    foreign key (order_no) references order
        on delete cascade on update cascade,
    foreign key (dept_no) references department
        on delete cascade on update cascade,
    foreign key (sales_name) references salesperson
        on delete cascade on update cascade);
```

This process of decomposition and reduction of tables moves us closer to a minimum set of 3NF tables. Additionally, we must consider the tables **job** and **department**. Because we have not defined other attributes in these tables, **job** and **department** are simple tables consisting of a single key attribute. When this occurs and the key attribute appears in other tables as a nonkey, we can consider the elimination of the simple table. The trade-off is between the decrease in storage space and update cost when we eliminate a table and the possible loss of data integrity as a side effect of deletions on another table in which the key of the eliminated table has become a nonkey. In our example, if we can justify this trade-off and eliminate the simple tables, we have the following minimum set of 3NF tables:

Table	*Primary key*	*Nonkey*
customer	cust_no	job_title
order	order_no	cust_no
salesperson	sales_name	dept_no
item	item_no	dept_no
order_item_sales	order_no,item_no	sales_name
order_dept_sales	order_no,dept_no	sales_name

In summary, the reductions shown in this section have decreased storage space and update cost and have maintained the normalization at a minimum of 3NF. But we have potentially higher retrieval cost—given the transaction "list all job_titles," for example—and have increased the potential for loss of integrity because we have eliminated simple tables with only key attributes.

7.3 Physical Design

7.3.1 Schema Refinement Based on Usage

Let us now look at the quantitative trade-offs of further refinement of tables to improve processing efficiency. Assume that each of the following transactions are to be executed once per fixed time unit.

Query: Select all order numbers assigned to customers who are computer engineers.

select o.order_no, c.cust_no, c.job_title
from **order** as o, **customer** as c
where c.cust_no=o.cust_no
and c.job_title=computer engineer;

Update: Add a new customer, a painter, with number 423378 and the customer's order number, 763521601, to the database.

insert into **customer** (cust_no, job_title)
values ('423378','painter');
insert into **order** (order_no, cust_no)
values ('763521601','423378');

Using the minimum set 3NF schema, the system query optimizer can choose from a number of different ways to execute the transaction. Let us first assume that the tables are all ordered physically by their primary keys. We use the sort/merge join strategy for the first transaction: Sort the **order** table by cust_no, then join tables **order** and **customer** with a single scan of each, and select only rows that have job_title of computer engineer. We then project on order_no to answer the query. To simplify the analysis, we assume that a sort of n rows takes n $\log_2$ n row (logical record, lra) accesses and that computer engineers make up 5% of the customers and orders in the database.

lra = sort **order** + scan **order** + scan **customer** + create **order_cust**
+ scan **order_cust** + create **comp_engr** + project **comp_engr**
= (200,000 $\log_2$ 200,000) + 200,000 + 80,000
+ 200,000 + 200,000 + 200,000*.05 + 200,000*.05
= 200,000*(17.61+3.10) + 80,000
= 4,222,000 row accesses

All row accesses are sequential in this strategy. We also assume 30 ms for a sequential block access, 60 ms for a random block access, a block size of 4 KB

(4096 bytes) and a prefetch buffer size of 64 KB (as done in DB2). We can estimate the I/O service time by first computing the effective prefetch blocking factors for the tables **order**, **customer**, **order_cust**, and **comp_engr**: 4368, 2176, 1680, and 1680, respectively. We compute the sequential block accesses as follows.

sba = ceiling(200,000*(17.61 +1)/4368) + ceiling(80,000/2176)
+ ceiling(420,000/1680)
= 1140

iotime = 1140*30 ms = 34.2 sec

The strategy to execute the second transaction, using the same schema, is to scan each table (**order** and **customer**) and rewrite both tables in the new order.

sba = ceiling(200,000/4368)*2 + ceiling(80,000/2176)*2
= 166

iotime = 166*30 ms = 5.0 sec

If we refine the minimum set 3NF schema to avoid the join in the first transaction, the resulting schema will have a single table **order_cust**, with primary key order_no and nonkey attributes cust_no and job_title, instead of separate tables **order** and **customer**. This not only avoids the join, but also the sort needed to get both tables ordered by cust_no. The strategy for the first transaction is now to scan **order_cust** once to find the computer engineers, write the resulting data on disk, and then read back from disk to project the resulting temporary table, **comp_engr**, to answer the query.

sba = ceiling(200,000/1680) + [ceiling(200,000*.05/1680)]*2 = 132

iotime = 132*30 ms = 4.0 sec

The strategy for the second transaction, using this refined schema, is to scan **order_cust** once to find the point of insertion and then to scan again to reorder the table.

sba = ceiling(200,000/1680)*2 = 240

iotime = 240*30 ms = 7.2 sec

Common to both strategies is the addition of an order record to the tables **order_item_sales** and **order_dept_sales**. For the sake of simplicity, we will assume these tables to be unsorted, so the addition of a new order will require only one record access at the end of the table and, thus, negligible I/O time.

The basic performance and normalization data for these two schemas and the two transactions given previously are summarized in Table 7.1.

The refined schema dramatically reduces the I/O time for the query transaction, but the cost is the loss of performance for the update, more storage space, and significant reduction in the degree of normalization. The normalization is reduced because we now have a transitive FD: order_no –> cust_no –> job_title in table **order_cust**. The implication of this is, of course, that there is a delete anomaly for job_title when a customer deletes an order or the order is filled.

The significance of these performance and data integrity differences depends upon the overall objectives as well as the computing environment for the database, and it must be analyzed in that context. For instance, the performance differences must be evaluated for all relevant transactions, present and projected. Storage space differences may or may not be significant in the computing environment. Integrity problems with the deletion commands need to be evaluated on a case-by-case basis to determine whether the side effects of certain record deletions are destructive to the objectives of the database. In summary, the database designer now has the ability to evaluate the trade-offs among query and update requirements, storage space, and integrity associated with normalization. This knowledge can be applied to a variety of database design problems.

Table 7.1. Comparison of performance and integrity of original tables and join table

	Minimum set 3NF schema (order and customer)	*Refined schema (order_cust)*
Query	34.2 sec	4.0 sec
Update	5.0 sec	7.2 sec
Storage space (relevant tables)	5.4 MB	7.8 MB
Normalization	3NF	2NF

7.3.2 Index Selection Problem

The usage refinement solution can be further improved by a careful selection of indices. If we create a secondary index to access the **order_cust** table for the 5% of customers with orders who are computer engineers, we then will have 5% of 200,000 records or 10,000 records to randomly access at 60 ms each. This will take 600 seconds, which is clearly unacceptable compared to the previously mentioned solutions (Table 7.1). Building a secondary index on job_title to the **customer** table is similarly poor in performance.

On the other hand, the performance of the update to **customer** and **order** would significantly improve with a primary index to each table. In each case, access via hashing is typically one random block access to each table plus a sequential rewrite, while access via B^+-tree is one to two random block accesses plus a sequential rewrite. In either case, the total time to perform the update is well under one second. Similarly, with the join table **order_cust**, a primary index can be built for the composite key order_no, cust_no which results in less than one second update time. Thus, creation of two primary indices clearly improves update performance, and hence improves overall performance.

In general, picking an optimal index is known to be NP-complete, so we usually use heuristic approaches such as the one illustrated above. It should also be noted that adding an index can sometimes fool a query optimizer and actually degrade performance instead of improve it. To avoid this type of problem, one should always investigate the side effects of implementing an index by testing the dominant transactions for the database.

7.4 Summary

In this chapter we developed a global (logical) schema for a centralized relational database, given the requirements specification for a retail store database. The example illustrates the life-cycle steps of ER modeling, global schema design, normalization, and schema refinement based on processing efficiency. It summarizes the techniques presented in Chapters 1 through 6. Next we turn to distributed databases as the next part of our analysis of database design.

CHAPTER 8

DATA ALLOCATION STRATEGIES

Distributed and multidatabase design is an integral part of the database life cycle. Design components that apply to both homogeneous distributed and heterogeneous multidatabases include data fragmentation, data distribution methods, and data allocation strategies. In this chapter we look at each of these components briefly and then examine two data allocation methods in detail, one in which no data redundancy is allowed and another with data redundancy. These methods are easily computable by hand for small to medium configurations or implementable in software for large configurations.

8.1 Introduction

Advances in the computer and communications technologies have led to distributed computer systems, which interconnect mainframes, minicomputers, and workstations through various communications media. This was accompanied by the development of distributed operating systems, distributed languages, and distributed database management systems. A distributed database management system (DDBMS) is a software system that supports the transparent creation, access, and manipulation of interrelated data located at the different sites of a computer network. Each site of the network has autonomous processing capability and can perform local applications. Each site also participates in the execution of at least one global application, which requires network communication [Chu84, CePe84]. The goal of a DDBMS is to improve the accessibility, sharability, and performance of a DBMS while preserving the appearance of a centralized DBMS.

Because of the nature of the loosely coupled network of computers, the database design issues encountered in distributed database systems differ from those encountered in centralized database systems [Heba77, FHS80]. In centralized databases, access efficiency is achieved through local optimization by using complex physical structures. In distributed databases, the global optimization of processing, including cost of network communication and local processing, is of major concern. Total cost is a function of the network configuration, the user work load, the data allocation strategy, and the query optimization algorithm.

DDBMSs may be homogeneous or heterogeneous, semiautonomous (federated) or autonomous (multidatabase). We will first look at the basic data allocation problem common to the variety of DDBMSs and then illustrate two easily computable methods, or strategies, for allocating data (files, tables, or fragments of tables) in a distributed database system.

8.2 Distributed and Multidatabase Design

Once a DDBMS has been developed or purchased, the database designers or administrators need to know how to design and allocate the distributed database. This is significantly influenced by the architecture and the facilities of the DDBMS; it, in turn, significantly impacts the query processing, concurrency control, and availability of the database.

The three most common objectives of distributed database design are the

- separation of data fragmentation from data allocation,
- control of data redundancy, and
- independence from local DBMSs.

The distinction between designing the fragmentation and allocation schema is conceptually relevant: The first is a logical mapping but the second is a physical mapping. In general, it is not possible to determine the optimal fragmentation and allocation by solving the two problems independently; they are interrelated.

8.2.1 Fragmentation

A table r is fragmented by partitioning it into a minimal number of disjoint subtables (fragments) r1,r2, . . .,rn. These fragments contain sufficient information to reconstruct the original table r. Basically, there are two different schemes for fragmenting a table: horizontal and vertical.

Horizontal fragmentation partitions the records of a global table into subsets. A fragment, ri, is a selection on the global table r using a predicate Pi, its qualification. The reconstruction of r is obtained by taking the union of all fragments.

Vertical fragmentation subdivides the attributes of the global table into groups. The simplest form of vertical fragmentation is decomposition. A unique record-id may be included in each fragment to guarantee that reconstruction through a join operation is possible. Note that mixed fragmentation is the result of the successive application of both fragmentation techniques.

Rules for Fragmentation

- Fragments are formed by the select predicates associated with dominant database transactions. The predicates specify attribute values used in the conjunctive (AND) and disjunctive (OR) form of select commands and in records containing the same values they form fragments.
- Fragments must be disjoint and their union must become the whole table. Overlapping fragments are too difficult to analyze and implement.
- The largest fragment is the whole table. The smallest fragment is a single record. Fragments should be designed to maintain a balance between these extremes. The whole table as a fragment disallows the potential efficiency of partitioning the table across local sites by usage. Single records as fragments, on the other hand, introduce undue complexity into the data allocation problem, extreme sensitivity to changing applications, and potentially too much overhead to execute joins between tables.

8.2.2 Data Allocation

The constraints under which data allocation strategies may operate are determined by the system architecture and the available network database management software. The four basic approaches are

- centralized,
- partitioned,
- replicated data, and
- selective replication.

In the centralized approach, all the data are located at a single site. The implementation of this approach is simple. However, the size of the database is limited by the availability of the secondary storage at the central site. Furthermore, the database may become unavailable from any of the remote sites when communication failures occur, and the database system fails totally when the central site fails.

In the partitioned approach, the database is partitioned into disjoint fragments, and each fragment is assigned to a particular site. This strategy is particularly appropriate where local secondary storage is limited compared to the database size, the reliability of the centralized database is not sufficient, or operating efficiencies can be gained through the exploitation of the locality of references in database accesses.

The completely replicated data approach allocates a full copy of the database to each site in the network. This completely redundant distributed data strategy is only appropriate when reliability is critical, the database is small, and update inefficiency can be tolerated. It is much less commonly used than selective replication.

The selective replication approach partitions the database into critical and noncritical fragments. Noncritical fragments need only be stored once, while critical fragments are replicated as desired to meet the required level of availability and performance. This is the most commonly used strategy because of its great flexibility; some fragments may be small, while others can be quite large, possibly entire tables.

The cost/benefit of the replicated database allocation strategy can be estimated in terms of storage cost, communication costs (query and update time), and data availability. Figure 8.1 briefly illustrates the trade-off by showing the data replication on the horizontal axis and costs on the vertical axis. It can be seen from Figure 8.1 that

- the query communication cost decreases as the number of copies increases because most data can be found at local sites, thus eliminating the need for communication calls.
- the update communication cost increases with the number of copies because duplicated data will need to be updated.
- the storage cost and local processing cost increase as the number of copies increases.
- the read availability increases with the number of copies in the system, while the write availability generally decreases; a write requires most or all copies to be available.

An optimal data allocation can be theoretically determined to minimize the total cost (storage+communication+local processing) subject to some response time and availability constraints. This problem, traditionally referred to as the File Allocation Problem (FAP) in computing networks, was first addressed by Wesley Chu [Chu69]. Since then, many different file allocation algorithms have appeared in the literature [Case72, MaRi76, MoLe77, CoGe80, FiHo80]. Earlier allocation resolutions were simple, but more recent methods are actual design methodologies that utilize the allocation techniques for one of the decisions [CPW87]. Application of the FAP problem depends on the nature of the problem, the availability of information needed to reach an exact solution, and the need to determine optimal versus approximate solu-

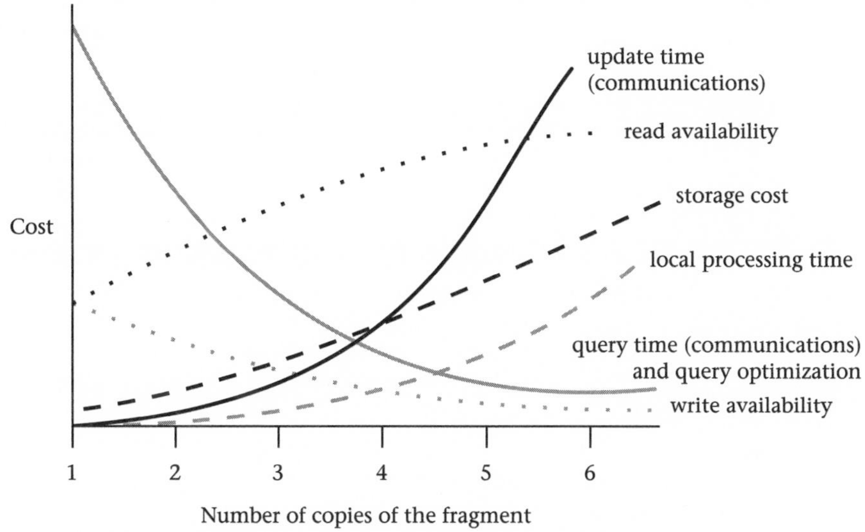

Figure 8.1 Trade-offs in database distribution due to data replication

tions in real life. It has often been found that, for real-life situations, sophisticated FAP solutions are rarely needed. In most cases, data allocation decisions can be made by exercising judgment and using real-life constraints of security and management. However, it is preferable to use simple analytical models to support the decisions and improve insights.

8.3 The General Data Allocation Problem

Assume knowledge of application system specifications and distributed system configuration as outlined in the list that follows.

- *Application system specifications:*

  A database global schema and fragmentation schema

  A set of user transactions and their frequencies

  Security: data ownership (who can update) and access authorization (who can query) for each transaction

  Recovery: estimated frequency and volume of backup operations

  Integrity: referential integrity, boundary value integrity rules, journaling overhead

- *Distributed or multidatabase system configuration and software:*

  The network topology, network channel capacities, and network control mechanism

  The site locations and their processing capacity (CPU and I/O processing)

  Sources of data (where data can be located) and sinks of data (where user transactions can be initiated and data transferred)

  The transaction processing options and synchronization algorithms

  The unit costs for data storage, local site processing, and communications

Find the allocation of programs and database fragments to sites that minimizes C, the total cost. Keep in mind that

$$C = C_{comm} + C_{proc} + C_{stor}$$

where

C_{comm} = communications cost for message and data

C_{proc} = site processing cost (CPU and I/O)

C_{stor} = storage cost for data and programs at sites

are subject to possible additional constraints on

- transaction response time, which is the sum of communication delays, local processing, and all resource queuing delays, and
- transaction availability, which is the percentage of time the transaction executes with all components available.

In some cases, the total cost (possibly including equipment cost) could be considered a constraint and minimum response time the objective. In other cases, the network topology and/or local site processing capacity is to be analyzed as well as the data distribution.

8.4 Data Allocation Strategies

A general rule for data allocation states that data should be placed as close as possible to where it will be used, and load balancing should be used to find a global optimization of system performance. In the following sections we describe two methods originally defined by Ceri and Pelagatti [CePe84] and extend the discussion by adding illustrative examples and practical interpretation of the important parameters.

8.4.1 The Nonredundant Best Fit Method

The nonredundant *best fit* method determines the single site most likely to allocate a fragment (which may be a file, table, or subset of a table) based on maximum benefit, where benefit is interpreted to mean total query and update references. In particular, place fragment ri at the site s*, where the number of local query and update references by all the user transactions is maximized.

Let us illustrate the application of this method with a simple example of a global schema and its processing characteristics. In this example each fragment to be allocated is an entire table. The average disk I/O service times are given for a query or update originating from the same site in the network (local) or combined disk and network service times from different sites (remote).

System Parameters

Table size		*Avg local query (update) time (milliseconds)*	*Avg remote query (update) time (milliseconds)*
R1	300 KB	100 (150)	500 (600)
R2	500 KB	150 (200)	650 (700)
R3	1.0 MB	200 (250)	1000 (1100)

User transactions are described in terms of their frequency of occurrence, which tables they access, and whether the accesses are reads or writes.

Transaction	*Site(s)*	*Frequency*	*Table accesses (reads, writes)*
T1	S1, S4, S5	1	Four to **R1** (3 reads, 1 write), two to **R2** (2 reads)
T2	S2, S4	2	Two to **R1** (2 reads), four to **R3** (3 reads, 1 write)
T3	S3, S5	3	Four to **R2** (3 reads, 1 write), two to **R3** (2 reads)

Security: User transactions T1, T2, and T3 can either query or update (no restrictions)

Sources of data: All sites—S1, S2, S3, S4, S5

Sinks of data (possible locations of transactions): All sites—S1, S2, S3, S4, S5

Local Reference Computations

Our goal is to compute the number of local references to each table residing at each site, one by one. The site that maximizes the local references to a given table is chosen as the site where that table should reside.

The preceding tables tell us that table **R1** has the following local references: At site S1 it has only transaction T1 with four references at a frequency of one, and thus four total references; at site S2 it has transaction T2 with two references at a frequency of two, and thus four total references; at site S3 it has no transaction references; at site S4 it has both transactions T1 and T2 for a total of eight references; and at site S5 it has transaction T1 for a total of four references. A maximum of eight local references to table **R1** occurs at site S4 (see Table 8.1).

Table **R2** has the following local references: at site S1 it has only transaction T1 for a total of 2 references; at site S2 it has no references by any transaction; at site S3 it has 4 references by transaction T3 and a frequency of three, thus 12 total references; at site S4 it has only transaction T1 for a total of 2 references; at site S5 it has transactions T1 and T3 for a total of 14 references. A maximum of 14 local references to table **R2** occur at site S5 (see Table 8.1).

Table **R3** local references are computed in a similar fashion: At sites S2 and S4 there are a maximum of eight references.

Table 8.1 Local references for each table at each of five possible sites

Table	*Site*	*Transactions T1 (frequency)*	*T2 (frequency)*	*T3 (frequency)*	*Total local references*
R1	S1	3 read, 1 write (1)	0	0	4
	S2	0	2 read (2)	0	4
	S3	0	0	0	0
	S4	3 read, 1 write (1)	2 read (2)	0	8 (max.)
	S5	3 read, 1 write (1)	0	0	4

Table 8.1 Continued

R2	S1	2 read (1)	0	0	2
	S2	0	0	0	0
	S3	0	0	3 read, 1 write (3)	12
	S4	2 read (1)	0	0	2
	S5	2 read (1)	0	3 read, 1 write (3)	14 (max.)
R3	S1	0	0	0	0
	S2	0	3 read, 1 write (2)	0	8 (max.)
	S3	0	0	2 read (3)	6
	S4	0	3 read, 1 write (2)	0	8 (max.)
	S5	0	0	2 read (3)	6

Allocation Decision

Figure 8.2 presents the allocation decision. Allocate table **R1** at site S4 and table **R2** at site S5. At these sites the number of local references to these tables is clearly maximized. However, table **R3** is maximized at both sites S2 and S4, so additional information is needed to choose the allocation. For instance, if maximum availability of data is a major consideration, then choose site S2 for table **R3** because site S4 already has table **R1** allocated to it; putting **R3** there as well would decrease the potential availability of data should site S4 crash. The final allocation under these assumptions: S1 is empty, S2 has table **R3**, S3 is empty, S4 has table **R1**, and S5 has table **R2**.

The advantage of the best fit method is its computational simplicity. The main disadvantage is in accuracy: Computing the number of local references does not accurately characterize disk service time or response time. Furthermore, it does not give any insights regarding data replication. A better approach is to compute total block accesses or total I/O time.

8.4.2 The Redundant "All Beneficial Sites" Method

The redundant *all beneficial sites* method (ABS) can be used for either the redundant or nonredundant case. It selects all sites for a fragment allocation where the benefit is greater than the cost for one additional copy of that fragment. You are assumed to start with no copy or one copy of each table or fragment of a table.

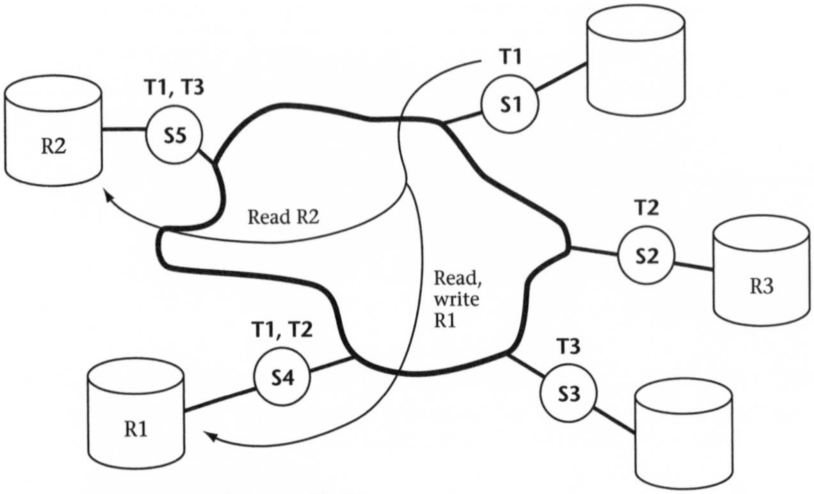

Figure 8.2 Nonredundant "best fit" method for data allocation, showing remote query and update for transaction T1 originating at site S1

The benefit for an additional copy of a given fragment F at site S is measured by the difference in elapsed time between a remote query (i.e., no replicated copy) and a local query (i.e., replicated copy available), multiplied by the frequency of queries to fragment F originating from site S.

The cost for an additional copy of a given fragment F at site S is the total elapsed time for all the local updates for fragment F from transactions originating at site S, plus the total elapsed time for all the remote updates of fragment F at site S from transactions originating at other sites.

Cost/Benefit Computations

The cost/benefit computations described in this section are summarized in Table 8.2.

Table R1

Table **R1** at site S1 has the following cost: two remote updates (writes) by transaction T1 (frequency of one), one each from sites S4 and S5, multiplied by 600 ms per write, totaling 1200 ms; plus one local update by T1 at site S1 at 150 ms for a grand total of 1350 ms. The benefit is from three queries (reads) by transaction T1 at site S1, multiplied by the difference between a remote and local query (500–100=400 ms), totaling 1200 ms.

Table **R1** at site S2 has the cost of three remote updates by transaction T1 (frequency of one)—one each from sites S1, S4, and S5—multiplied by 600 ms per write, totaling 1800 ms. The benefit is from two queries (reads) by transaction T2 at site S2 (frequency of two), multiplied by the difference between a remote and local query (400 ms), totaling 1600 ms.

Table **R1** at site S3 has the cost of three remote updates by transaction T1 (frequency of one)—one each from sites S1, S4, and S5—multiplied by 600 ms per write, totaling 1800 ms. There is no benefit, because no transaction accesses table **R1** locally at site S3.

Table **R1** at site S4 has the cost of two remote updates by transaction T1 from sites S1 and S5 (frequency of one), multiplied by 600 ms per write, totaling 1200 ms; plus one local update by T1 at site S4 at 150 ms, for a grand total of 1350 ms. The benefit is three queries by transaction T1 (frequency of one) and two queries by transaction T2 (frequency of two), multiplied by 400 ms, totaling 2800 ms.

Table **R1** at site S5 has the cost of two remote updates by transaction T1 from sites S1 and S4 (frequency of one), multiplied by 600 ms per write, totaling 1200 ms; plus one local update by T1 at site S5 at 150 ms, for a grand total of 1350 ms. The benefit is three queries by transaction T1 (frequency of one), multiplied by 400 ms, totaling 1200 ms.

In summary, for table **R1** benefit exceeds cost only at site S4; thus, only one copy of **R1** is allocated to this network.

Tables R2 and R3

With similar computations we obtain the results for tables **R2** and **R3** as shown in Table 8.2.

In summary, for table **R2**, benefit exceeds cost at sites S3 and S5. For table **R3**, benefit exceeds cost at all sites except S1.

Allocation Decision

Figure 8.3 presents the allocation decision. Allocate table **R1** to site S4. Allocate table **R2** to sites S3 and S5. Allocate table **R3** to sites S2, S3, S4, and S5.

In the cases where benefit and cost are equal, consider whether either cost or benefit (or both) is likely to change in the near future or if greater availability is important. Adjust the allocation accordingly. If cost exceeds benefit at all sites for a given fragment, then pick the site for a single allocation where the difference between cost and benefit is minimized.

Note that there exist many more elaborate fragmentation and data allocation strategies than are covered here; however, this text has highlighted the major issues to provide a simple method when quick analysis is needed.

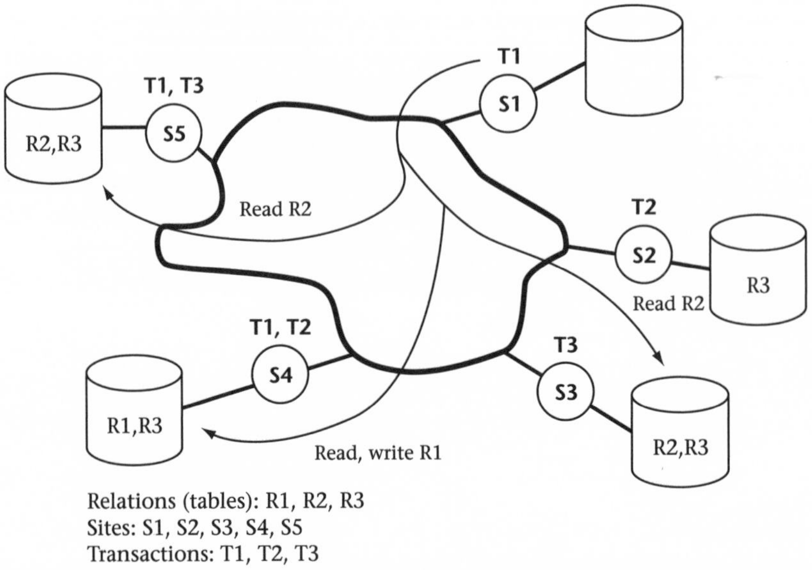

Figure 8.3 Redundant "all beneficial sites" method for data allocation, showing remote query and update for transaction T1 originating at site S1

Table 8.2 Cost and benefit for each table located at five possible sites

Table	*Site*	*Remote update (local update) transactions*	*No. of writes*freq*time (ms)*	*Cost (ms)*
R1	S1	T1 from S4 and S5 (T1 from S1)	2*1*600 +1*1*150	1350
	S2	T1 from S1, S4, S5	3*1*600	1800
	S3	T1 from S1, S4, S5	3*1*600	1800
	S4	T1 from S1 and S5 (T1 from S4)	2*1*600 +1*1*150	1350
	S5	T1 from S1 and S4 (T1 from S5)	2*1*600 +1*1*150	1350
R2	S1	T3 from S3 and S5	2*3*700	4200
	S2	T3 from S3 and S5	2*3*700	4200
	S3	T3 from S5 (T3 from S3)	1*3*700 +1*3*200	2700
	S4	T3 from S3 and S5	2*3*700	4200
	S5	T3 from S3 (T3 from S5)	1*3*700 +1*3*200	2700

Table 8.2 Continued

R3	S1	T2 from S2 and S4	2*2*1100	4400
	S2	T2 from S4 (T2 from S2)	1*2*1100 +1*2*250	2700
	S3	T2 from S2 and S4	2*2*1100	4400
	S4	T2 from S2 (T2 from S4)	1*2*1100 +1*2*250	2700
	S5	T2 from S2 and S4	2*2*1100	4400

Table	*Site*	*Query (read) sources*	*No. of reads*frequency *(remote–local time)*	*Benefit (ms)*
R1	S1	T1 at S1	3*1*(500 – 100)	1200
	S2	T2 at S2	2*2*(500 – 100)	1600
	S3	None	0	0
	S4	T1 and T2 at S4	(3*1 + 2*2)*(500 – 100)	2800
	S5	T1 at S5	3*1*(500 – 100)	1200
R2	S1	T1 at S1	2*1*(650 – 150)	1000
	S2	None	0	0
	S3	T3 at S3	3*3*(650 – 150)	4500
	S4	T1 at S4	2*1*(650 – 150)	1000
	S5	T1 and T3 at S5	(2*1 + 3*3)*(650 – 150)	5500
R3	S1	None	0	0
	S2	T2 at S2	3*2*(1000 – 200)	4800
	S3	T3 at S3	2*3*(1000 – 200)	4800
	S4	T2 at S4	3*2*(1000 – 200)	4800
	S5	T3 at S5	2*3*(1000 – 200)	4800

The all beneficial sites method can be derived from exhaustive enumeration of total cost for the initial allocation configuration and the total cost for a new allocation configuration after the replication of a fragment (or table) at a given site. The decision is made to replicate the fragment (or table) if the total cost after replication is lower than total cost before replication.

For example, let fragment F1 be initially allocated to site S1. We need to decide whether to replicate F1 at site S2. Let query Q1 and update U1, both originating at site S1, access F1; and let query Q2 and update U2, both originating at site S2, also access F1.

Total-cost$_1$(initial allocation of F1 to S1) = Q1(local) + U1(local)
+ Q2(remote) + U2(remote)

Total-cost$_2$(after replication of F1 at S2) = Q1(local) + U1(local)
+ U1(remote) + Q2(local) + U2(local) + U2(remote)

where queries Q1 and Q2 are made to the closest copy of F1, and updates U1 and U2 must be made to both copies of F1. We allow F1 to be replicated at S2 if the following condition holds:

$$\text{Total-cost}_2 < \text{Total-cost}_1$$

$$\text{Q1(local)} + \text{U1(local)} + \text{U1(remote)} + \text{Q2(local)} + \text{U2(local)} + \text{U2(remote)} < \text{Q1(local)} + \text{U1(local)} + \text{Q2(remote)} + \text{U2(remote)}$$

$$\text{U1(remote)} + \text{Q2(local)} + \text{U2(local)} < \text{Q2(remote)}$$

$$\text{Q2(remote)} - \text{Q2(local)} > \text{U1(remote)} + \text{U2(local)}$$

which is the relationship that defines the all beneficial sites method—that is, the benefit is the difference between a remote and local query time to F1, and the cost is the sum of the local and remote update times for the new copy of F1.

8.4.3 Progressive Fragment Allocation

A practical extension of the all beneficial sites method, called the *progressive fragment allocation method* [JWBT91], allocates the first copy of each fragment on the basis of maximum value of benefit minus cost. It remembers where that copy is, and bases the next allocation decision on the location of that first copy and the maximum value of benefit minus cost for the remaining sites. This procedure is continued, one allocation at a time, until benefit no longer exceeds cost for any of the remaining sites. Note that for this method, cost stays constant for each decision because the update for an additional fragment is independent of previous allocations. However, benefit does not stay constant; it decreases each time a new copy is allocated that is closer to a given site than the previous set of allocations. The decrease in the benefit at a given site, which must have at least one query to this fragment, is measured by the decrease in propagation delay between the former closest copy and the proposed new copy of the fragment, relative to that given site. In the worst case, when a new copy is no closer than any previous copies, the benefit stays the same, but does not increase.

This approach gives a more realistic allocation based on a progressive set of allocations, rather than a set of independent allocation decisions. It is also a fast method because sites where benefit is less than cost need no longer be evaluated in future iterations.

As an example, let us assume that two fragments, F1 and F2, are to be allocated to either or both sites S1 and S2. The costs and benefits are computed to be:

F1	S1	cost = 150	benefit = 200
	S2	cost = 170	benefit = 175
F2	S1	cost = 60	benefit = 30
	S2	cost = 50	benefit = 45

Using the all beneficial sites method, F1 is allocated to both S1 and S2 because benefits exceed costs at both sites. F2 is allocated to S2 because it minimizes the amount by which cost exceeds benefit.

Using the progressive fragment allocation method, F1 is initially allocated to site S1 where benefit exceeds cost by the greatest amount; and F2 is initially allocated to site S2 where the differential between benefit and cost is minimized, although cost exceeds benefit at all sites. After this initial allocation, let us assume the benefit of F1 at S2 is decreased due to the presence of a copy of F1 at S1:

F1	S2	cost = 170	benefit = 165

At this point no further allocations can be made for F1 (beyond site S1) because cost now exceeds benefit. This decision is based on more precise data than the all beneficial sites method, and is therefore more accurate.

8.5 Summary

We have seen that distributed database design requires much more analysis than centralized databases, but that there exists a set of basic principles we can use for everyday design decisions. We have also seen that both nonredundant and redundant data allocation methods can be simply expressed and implemented to minimize the time needed to execute a collection of transactions on a distributed database. These methods take into account the execution times of remote and local database transactions for query and update and the frequencies of these transactions.

The advantages of the all beneficial sites method, compared to the best fit method, are its computational simplicity, its greater attention to the relative weights of service time for reads and writes, and its applicability to either the nonredundant or redundant data alternatives. It has no disadvantages relative to best fit, but it does have some general limitations regarding the difficulty of obtaining the average query and update times over all applications and the fact that it ignores the details of network topology and protocols. In a new case study in Chapter 9, we will look at a practical extension of all beneficial sites that overcomes these limitations.

Literature Summary

[ACM90] "Special Issue on Heterogeneous Databases," *ACM Computing Surveys* 22,3 (Sept. 1990), pp. 173–293.

[Case72] Casey, R.G. "Allocation of Copies of a File in an Information Network," *Spring Joint Computer Conf., 1972,* AFIPS Press, Vol. 40, 1972.

[CNP82] Ceri, S., Negri, M., and Pelagatti, G. "Horizontal Data Partitioning in Database Design," *Proc. ACM-SIGMOD Int'l. Conf. on Management of Data,* Orlando, FL, June 2–4, 1982, pp. 128–136.

[CePe84] Ceri, S. and Pelagatti, G. *Distributed Databases: Principles and Systems,* McGraw-Hill, New York, 1984.

[CPW87] Ceri, S., Pernici, B., and Wiederhold, G. "Distributed Database Design Methodologies," *Proc. of the IEEE,* May 1987, pp. 533–546.

[Chu69] Chu, W.W. "Optimal File Allocation in a Multiple Computer System," *IEEE Trans. on Computers,* C-18,10 (Oct. 1969), pp. 885–889.

[Chu84] Chu, W.W. *Distributed Data Bases, Handbook of Software Engineering,* C.R. Vick and C.V. Ramamoorthy (editors), Van Nostrand Reinhold, New York, 1984.

[CoGe80] Coffman, E.G., et al. "Optimization of the Number of Copies in Distributed Databases," *Proc. of the 7th IFIP Symposium on Computer Performance Modelling, Measurement and Evaluation,* Springer-Verlag, New York, May 1980, pp. 257–263.

[FiHo80] Fisher, M.L. and Hochbaum, D. "Database Location in Computer Networks," *J ACM* 27, 4 (Oct. 1980).

[FHS80] Fisher, P., Hollist, P., and Slonim, J. "A Design Methodology for Distributed Databases," *Proc. IEEE Conf. Distributed Computing,* Sept. 1980, IEEE, pp. 199–202.

[Heba77] Hebalkar, P.G. "Logical Design Considerations for Distributed Database Systems," *IEEE COMPSAC,* Nov. 1977, pp. 562–580.

[HsKa89] Hsiao, D.K. and Kamel, M.N. "Heterogeneous Databases: Proliferations, Issues, and Solutions," *IEEE Trans. on Knowledge and Data Engineering* 1,1 (March 1989), pp. 45–62.

[JWBT91] Janakiraman, J., Warack, C., Bhal, G., and Teorey, T.J. "Progressive Fragment Allocation," *Proc. 10th Int'l. Conf. on the Entity Relationship Approach,* San Mateo, CA, October 23–25, 1991, pp. 543–560.

[MaRi76] Mahmood, S. and Riordan, J . "Optimal Allocation of Resources in Distributed Information Networks," *ACM Trans. Database Systems* 1,1(March 1976), pp. 66–78.

[MoLe77] Morgan, H.L. and Levin, K.D. "Optimal Program and Data Allocation in Computer Networks," *Comm. ACM* 32,5 (May 1977), pp. 345–353.

[TCOU89] Teorey, T.J., Chaar, J., Olukotun, K., and Umar, A. "Distributed Database Design: Some Basic Concepts and Strategies," *Database Programming and Design* 2,4 (April 1989), 34–42.

EXERCISES

Problem 8-1

First use the best fit method based on frequency of applications to determine a feasible nonredundant allocation for the three unfragmented tables (**R1**, **R2**, **R3**) among the three equidistant sites (S1, S2, S3). Then use the all beneficial sites approach to determine where to replicate the tables, using the following workload and configuration parameters. Assume that each site has adequate sequential and random (hashing) access methods for disk files.

Workload (applications)

Query 1: requires a 3-way join (single full scan, no sort required) of tables **R1**, **R2**, and **R3**.

Query 2: requires a random access to one record in **R2**.

Update 1: requires a random access to one record in **R1**, and a rewrite of that record.

Update 2: sequential scan of table **R2** and a rewrite of every record.

Type of application	*Origin of application*	*Application frequency*
Query 1	(on **R1**, **R2**, **R3**)	Site S1
Query 2	(on **R2** only)	Sites S1, S2, S3
Update 1	(on **R1** only)	Site S2
Update 2	(on **R2** only)	Site S3

Tables

R1 fits exactly into 100 blocks. Blocking factor=20.

R2 fits exactly into 100 blocks. Blocking factor=10.

R3 fits exactly into 100 blocks. Blocking factor=50.

Critical disk and network times

Trba = 40 ms at all sites (disk I/O time for a random block access)

Tsba = 10 ms at all sites (disk I/O time for a sequential block access)

network propagation delay = 10 ms; transmission delay for one packet (or block) = 100 ms

Problem 8-2

Repeat Problem 8-1 using the best fit method based on total block accesses for each application (block accesses per application execution times frequency) instead of just frequency of the application. Why does this give a different result from Problem 8-1?

Problem 8-3

Apply the all beneficial sites approach to determine an optimal redundant allocation for the three fragments (F1, F2, F3) across the four sites given in the figure below. Assume that each allocation decision can be made independently of the other decisions. To determine where to replicate the fragments, use the following workload and configuration parameters. Assume that each site has adequate sequential and random (hashing) access methods for disk files.

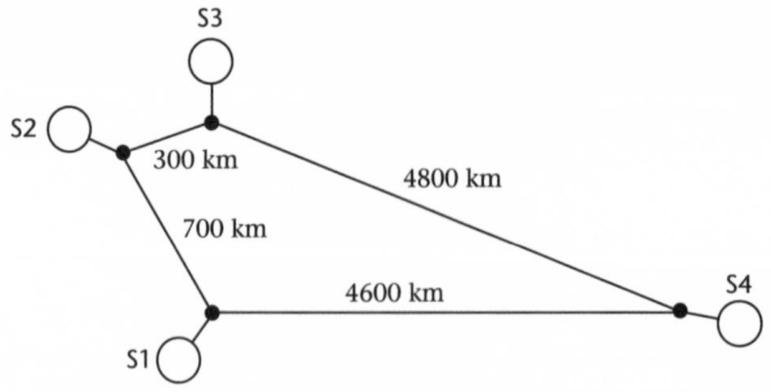

Workload (transactions)

Query 1: requires a 3-way join (single full scan, no sort required) of fragments F1, F2, and F3.

Query 2: requires a random access to one record in F2, then to one record in F1.

Query 3: requires a random access to one record in F3.

Update 1: requires a random access to one record in F1, and a rewrite of that record.

Update 2: sequential scan of fragment F2 and a rewrite of each record updated.

Type of transaction	*Origin of transaction*	*Transaction frequency*	*Size of reply*
Query 1 (on F1, F2, F3)	Site S1	1	whole table
Query 2 (on F2, F1)	Sites S2, S3, S4	100 (each site)	1 packet
Query 3 (on F3)	Site S3	5	1 packet
Update 1 (on F1 only)	Site S2	50	1 packet
Update 2 (on F2 only)	Sites S1, S3, S4	50 (each site)	1 packet

Fragments

F1 has 20,000 records, blocking factor=20.

F2 has 10,000 records, blocking factor=100.

F3 has 50,000 records, blocking factor=25.

Block size = 10,000 Bytes.

Packet size = 1000 Bytes.

Critical disk and network times

Trba = 40 ms at all sites (disk I/O time for a random block access)

Tsba = 10 ms at all sites (disk I/O time for a sequential block access)

network propagation delay is based on degraded speed of light estimate (200 km/ms)

network transmission rate is based on T1 speed (1.544 Mbps)

Problem 8-4

Redo Problem 8-3 with a variation of ABS called *progressive fragment allocation* that first allocates an initial copy of each fragment as the one that has the maximum value of benefit minus cost, then remembers where that copy is (e.g., has memory) and successively determines where each of the next copies should go on the basis of maximum value of benefit minus cost, one at a time, so long as benefit exceeds cost. Note that after each specific fragment allocation, the benefit decreases because additional copies make the query times decrease, and it is assumed that the benefit is a function of a closer copy, not just a local copy being created.

Problem 8-5

Consider how your allocation strategy in Problem 8-3 would change under the two extremes of network configuration:

a. Every link is 56 Kbps, so that packet transmission is dominant.
b. Every link uses a future technology of Gbps, so that packet transmission delays are minimal.

CHAPTER 9

OPTIMAL DISTRIBUTED DATA ALLOCATION

This chapter presents a distributed database design problem that involves the development of a global schema and a fragmentation and allocation of data. An ER model for the database is first developed from a simple set of logical database requirements. We note that the ER model is derived as if the entire database were a single centralized database. This model applies to any form of data distribution because the ER model is independent of data distribution parameters. The requirements also include a description of the transactions and a proposed network environment. A stepwise solution to this problem is then given in detail, based on mean value assumptions about work load and service.

Most textbooks and courses on distributed database systems lack concrete examples of how the database design process can be extended to include data fragmentation and data allocation strategies. The problem presented here has been carefully designed to provide enough complexity to challenge the advanced database student or practitioner, but to be small enough to avoid the drudgery of repetitive hand computation. On this latter point, as the solution is developed, it should become obvious where software tools would be helpful to evaluate large-scale designs.

9.1 A Distributed Database Design Problem

Given the database description that follows [Spro76], an ER diagram representation of that description is shown in Figure 9.1, and from this diagram we develop a global schema of 3NF (and BCNF) tables. Then we design a data fragmentation and an initial nonredundant data allocation based on the needs of individual users at remote sites, given the network topology in Figure 9.2. Finally, we design an optimal data allocation schema using the all beneficial sites method for allocating redundant data [CePe84, CPW87, TCOU89], weighing the design decisions against an exhaustive enumeration of transaction costs and feasible allocations.

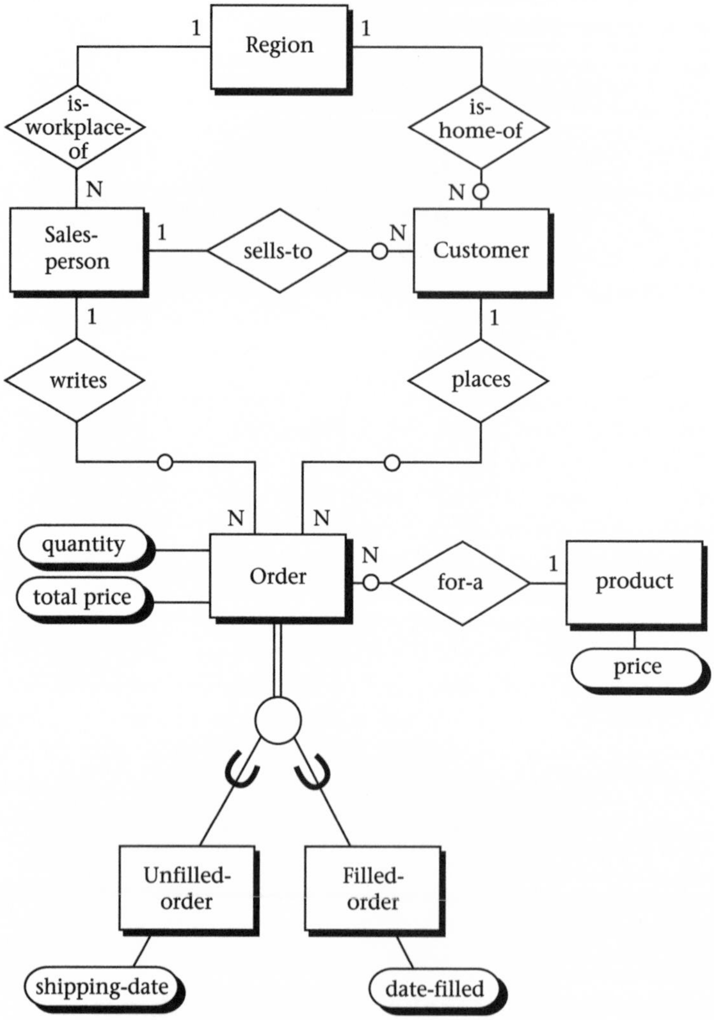

Figure 9.1 ER diagram for the "order" database example

9.1.1 Database Description

A customer places an order through a particular salesperson for a given quantity of a specific product that is to be shipped by a certain date. Once the order is filled, the data is saved for future reference, possibly at a site where data about the active (unfilled) orders is saved. Customers are considered to

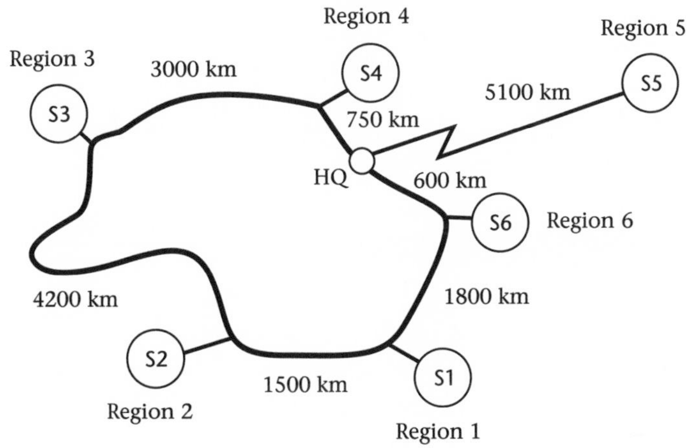

Figure 9.2 Network topology for the "order" database

be located in certain marketing regions, and a salesperson serves customers within a particular region. The headquarters (HQ) of the company is located at a site that is separate from any regional office.

The database serves to provide information for management decision making—marketing and sales planning, for example—as well as to track orders, customers, and salespersons so that customer service is maximized. It also helps management make decisions regarding shipping.

Cardinalities (Initially)

Regions=6

Salespersons=1200

Customers=240,000

Orders (filled)=2,000,000

Orders (unfilled) average level of 2000 (per region)

Products=10,000

Entities and Their Attributes (Average Field Width)

Region	reg-no(2), reg-name(15), mgr-name(20), addr(30), phone(10)
Salesperson	sales-id(6), sales-name(20), addr(30), phone(10)
Customer	cust-id(8), cust-name(20), addr(30), phone(10), company(20)

Product	prod-no(10), prod-type(15), prod-name(20), price(10)
Order	order-no(12), ord-date(6), prod-no(10), quantity(5), shipping-date(6), date-filled(6), total-price(10)

Note: The designer is allowed to extend these entities and attributes in any way—by adding foreign keys, for example.

9.1.2 Database Transactions

Database transactions are relatively simple queries and updates. After each transaction a frequency is specified, and the source is given as either the HQ or one of the regions. If the regional frequency is given, the total frequency is that number multiplied by six, the total number of regions. Assume that the search key value is known when the query is made.

Database Queries

Q1. Which salespersons service a particular region? [20/day/HQ]

Q2. What are the unfilled orders for a particular salesperson? [50/day/region]

Q3. Who are the customers in a particular region? [20/day/HQ]

Q4. To which customers has a particular salesperson sold in a particular region? [50/day/region]

Q5. What are the details of the unfilled orders for a particular customer? [100/day/region]

Q6. How many new orders have there been this past month for all products in each region? [1/month/HQ]

Q7. What unfilled orders are for more than $10,000 and who sold those orders? [1/day/HQ]

Q8. For a given order, filled or unfilled, what is the name and address of the customer and the salesperson? [150/day/region]

Q9. For a given customer, who is the salesperson? [200/day/region]

Q10. Which unfilled orders are currently past any of their shipping dates, and for what products are they? [1/day/HQ]

Database Updates

U1. Add a new customer. [one batch of 50/day/region]

U2. Move a salesperson to a different region. [2/week/HQ]

U3. Place a new order. [400/day/region]

U4. Mark an order as filled (shipped). [2400/day/HQ]

U5. Update the product catalog with new products. [one batch of 100/quarter/HQ]

Note 1: Assume that a deletion results in setting the data to null, but no reorganization.

Note 2: week=5 days, month=21 days, quarter=63 days, year=252 days (shipping dates).

9.1.3 Network and Local Site Specifications

A variety of simplifying assumptions are given so that gross estimates of transaction response times can be made. Network contention is assumed to be nil because database design decisions are normally independent of total network load.

1. The generic packet switched network, including an overseas site, S5, runs at 56 kilobits per second (see Figure 9.2). Pick the shortest distance between two sites and assume a simple protocol with no overhead: Send a one-packet query or update and receive a result of one packet or more with no processing overhead, only disk and transmission delays. Packet size=block size=2000 bytes.
2. The ideal propagation delay is the speed of light, approximately 300 kilometers per millisecond. We assume a lower speed of 200 kilometers per millisecond which is commonly used to take cable degradation into account. We also assume that station latency overhead is negligible.
3. Trba (random block access)=40 ms, Tsba (sequential block access)=10 ms for a 2000-byte block. Local disk capacity: Assume it is sufficient to hold all the allocated data.
4. Local query and update: Compute access times based on disk I/O for read and rewrite.
5. Remote query and update: Compute access times based on disk I/O for read and rewrite, plus network propagation and transmission delays for the query/update, including the actual data being transferred to answer the query/update. Pick an intelligent (near-optimal) query processing strategy for each query and update; absolute optimality is not necessary.
6. Assume that all tables are initially sorted by the primary key.

7. Assume that the local database systems contain sufficient indexing so that all searches for individual records (rows), based on the key value, take one random block access; if a rewrite is necessary for an update, it takes one sequential block access. When joins of tables are required, do appropriate selections and projections first to reduce the cost of a join. If necessary, one or both tables may need to be sorted on the attribute used in the join; however, you can specify any attribute for sorting a table before it is initially stored. Assume that all data is uniformly distributed over the six regions.

9.2 Global Schema and Fragmentation Design

In this part of the design problem we will

- erform an analysis of the transactions;
- make global schema design decisions;
- perform normalization; and
- implement fragmentation and nonredundant allocation.

9.2.1 Analysis of the Transactions

Two methods are commonly used to determine which transactions to consider in the design process: either all transactions or a dominant subset. A dominant subset is frequently used when an exhaustive enumeration would be prohibitive; it is selected on such criteria as high frequency of execution, high volume of data accessed, response time constraints, and explicit priority. We will look at the exhaustive enumeration approach first to create a standard for comparison with approximation method, such as dominant subsets of transactions.

Since at this point we are not considering time constraints or priorities of transactions, our selection of a dominant subset will be based primarily on frequency of execution and volume of data searched. Our initial analysis will be to estimate the number of records accessed during each transaction, given some simplifying assumptions about database retrievals and updates (see Table 9.1). Later, as we know more details about physical storage and network distribution parameters, the analysis can be refined.

The dominant transactions in this group are queries Q2 through Q5 and update U1. All other transactions appear to have a significantly lower data volume than this subset. We will test this method and its refinements against exhaustive enumeration in Section 9.3.3.

Table 9.1 Analysis of all transactions

Tr.	*Tr./day*	*Approx. number of records accessed (per region)*	*Total records/day*
Q1.	20	1200 salesperson records (get all salespersons per region)	24K
Q2.	50*6	2000 unfilled_order records (get all unfilled_orders per reg.)	600K
Q3.	20	40,000 customer records (get all customers per region)	800K
Q4.	50*6	40,000 customer records (scan all customers, check salesperson)	12M
Q5.	100*6	2000 unfilled_order records (scan all unfilled_orders, check customer)	1.2M
Q6.	1/21	10,000 product count records. . . . assume a 20B count record for each product is maintained by U3 for each new order (scan all count records, check product number and region number)	.5K
Q7.	1	[2000 unfilled_order records]*6 (scan unfilled_orders, check total price and salesperson)	12K
Q8.	150*6	1 order record, filled or unfilled + 1 salesperson record + 1 customer record (access order based on key, check customer and salesperson names and addresses)	2.7K
Q9.	200*6	1 customer record + 1 salesperson (access customer based on key, check salesperson)	2.4K
Q10.	1*6	[2000 unfilled_order records] (scan unfilled_orders, check shipping date)	12K
U1.	1*6	40,000 + 40,050 customer records (scan all customers, rewrite to maintain sort by primary key)	480.3K

(Table continues on following page)

Table 9.1 Continued

U2. .4	100 salesperson records + 1 rewrite + 401 salesperson records (scan half of salespersons in a region, delete with one rewrite; scan all salespersons to do the insert, then rewrite whole table)	.3K
U3. 400*6	1 unfilled_order record + 1 rewrite + 1 count record + rewrite (access last unfilled_order and rewrite with new order, then update the product count per month) + access product for price	12K
U4. 2400	1 unfilled_order record + 1 rewrite + 1 filled_order record + 1 rewrite (index to an unfilled_order, delete and rewrite; index to a filled_order and rewrite)	9.6K
U5. 1/63	10,000 + 10,100 product records (scan all products and rewrite with 100 more products) + write 100 product_count records	.3K

9.2.2 Global Schema Design Decisions

The transformation from the entity-relationship model to the relational model is very straightforward in most cases, since the relationships in Figure 9.1 are, for the most part, binary and one-to-many. In such cases we create a table from each entity in the relationship and add a foreign key in tables that represent the "many" side. The foreign key is the primary key of the parent entity, that is, the entity on the "one" side of the relationship.

The only additional relationship to consider is the generalization of order from the unfilled-order and filled-order entities. In this case we make the simplifying decision that both tables unfilled_order and filled_order will have the same scheme, with the attribute date_filled set to null in unfilled_order. We will also assume that filled orders will be physically near each other and unfilled_orders physically near each other on each local computers disk subsystem. Alternatively, we could have consolidated both types of order into a single table, order, to be separated physically by whether or not date_filled has a null value. Analysis of the trade-offs between these two alternative designs would occur at the physical level, using the parameters discussed in Section 9.1.

Following is a feasible set of table definitions in standard SQL. All tables are assumed to be sorted by primary key as noted in the assumptions.

Initial Table Definitions (SQL)

```
create table region (reg_no char(2),
        reg_name varchar(256),
        mgr_name varchar(256),
        mgr_addr varchar(256),
        mgr_phone char(10),
        primary key (reg_no));
create table salesperson (sales_id char(6),
        sales_name varchar(256),
        sales_addr varchar(256),
        sales_phone char(10),
        reg_no char(2) not null,
        primary key (sales_id),
        foreign key (reg_no) references region
            on delete set default on update cascade);
create table customer (cust_id char(8),
        cust_name varchar(256),
        cust_addr varchar(256),
        cust_phone char(10),
        company varchar(256),
        reg_no char(2) not null,
        sales_id char(6) not null,
        primary key (cust_id),
        foreign key (reg_no) references region,
            on delete set default on update cascade,
        foreign key (sales_id) references salesperson
            on delete set default on update set default);
create table product (prod_no char(10),
        prod_type varchar(256),
        prod_name varchar(256),
        price decimal (10,2) not null,
        primary key (prod_no));
```

```
create table product_count (prod_no char(10),
        prod_count char(10),
        primary key(prod_no),
        foreign key (prod_no) references product
                on delete cascade on update cascade);
create table unfilled_order (order_no char(12),
        ord_date date,
        quantity char(5) not null,
        total_price decimal (10,2) not null,
        shipping_date date not null,
        date_filled date default ' ',
        prod_no char(10) not null,
        cust_id char(8) not null,
        sales_id char(6) not null,
        primary key (order_no),
        foreign key (prod_no) references product
                on delete set default on update cascade,
        foreign key (cust_id) references customer
                on delete cascade on update cascade,
        foreign key (sales_id) referencessalesperson
                on delete set default on update cascade);
create table filled_order (order_no char(12),
        ord_date date,
        quantity char(5) not null,
        total_price decimal (10,2) not null,
        shipping_date date, not null,
        date_filled date not null,
        prod_no char(10) not null,
        cust_id char(8) not null,
        sales_id char(6) not null,
        primary key (order_no),
        foreign key (prod_no) references product
                on delete set default on update cascade,
        foreign key (cust_id) references customer
                on delete cascade on update cascade,
        foreign key (sales_id) references salesperson
                on delete set default on update cascade);
```

9.2.3 Normalization of the Global Schema

Normal forms were derived from the FDs in the table that follows.

Table	*FDs*
region	reg_no->reg_name, mgr_name, mgr_addr, mgr_phone
salesperson	sales_id->sales_name, sales_addr, sales_phone, reg_no
customer	cust_id->cust_name, cust_addr, cust_phone, company, sales_id, reg_no sales_id->reg_no
product	prod_no->prod_type, prod_name, price
product_count	prod_no->prod_count
unfilled_order (*or filled_order*)	order_no->ord_date, quantity, total_price, shipping_date

The **region**, **salesperson**, **product**, and **product_count** tables are in BCNF. The **customer**, **unfilled_order**, and **filled_order** tables are considered to be in 2NF because of the existence of a transitive FD. There is no delete anomaly because of the replication of the dependent attributes elsewhere.

9.2.4 Fragmentation and Nonredundant Allocation

Only horizontal data fragmentation is considered here. Vertical fragmentation involves modifications to the relational schema, and its methods are well documented in [CePe84]. In general, horizontal fragmentation decisions can be made by studying the relationships between transactions and the relational schema. In a variation of the best fit method, we analyze each table in terms of the data volume (records/day) for all transactions that use that table, and note where the transactions originate. From Table 9.1 we can make the following nonredundant data allocations, noting in parenthesis the transactions that use each table.

The **region** (no transactions) table is very small and is used only by the HQ; therefore, it is left whole and unfragmented at the HQ site.

The **product** (Q6, U3, U5) and **product_count** (Q6, U3, U5) tables are used mostly at the regions by the dominating transaction U3. However, there is no obvious need to partition them because each application needs to access the whole tables. Thus, they are left unfragmented at each of the regions (see alternative 2A below which is an exception to nonredundancy when fragmentation is not needed and the regions are symmetric).

The **salesperson** (Q1, U2) table should remain unfragmented at HQ since it is used only for a full table scan in Q1 by the HQ. Although the salespersons id is imbedded in other tables in the various regions for use in queries Q2, Q4, Q8, and Q9, any retrieval of further salesperson information can be made in a single random access, since the primary key is known in each case. The HQ allocation would have the additional benefit of making update U2 much easier, since only the region number (reg_no) would have to be changed to affect a location change for a salesperson.

The **filled_order** (Q8, U4) table should remain unfragmented at HQ because the data volume for U4 at HQ dominates the data volume for Q8 at the regions.

The **customer** (Q3, Q4, Q9, U1) table is used more at the regional level (Q4, Q9, U1) than at the HQ level (Q3). Therefore, we initially fragment the customers by regions.

The **unfilled_order** (Q2, Q5, Q7, Q8, Q10, U3, U4) table has many transactions at the HQ and at the regional level. If we total the data volume for HQ (Q7, Q10, U4) and regions (Q2, Q5, Q8, U3), we find that the regional activity is much higher. Therefore, we initially fragment the unfilled_orders by regions.

Fragmentation done in this manner is clearly heuristic. In this problem, we wish to study the most obvious alternative data allocation strategies for **product** and **product_count**, **salesperson**, **customer**, **unfilled_order**, and **filled_order**.

Alternative allocation strategies (cases):

1. Keep unfragmented and store only at headquarters (HQ).
2. Fragment and store by region.

2A. Keep unfragmented and replicate at each region.

3. Combine cases 1 and 2: store unfragmented at HQ; replicate fragments at the regions.

3A. Combine cases 1 and 2A: store unfragmented at HQ and replicate at all regions.

9.3 Redundant Data Allocation Methods

In this section we will consider cost/benefit analysis, exhaustive enumeration, dominating transactions, and the all beneficial sites method and variations of it.

9.3.1 Cost/Benefit Analysis: Basic Performance Statistics

To produce a redundant data allocation, one need only consider allocating additional copies of a table at sites where there are queries that use that table. Thus, one need not consider, for example, placing a copy of region 1's **salesperson** table at site 2, since site 2 would never query or update this information. This results in the following regional fragments being considered for redundant allocation: **salesperson**, **customer**, **unfilled_order**, and **filled_order**.

First, we convert the logical schema specification into 2000-byte block allocations, which are shown in Table 9.2. As an example of how the computations are conducted, let us analyze the I/O time to execute Q1, "Which salespersons service a particular region?"

Application Q1

Case 1: Salesperson data stored unfragmented at HQ

This query requires a scan of 1200 salesperson records (42 blocks) at the HQ and a selection of only those from the targeted region. Ignoring the processing overhead and system contention, we calculate simple elapsed time in terms of I/O service time for the 42 blocks:

Simple elapsed time = 42 blocks*Tsba = 42*10 ms = 420 ms

Note that SQL query optimizers will do these computations automatically. It is recommended that you use the SQL optimizer, if possible, to explain the query plan before analyzing it. The system plan could be quite different from a plan based on your assumptions.

Case 2: Salesperson data fragmented and stored by region only

Since the query is initiated by HQ, the targeted region must be accessed and its fragment fully scanned and transmitted to HQ. This involves transmission of a single packet from HQ to that region, followed by transmission of seven packets of salesperson data from the region to HQ. Our simplified model of wide area networks assumes that each regional request and reply is done sequentially, and that within each regional reply, the propagation delay occurs exactly once and multiple-packet replies occur serially. Propagation and transmission delays for this simple network are summarized in Table 9.3; the average propagation delay is 13.8 ms.

Table 9.3 Network topological features and delays

Region	*Distance to HQ (in km)*	*Prop. delay to HQ (in ms)*	*Trans. delay to HQ (in ms)*
1	2400	12	285.7
2	3900	19.5	285.7
3	3750	18.25	285.7
4	750	3.75	285.7
5	5100	25.5	285.7
6	600	3	285.7
		(Average = 13.8 ms)	

Block size (packet size) = 2000 Bytes

Transmission speed = 56 Kbps

simple elapsed time

= propagation delay from HQ to the targeted region

+ request packet transmission delay from HQ to the targeted region

+ local disk I/O time for the query at the targeted region

+ propagation delay back to HQ

+ reply packet transmission delay back to HQ

=13.8 ms+285.7 ms+7 blocks*10 ms/block +13.8 ms+7 packets*285.7 ms

=2383.2 ms

Case 3: Salesperson stored at HQ and replicated in fragments in each region

This query takes the minimum of cases 1 and 2 because case 3 provides for two paths to the same data.

Obviously, if Q1 were the only transaction, storing the unfragmented salesperson data at HQ (case 1) would minimize simple elapsed time, disregarding any reliability constraints. On the other hand, if the link were improved to T1 speed (1.544 megabits per second), then fragmenting the data at the regions (case 2) would produce the best performance. However, there are many more query and update transactions to consider; Table 9.4 summarizes the cost of each transaction for each of the three data allocation cases. Since U4, "Mark an order as filled (shipped)," is among the more complex transactions, the details of its simple elapsed time computation are shown.

Application U4

Case 1: Unfilled_orders and filled_orders stored unfragmented at HQ

We first assume that **unfilled_order** and **filled_order** are physically separated at the HQ. This update involves strictly local accesses, using an index to find the appropriate unfilled order, marking the deletion, and rewriting the block. Then another index is consulted to find the appropriate point in **filled_order** to insert the new record. This involves one access to get the appropriate block and another to rewrite that block with the new record.

simple elapsed time
= access **unfilled_order** block + rewrite block
+ access **filled_order** block + rewrite block
= 1 Trba + 1 Trba + 1 Trba + 1 Trba
= 40 ms + 40 ms + 40 ms + 40 ms
= 160 ms

Case 2: Unfilled_orders and filled_orders fragmented and stored by region only

In this case the local update time is the same as in case 1 because the updates involve only random accesses to data, followed by sequential rewrites. We assume that the reply from an update is a single packet.

simple elapsed time
= request propagation delay + request transmission delay
+ local update time + reply propagation delay
+ reply transmission delay
= 13.8 ms + 285.7 ms + 160 ms + 13.8 ms + 285.7 ms
= 759 ms

Case 2A: Unfilled_orders fragmented at regions and filled_order unfragmented at HQ

This case represents the original fragmentation and nonredundant allocation decision. Note that it produces the same simple elapsed time as case 2.

simple elapsed time
= remote update to **unfilled_order** at region
+ local update of **filled_order** at HQ
= (13.8 ms + 285.7 ms + 80 ms + 13.8 ms +
285.7 ms) + (80 ms)
= 759 ms

Case 3: Unfilled_orders and filled_orders stored at HQ and replicated in fragments in each region

This case requires that both copies of the data be updated.

simple elapsed time
= simple elapsed time for the HQ update
+ simple elapsed time for the regional update
= 160 ms + 759 ms
= 919 ms

Thus, U4 would be best served by the data allocation scheme for case 1. Table 9.4 summarizes all costs for each of the transactions.

Table 9.4 Simple elapsed time, in ms, for three data allocation schemes (cases) for a single execution of each transaction

Trans.	*Freq./day*	*Case 1: Unfrag. @ HQ*	*Case 2: Frag. @ reg.*	*Case 3: Replicated @ HQ&reg.*
Q1	20 @ HQ	42 blk*10 =420 ms	13.8+285.7+7*10 +13.8+7*285.7 =2383.2 ms	minimum (1&2)=420 ms
Q2	50*6 reg.	local: 72 blk*10 =720 remote: 13.8+285.7 +13.8+12*285.7 =3741.7 total: 4461.7	12 blk*10 =120	minimum (1&2)=120
Q3	20 @ HQ	12,000 blk*10 =120,000	local: 2000 blk*10 =20,000 remote: 13.8+285.7 +2000*285.7+13.8 =571,713.3 total=591,713.3	minimum (1&2) = 20,000
Q4	50*6 regs.	local: 12,000*10 remote: 13.8+285.7 +10*285.7 =3156.5 total=123,156.5	2000 blk*10 =20,000	minimum (1&2) = 20,000
Q5	100*6 reg.	same as Q2	same as Q2	same as Q2

Table 9.4 Continued

Q6	1/21 @ HQ (20B count per product)	100 blk*10 =1000	local: 6*100 blk*10 =6000 remote: 6*(13.8+285.7 +13.8+100*285.7) =173,299.8	minimum (1&2)=1000 (Case 3A)
Q7	1 @ HQ	72 blk*10 =720 remote: 6*(13.8+285.7 +13.8+285.7)=359 total: 4314	local: 6*72*10 =720	minimum (1&2)=720
Q8	150*6 reg.	local: 3 Trba=120 remote: 13.8+285.7 +13.8+285.7=599 total: 719	3 Trba=120	minimum (1&2)=120
Q9	200*6 reg.	local: 2 Trba=80 remote: 599 total: 679	2 Trba=80	minimum (1&2)=80
Q10	1 @ HQ	same as Q7	same as Q7	same as Q7
U1	1 @ regs.	local: (12,000 +12,014)*10 =240,140 remote: 599 total: 240,739	6*(2000+2003) blks*10=240,180	sum (1&2)= 480,919
U2	.4 @ HQ	24 blk*10+40 +84 blk*10 = 1120	local: 4 blk*10+40 +14 blk*10=220 remote: 599 total: 819	sum (1&2)=1939
U3	400*6 regs.	local: 3 Trba +2 Trba= 200 remote: 599 total: 799	3 Trba +2 Trba =200 (Case 2A)	sum (1&2)=999 (Case 3A)
U4	2400 @ HQ	2*(Trba+Trba) =160	local: 160 remote: 2*(13.8+285.7)=599 total: 759	sum (1&2)=919

(Table continues on following page)

Table 9.4 Continued

U5	1/63 @ HQ	(278+281)*10 +1*40=5630	local: 6*(278+281) *10+6*1*40 =33,780 remote: 6*599 =3594 total: 37,374 (Case 2A)	sum(1&2) =43,004 (Case 3A)

Table 9.5 Cumulative simple elapsed time, in seconds, for three data allocation schemes for total transaction executions per day

Trans.	*Freq./day*	*Case 1 Unfrag. @ HQ*	*Case 2 Frag. @ regs*	*Case 3 Replicated*
Q1	20 @ HQ	8.40	47.66	8.40
Q2	50*6 reg.	1338.51	36.00	36.00
Q3	20 @ HQ	2400.00	11834.27	2400.00
Q4	50*6 regs.	36937.95	6000.00	6000.00
Q5	100*6 reg.	2677.02	72.00	72.00
Q6	1/21 @ HQ	0.05	8.54	0.05
Q7	1 @ HQ	0.72	4.31	0.72
Q8	150*6 reg.	647.10	108.00	108.00
Q9	200*6 reg.	814.80	96.00	96.00
Q10	1 @ HQ	0.70	4.31	0.70
U1	1 @ regs.	240.74	240.18	480.92
U2	.4 @ HQ	0.45	0.33	0.78
U3	400*6 reg.	1917.60	480.00	2397.60
U4	2400 @ HQ	384.00	1821.69	2205.60
U5	1/63 @ HQ	0.089	0.593	0.683

9.3.2 Exhaustive Enumeration Method

The exhaustive enumeration method computes the entire cost of executing all transactions that use a particular table for each allocation strategy and then chooses the strategy that minimizes total cost. In this case cost is measured in simple elapsed time for queries and updates, assuming no contention either on the network or at the local sites. Cost computations are summarized for each table in Table 9.6.

Thus, our allocation decision is:

1. Allocate **unfilled_order** and **filled_order** to each region, fragmented by region.
2. Replicate **salesperson** and **customer** unfragmented at the HQ and fragmented at the regions.
3. Allocate **product** and **product_count** unfragmented to each of the regions. Replication at the HQ is not recommended due to higher cost.
4. Allocate **region** to the HQ (unfragmented), based on previous knowledge.

Note in Table 9.6 that several of the values are actually value ranges, for example, those associated with Q8 and U4. In most cases (in this example) the allocation decision for a given table can be made independently of the allocation decisions for the other tables because the transactions for those tables are either single table transactions or they are multiple table transactions with the initial nonredundant allocation of the tables at the same place(s). When this occurs we simply assume that our initial allocation will hold under further analysis. Conversely, Q8 and U4 are multiple table transactions where the nonredundant allocations are at different places. For instance, in Q8, **filled_order** and **salesperson** are initially at the HQ, but **customer** and **unfilled_order** are fragmented at the regions. For such transactions the allocation decisions for their associated tables are highly dependent on the locations of all the tables in each transaction. When this occurs we cannot make the assumption that the initial allocation will always hold. The lower bound value represents the best case where all the associated tables for that transaction are clustered for local accesses only, while the upper bound value represents the worst case allocation causing the maximum of remote accesses across the network.

In Table 9.6 the range of cost values for a given table and decision case can either be the minimum cost, greater than the minimum cost, or an overlapping cost with one or more other cases. For **salesperson**, the cost for Case 3 (replicated) is very close to the lower bound of Case 1 (HQ) and completely below the range of costs for Case 2 (fragmented at regions); thus, we pick Case 3 because of the near tie on minimum cost and greater availability. This decision is justified later when we observe that **filled_order** and **unfilled_order** are both fragmented at regions, putting Case 1 nearer the upper bound.

For **filled_order**, the cost of Case 3 falls between the range of costs for both Case 1 and Case 2. However, the upper bound cost in Case 1 and the lower bound cost in Case 2 occur due to the previous decisions of **unfilled_order** fragmented at the regions and both **salesperson** and **customer** are replicated at the HQ and regions. Therefore, we revise the **filled_order** statistics with this additional information (Table 9.6) and see that Case 2 (fragmented at regions) now minimizes cost.

Table 9.6 Exhaustive enumeration of simple elapsed times for all transactions for each table

Table & trans.	*Case 1: Unfragmented at HQ only*	*Case 2: Fragmented at regions only*	*Case 3: Replicated*
salesperson			
Q1	8.4	47.7	8.4
Q8	108 – 647.1	108 – 647.1	108
U2	.4	.3	.7
	116.8 – 655.9 sec	156 – 695.1 sec	**117.1 sec**
customer			
Q3	2400	11834.3	2400
Q4	36947.0	6000	6000
Q8	108 – 647.1	108 – 647.1	108
Q9	814.8	96	96
U1	240.7	240.2	480.9
	40510.5–41049.6 sec	18278.5–18817.6 sec	**9084.9 sec**
unfilled_order			
Q2	1338.5	36.0	36.0
Q5	2677.0	72.0	72.0
Q7	.7	4.3	.7
Q8	108 – 647.1	108 – 647.1	108.0
Q10	.7	4.3	.7
U3	1773.6	336	2109.6
U4	240 – 1677.6	1677.6	1917.6
	6138.5 – 8115.2 sec	**2238.2 – 2777.3 sec**	4244.6 sec
filled_order			
Q8	108 – 647.1	108 – 647.1	108
U4	240 – 1677.6	1677.6	1917.6
	348 – 2324.7 sec	1785.6 – 2324.7 sec	**2025.6 sec**

Table 9.6 Continued

filled_order (2nd iteration, using decisions from the first iteration)			
Q8	647.1	108	108
U4	1677.6	1677.6	3355.2
	2324.7 sec	**1785.6 sec**	3463.2 sec
product and *product_count*		*Case 2A*	*Case 3A*
Q6	.05	8.5	.05
U3	1773.6	336	2109.6
U5	.1	.6	.7
	1752.15 sec	**345.1 sec**	2110.35 sec

9.3.3 All Beneficial Sites Method

The all beneficial sites method can be used for either redundant or nonredundant data allocation design decisions. It is particularly useful when the number of alternative strategies (cases) for the exhaustive enumeration method is prohibitively large. The all beneficial sites method selects all sites for a fragment allocation where the benefit is greater than the cost of one additional copy of that fragment. You may start with either no copies or one nonredundant copy. In this network, individual remote query and update times can be calculated instead of the average as used in [TCOU89]. The benefit at a specific site is measured by the difference in cost to do a remote query (i.e., having no additional copy for a given fragment) and to do a local query (i.e., having one additional copy of the fragment so the same query can be done locally). The cost at a specific site is the cost of all the additional local and remote update references for the fragment at that site.

Total cost for an additional copy of a fragment at a specific site is the elapsed time for local and remote update references multiplied by their relative number of write requests by the various user transactions at all sites. Total benefit for the same additional copy of a fragment at that site is the difference between remote and local query time per request, multiplied by the total number of queries (reads).

In this example, we determined that the initial allocation was

1. **region**, **salesperson**, and **filled_order** at the HQ;
2. **customer** and **unfilled_order** fragmented by region; and
3. **product** and **product_count** unfragmented at all regions.

We now determine whether or not to replicate data by computing costs and benefits for each table (see Table 9.7).

From Table 9.7 we see that costs exceed benefits for **product**, **product_count**, and **unfilled_order**; thus, no replication of data is needed.

Table 9.7 Computation of costs and benefits for all beneficial sites

Table(initiallyat) & transaction(from)	*Cost of replicating*	*Benefit of replicating*	*Decision*
salesperson(HQ)			
Q1(HQ)		0(no query at regions)	replicate
Q8(regions)		**599 ms*900/day**	at regions
U2(HQ)	789 ms*.4/day		
filled_order(HQ)			
Q8(regions)		599 ms*150/day*6 reg.	replicate
		= **539,100 ms**	at regions
U4(HQ)	50 ms*2400/day		
	= 120,000 ms		
customer(regions)			
Q3(HQ)		**571,713 ms*20/day**	replicate
Q4(regions)		0(no queries at HQ)	at HQ
Q8(regions)		0(no queries at HQ)	
Q9(regions)		0(no queries at HQ)	
U1(regions)		240,730 ms*1/day	
unfilled_order(regions)			
Q2(regions)		0(no queries at HQ)	do not
Q5(regions)		0(no queries at HQ)	replicate
Q7(HQ)		3594 ms*1/day at HQ	
Q8(regions)		0(no queries at HQ)	
Q10(HQ)		3594 ms*1/day	
U3(regions)	**739 ms*400/day *6 reg**		
U4(HQ)	**50 ms*2400/day**		
product and **product_count** (unfragmented at all regions)			
Q6(HQ)		(173,299.8)*(1/21)	do not
		=8252.4 ms	replicate
U3(regions)	**739*2400/day**		at HQ
	=1773.6 sec		
U5(HQ)	5630 ms*(1/63)		
	=89.4 ms		

However, for **salesperson**, **customer**, and **filled_order** the benefits exceed costs and replication of the table at the HQ is justified. This result is consistent with the exhaustive enumeration method, and in fact selects from the same computations in Table 9.4.

As a minor extension of the original problem, consider the following availability constraint: A crash at one site should not cause the loss of data to any of the other sites that may need it now or in future transactions. This is partly met by redundancy in the network ring architecture, but data redundancy is also required. Because the **customer** table is the only table replicated in the unconstrained problem, we must now create additional copies of all other tables by fragmenting them at the regions and maintaining an unfragmented copy at the HQ. This satisfies the availability constraint and maximizes the local query performance at each site.

9.3.4 Variations of All Beneficial Sites

Numerous variations of the all beneficial sites method have been suggested, and some of the more practical ones are mentioned in this section [JWBT91].

In the previous section we assumed an initial nonredundant allocation and looked at one-step variations from this initial allocation. Using a cumulative approach instead, we can make an allocation decision regarding a particular table, then assume that the next decision must be made based on the new state of the configuration, which no longer resembles the initial allocation. The cumulative approach tends to give a more accurate solution, but it requires more computation since several starting points must be used so the best sequence of replications can be chosen methodically. Although both the one-step and cumulative approaches are "local optimization" methods, and cannot guarantee global optimal solutions, the cumulative approach tends to be much closer to the global optimal case.

A significant improvement in accuracy can be made by noting that the difference between a remote and local query from site s is nonzero for any new data replication that brings the closest copy to site s nearer than before (even though it is still not local). Therefore, if we use the cumulative approach described above, each new replication may result in a reduction in the benefit received between a remote and local query. This must be updated for each step in the cumulative approach.

Another practical approach involves computing actual wait times in the network and local sites rather than just I/O service times. This results in more realistic elapsed times instead of simple elapsed times for use in comparing different allocation decisions. However, it requires much more knowledge about system contention, which may not be available. Extensions of all beneficial sites to account for data availability in a partially reliable network are discussed in [CePe84].

9.4 Summary

A distributed data allocation optimization problem can be solved by a step-by-step solution approach that includes conceptual ER modeling; transformation to normalized tables; fragmentation for a nonredundant data allocation; and, finally, determination of a redundant data allocation scheme. A variety of practical data allocation strategies can be evaluated using a simple block access analysis of local databases and a packet propagation and transmission analysis of a simple network configuration for distributed databases. The all beneficial sites method has the most potential to be an effective substitute for exhaustive enumeration when scaling up for large complex databases.

Literature Summary

[CePe84] Ceri, S. and Pelagatti, G. *Distributed Databases: Principles and Systems,* McGraw-Hill, New York, 1984.

[CPW87] Ceri, S., Pernici, B., and Wiederhold, G. "Distributed Database Design Methodologies," *Proc. IEEE,* May 1987, pp. 533–546.

[JWBT91] Janakiraman, J., Warack, C., Bhal, G., and Teorey, T.J. "Progressive Fragment Allocation," *Proc. 10th Int'l. Conf. on the Entity Relationship Approach,* San Mateo, CA, October 23–25, 1991, pp. 543–560.

[Spro76] Sprowls, R.C. *Management Data Bases,* Wiley/Hamilton, Santa Barbara, CA, 1976.

[Teor89] Teorey, T.J. "Distributed Database Design: A Practical Approach and Example," *SIGMOD Record* 18,4 (Dec. 1989), pp. 23–39.

[TCOU89] Teorey, T.J., Chaar, J., Olukotun, K., and Umar, A. "Distributed Database Design: Some Basic Concepts and Strategies," *Database Programming and Design* 2,4 (April 1989), pp. 34–42.

EXERCISES

Problem 9-1

The following problem is a modification of a problem first presented in [TeFr82], a fictitious environment based roughly on the *Star Trek* concept. The database is now to be distributed over interplanetary space with nodes on the Earth, Mars, Jupiter's moon Io, and Neptune's moon Triton.

Data Requirements Description (processing independent)

The Space Federation governs 100 galactic sectors which it patrols with 25 starships assigned to approximately four sectors apiece. There are 100 cargo ships assigned the tasks of bringing fuel, equipment, and supplies to these starships. Because each starship is unique, cargo ships must be specially built to service each one and cannot service any other starship. More than one cargo ship is assigned to a starship to assure continued maintenance. To aid in dispatching cargo ships and assigning crew members for relief, the Federation keeps a record of all coordinates and crew rosters for each ship.

Each cargo ship belonging to the Space Federation is divided into five sections. These sections are assigned specific maintenance, navigation, and cargo manipulation duties. Each section performs an average of three different duties. Fifty crew members are assigned to a ship and each crew member works in two sections, on the average. The Federation maintains a set of personal information about each crew member.

The organization of the starship *Enterprise* is fairly simple. The starship is divided into several divisions, each of which has a division leader. Associated with each division are a number of tasks to be performed by crew members. Although a crew member will, in general, perform more than one task, no crew member performs tasks from more than one division. Some tasks require several crew members. Associated with each person on the ship (division leader and crew member) is a set of personal information. A rating of how well a task is performed is associated with the crew member and the tasks.

The sick bay of the starship *Enterprise* keeps the following information about its 10 physicians and the 1000 crew members they treat. Each physician treats an average of 400 crew members. For each one, the physician maintains a history of the diseases contracted and a record of the drug allergies. A crew member averages five of each of these sick log entries. The physician also notes the planets the crew member has visited (an average of 10). Associated with each planet is a list of known diseases indigenous to the planet and a description of their symptoms and treatment.

Space is not easy on starships. To keep them in top shape, the Federation maintains 10,000 space stations. Each is located at what has been determined to be an optimal set of coordinates for servicing the fleet, and each has been given the name of a famous captain or courageous cadet who died in battle. The starship manuals define 1000 standard starship repairs. Because of their complexity and special equipment requirements, each space station is constructed to handle only 50 of these repairs. Thus, any given repair can only take place at 500 of the stations. Approximately 100 mechanics work at each one. They are trained on 10 different repairs and are given a rating level associated with each specialty. The 25 Federation starships show up at these various stations for routine maintenance and whenever major difficulties that cannot be fixed by the starship engineering staff occur. The Federation keeps records of these repairs. About 1000 such repair stops have been made at each station.

Processing Requirements: Queries

1. Whenever a galactic sector appears to be having some difficulty such as an interplanetary war, the starship associated with that sec tor is found and called in to resolve the problem (freq=20%). Source: Triton, Earth.
2. The governing counsel often wants to know what galactic sectors are governed by a given starship, in particular, the starship Enterprise (freq=80%). Source: Earth.
3. When a starship needs servicing it is necessary to find the closest cargo ship capable of performing the service (freq=90%). Source: Mars, Triton.
4. Whenever a cargo ship is assigned a service operation, the Federation distributes notices to those crew members on both ships who will find relatives on the other ship. This is done by obtaining a report of all crew members with the same last names on both ships (freq=10%). Source: Earth.
5. The commander of the ship often wants to know the personal data about the individual assigned to a given section, such as id number, hometown, languages spoken, and hobbies (freq=90%). Source: local starship (not done on the network).
6. Every now and then, a cargo ship is short a crew member. Other crew members are examined for replacement possibilities. What is typically looked at is the set of duties the crew member already performs (freq=10%). Source: Earth.
7. Find the personal information and names of crew members capable of doing task T in division D, with a rating of R or better (freq=50%). Source: Earth.
8. Find the names of those crew members who are capable of doing all the tasks in a subset of division D's tasks (freq=10%). Source: Earth.

9. Find the names of all the crew members commanded by a specific leader (freq=40%). Source: Earth, Io, Triton.
10. Find the names of all the crew members that a given physician has treated (freq=20%). Source: Earth, Io.
11. Find the names of all the planets a given crew member has visited and list out their diseases, symptoms, and treatments (freq=50%). Source: Earth, Io.
12. Find the specified treatment for a given disease and list all crew members who are known to be allergic to this treatment (freq=30%). Source: Earth, Io.
13. A starship is due for maintenance on a specific control system. The captain wants to find the repair station closest to its coordinates that is capable of performing the repair (freq=30%). Source: Mars, Triton.
14. The Federation periodically checks usage patterns to see if its repair stations are appropriately distributed. It does this by listing all the starships that have had a given repair at a given station (freq=40%). Source: Mars, Triton.
15. The Enterprise needs a very tricky repair. The Federation office wants to find the best mechanic for this job and the station where the mechanic works (freq=30%). Source: Earth, Mars, Triton.

Processing Requirements: Updates

1. Occasionally a starship needs to be replaced. To insure continuity, the entire crew of the old ship is transferred to the new one, and all divisions and tasks remain the same (freq=1%). Source: Earth, Mars, Triton.
2. Similarly, cargo ships also need to be replaced and the crews remain (freq=15%). Source: Mars, Triton.
3. A starship that loses 10 or more crew members to battles, disease, rotation to Federation headquarters, or retirement receives an equal number of new crew members to replace them. The average number of replacements per visit (via cargo ship) is 25 (freq=5%). Source: Earth.
4. To keep crew members fresh, they are taught how to perform new tasks within their division. After every planet visitation, 20% of the crew changes one of their tasks (freq=25%). Source: Earth.
5. A new space station is built every few weeks (freq=10%). Source: Earth, Mars, Triton.

Networking Requirements

1. The database resides within the Earth's planetary system, with nodes on the Earth, Mars, Jupiter's moon Io, and Neptune's moon Triton. Planetary distances (approximate averages in M km) are:

	Earth	*Mars*	*Io*	*Triton*
Earth	0	216.8	777.9	4478.8
Mars	—	0	788.8	4489.7
Io	—	—	0	4479.0

2. Assume that the speed of light is the constraining speed: 300,000 km/second. Outside the Earth's solar system hyperspace starship speeds can take place, but they are not allowed within the solar system.
3. Assume that the interplanetary distances are so great that total response time is dominated by network propagation delay; network transmission delays and local CPU and I/O processing delays are considered negligible.
4. Frequencies are used as follows: a query or update with a frequency of 10% and two sources has 10% for each source or 20% overall.

The Problem

The goal of the distribution design is to allocate tables redundantly to a subset of the four processing centers to minimize total access time for the most dominant queries and updates. Let us define dominance by frequency of a query times the number of sources of the query greater than 60% and frequency of update times the number of sources of the update greater than 20%. This includes six of the queries and three of the updates. Note that access time is one-half the response time for any given query or update, given this simplified network model. If we extend this problem to include all queries and updates, does this result in a different allocation from the dominant application approach?

CHAPTER 10

DATABASE DEPENDABILITY

In this chapter we show how to estimate the availability, reliability, and mean transaction completion time for repairable centralized, distributed, and multidatabases in which each component is continuously available for repair. Reliability, the probability that the entire transaction can execute properly without failure is computed as a function of mean time to failure (MTTF) and mean time to repair (MTTR). Trade-offs between database queries and updates are then derived in terms of both performance and reliability.

It should be noted that database dependability is somewhat related to ER modeling. A good data model is needed to cluster together entities and attributes that have strong associations to each other, and this closeness will typically continue throughout the physical and distribution design steps. Thus, queries will tend to be clustered within subsets of the database and depend less on long distances in the network. This approach will tend to increase dependability and decrease the possibility of crashes and restarts of transactions.

10.1 Introduction

The increasing availability and importance of distributed and multidatabases raises serious concerns about their dependability in a fragile network environment, much more than with centralized databases. Although the major impetus for distributed data is to increase data availability, it is not always clear whether the dependability of the many hardware and software components of a distributed system is such that the level of availability desired is actually provided. Performance of a database system is closely related to dependability, and it cannot be good if the dependability is low.

Failures occur in many parts of a computer system: at the computer sites, the storage media (disk), communication media, and in the database transactions. Site failures may be due to hardware (CPU, memory, power failure) or software system problems. Disk failures may occur from operating system software bugs, controller problems, or head crashes. In the network, there may be errors in messages, including lost messages and improperly ordered messages, and line failures. Transaction failures may be due to bad data, constraint failure, or deadlock. Each of these types of failures contributes to the degradation of overall dependability of a system.

A significant amount of research has been reported on the subject of dependability of computer systems, and a large number of analytical models exist to predict reliability for such systems [JoMa88]. While these models provide an excellent theoretical foundation for computing dependability, there is still a need to transform the theory to practice for distributed databases running on real platforms in real distributed environments. Our goal is to provide that transformation with a realistic set of system parameters, test the model with a simulation tool, and make recommendations for validation testing with actual distributed database management systems.

Based on the definitions in [SiSw82, JoMa88], dependability of a system is composed of three basic characteristics: availability, reliability and serviceability. *Steady-state availability* is the probability that a system will be operational at any random point of time, and is expressed as the expected fraction of time a system is operational during the period it is required to be. *Reliability* is the conditional probability at a given confidence interval that a system will perform its intended function properly without failure and satisfy specified performance requirements during a given time interval [0,t] when used in the manner intended. *Serviceability* or *maintainability* is the probability of successfully performing and completing a corrective maintenance action within a prescribed period of time with the proper maintenance support.

In this chapter we will look at the issues of availability and reliability in the context of simple distributed or multidatabase transactions (and their subtransactions) in a network environment where the steady-state availability is known for individual system components: computers, networks, and the various network interconnection devices (and possibly their subcomponents). A transaction path is considered to be a sequential series of resource acquisitions and executions, with alternate parallel paths allowable. We assume that all individual system components, software and hardware, are repairable [JoMa88]. A *nonrepairable* distributed database is one in which transactions can be lost and the system is not available for repair. In a *repairable* distributed database all components are assumed to be continuously available for repair, and any aborted transaction is allowed to restart from its point of origin. We will only consider repairable databases here.

Serviceability is assumed to be deterministic in our model, but the model could be extended for probabilities less than 1 that the service will be successfully completed on time.

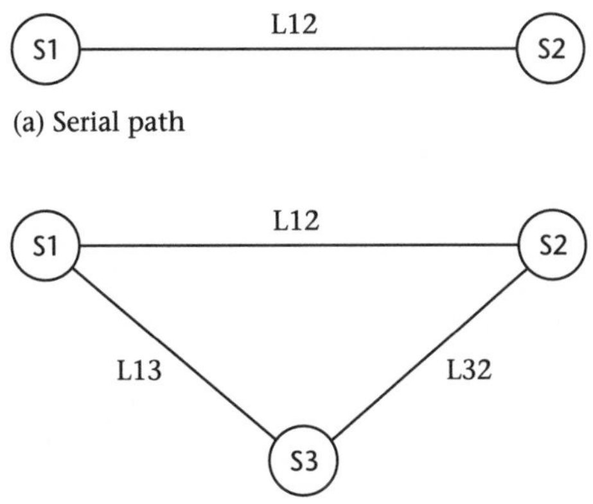

Figure 10.1 Simple network paths for a distributed database

10.2 Availability

Let us first look at the computation of steady-state availability in the network underlying the distributed or multidatabase. In Figure 10.1a, two sites, S1 and S2, are linked with the network link L12. Let A_{S1}, A_{S2}, and A_{L12} be the steady-state availabilities for components S1, S2, and L12, respectively.

Assuming that the availability of each system component is independent of the availability of all other components, the probability that path S1/L12/S2 is available at any randomly selected time t is the product of the individual (independent) availabilities in series:

$$A_{S1/L12/S2} = A_{S1}*A_{L12}*A_{S2} \qquad (10.1)$$

Extending the concept of availability to parallel paths (Figure 10.1b), we factor out the two components, S1 and S2, that are common to each path:

$$A_{S1//S2} = A_{S1}*A_{S2}* \qquad (10.2)$$

[availability of the connecting paths between S1 and S2]

Equation 10.2 states that the total path from site S1 to site S2 has three serial components: S1, S2, and the two possible connecting paths between the sites. We simply partition the whole path into three serial parts and apply Equation 10.1 to them to determine the total path availability. Now we need to determine the actual value of the third component of availability, the connecting paths. This is determined by the well-known relationship for parallel independent events that states that the total availability of a parallel path is the sum of the serial availability of each of the two independent paths, minus the product of their serial availabilities.

$$A_{S1//S2} = A_{S1}{*}A_{S2}{*}[A_{L12} + A_{L13}{*}A_{S3}{*}A_{L32} - A_{L12}{*}A_{L13}{*}A_{S3}{*}A_{L32}] \quad (10.3)$$

We note that if query optimizers pick the shortest path without regard to availability, the system could reverse the decision if the selected path is not available. We now have the basic relationships for serial and parallel paths for steady-state availability. This concept can easily be extended for more complex paths needed to satisfy the transaction due to larger networks or more complex data allocation strategies.

10.3 Reliability

An estimate of availability is limited to a single point in time. We now need to estimate the reliability for an entire transaction (including queries and/or updates), and (in Section 4) the mean transaction completion time for a repairable distributed or multidatabase that has automatic restarts. Let us assume that we are given the steady-state availability of each system component, the mean time to failure (MTTF), and the mean time to repair (MTTR) for each component. We are also given the mean delay experienced by the subtransaction on each component resource, derived from known characteristics of the network and database system. Note that from [SiSw82] we have the basic relationship for mean time between failures (MTBF):

$$MTBF = MTTF + MTTR \quad (10.4)$$

Reliability is the probability that the entire transaction can execute properly (over a given time interval) without failure. We first need to compute the estimated mean reliability over a time duration [0,t], where t is the mean delay experienced over the system during the transaction execution. For tractability we assume that the failure rate of each system component has a Poisson distribution

$$P_j(k,t) = (mt)^k * e^{-mt}/k! \quad (10.5)$$

which is the probability that there are exactly k failures of transaction j in time interval t, where m is the mean number of failures in time interval t. The probability that there are no failures in time interval t is:

$$P_j(0, t) = e^{-mt} \qquad (10.6)$$

We need to transform Equation 10.6 using real parameters from a distributed database system. Let

$MTTF_i$ = mean time to failure on component i,

$MTTR_i$ = mean time to repair for component i, and

MD_j = mean delay for transaction j

Note: MD_j is estimated here without contention. In a real system with contention for resources, the value of MD_j will increase dramatically as the system nears saturation, and thus the probability of failure will increase significantly (see Section 10.4).

The ratio $MD_j/MTTF_i$ represents the fraction of unit failure on component i for transaction j, where mt is normalized to 1, the unit (mean) time for the first failure. Substituting the ratio $MD_j/MTTF_i$ for mt in Equation 10.6, we obtain for any transaction j, the probability of no failures in the time interval [0, MDj] on component i. The probability that the transaction has no failures while actively using component i is the joint probability that the component is reliable over the interval, and that it is available at the beginning of the interval:

$$P_{j,i}(0, MD_j) = e^{-MD_j/MTTF_i} * A_i \qquad (10.7)$$

where the mean time to first failure of component i is $MTTF_i$ and the steady state availability of a single component i is given by

$$\begin{aligned} A_i &= MTTF_i/(MTTF_i + MTTR_i) \\ &= MTTF_i/MTBF_i \qquad (10.8) \end{aligned}$$

Note: This is a highly simplified model and should only be used to get preliminary insights about system performance.

10.3.1 Example 1: Query Reliability for a Simple Distributed Database

Let us now apply the relationship on Equation 10.7 to the simple distributed database over the network in Figure 10.1a. The probability that the whole transaction (i.e., query, in this case) succeeds is equal to the probability that the transaction can be completed without failure from initiation at site S1, local access to the data in site S2, and returning with the result to site S1. We assume that transaction j is successful only if all components are active the entire time required to service the transaction.

$$P(\text{success}) = P_{j,S1}(0, MD_j)*P_{j,L12}(0, MD_j)*P_{j,S2}(0, MD_j) \quad (10.9)$$

Let QIT = query initiation time (CPU)
PTT = packet transmission time
PD = packet propagation delay
QPT = query processing time (CPU & IO)
n=number of packets in the result of the query
QRDT = query result display time (CPU & IO)

We assume reasonable values for the above parameters, that is,

QIT = 1 ms
PTT = 8 ms (T1 link @ 1.544 MB/s, packet size 1544 Bytes)
PD = 10 ms (assumed 2000 km distance, degraded electronic speed 200 km/ms)
QPT = 200 ms
n = 5
QRDT = 60 ms
$MTTF_i$ = 300 sec for each component i
$MTTR_i$ = 5 sec for each component i ($MTBF_i$ = 305 sec)
$A_i = 300/(300+5) = .984$

Let us define the mean total (query) delay time as the sum of all the nonoverlapped delays from site S1 to site S2 and returning the result to site S1:

$$\begin{aligned} MD_j &= QIT + PTT + PD + QPT + n*PTT + PD + QRDT \\ &= 1 + 8 + 10 + 200 + 5*8 + 10 + 60 \text{ ms} \\ &= 329 \text{ ms} \end{aligned}$$

Applying Equation 10.9 we obtain:

$$\begin{aligned} P(\text{success for transaction } j) &= [e^{-329/300000}(.984)]^3 \\ &= [e^{-.00109667}(.984)]^3 \\ &= [(.998904)(.984)]^3 \\ &= [.982922]^3 \\ &= .9496 \end{aligned}$$

10.3.2 Example 2: Trade-offs Between Performance and Reliability

We now extend Example 1 (Figure 10.1b) to include updates so we can study the tradeoffs between performance and reliability for multiple copies of data. Let us assume that the frequency for this query is 10/tu where tu is the standard time unit for this discussion (e.g., hour, day, week, and so on). Let us also assume that we have an update transaction on the same data, with time UT1 = 329 ms and frequency of 2/tu. The corresponding query and update times, weighted by frequency of occurrence, are:

QT1(query time for a single copy)	= 329 ms * 10	= 3290 ms
UT1(update time for a single copy)	= 329 ms * 2	= 658 ms

Now, if we assume there are two copies of the data, one at S2 and another at S3, we obtain the following result, assuming that each update is initiated separately and takes the same time as the first update except with a smaller propagation delay (PD) due to the shorter distance (1200 km):

QT2 (min. query time for two copies)	= 325 ms * 10	= 3250 ms
UT2 (total update time for two copies)	= 654 ms *2	= 1308 ms

Using the all beneficial sites method to decide on whether to add another copy of the data [CePe84], the benefit from adding the second copy is the decrease in query time, and the cost is the added cost of updating the second copy:

Benefit (2nd copy)	= QT1 – QT2	= 3290 – 3250	= 40 ms
Cost (2nd copy)	= UT2 – UT1	= 1308 – 658	= 650 ms.

The cost exceeds the benefit for this case, so the decision, based purely on performance (query and update time), is not to replicate the data. However, the query reliability should increase as the second copy is placed in site S3, and the update reliability should decrease. If we compute the mean completion time for each query and update in both the one-copy and the two-copy cases, we should see the values of QT1, QT2, UT1, and UT2 all increase to QT1′, QT2′, UT1′, and UT2′ due to the probability of restarts. However, we also know that QT1′ – QT2′ > QT1 – QT2 because both values will increase proportionately, but UT2′ – UT1′ >> UT2 – UT1 because the degradation of update completion time is much more dramatic due to the decrease in update reliability as well as access time, thus driving the cost even higher than the benefit compared to the computation based on performance only.

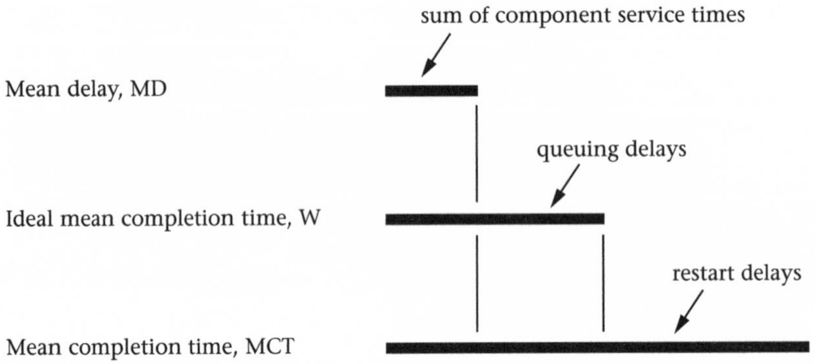

Figure 10.2 Components of mean completion time

In general, we see that adding more copies causes query time and update reliability to decrease and query reliability and update time to increase. Although the net effect tends to make the addition of extra copies look less favorable, the decision on when to add the copies depends on some crossover point between costs and benefits. As update frequencies become very small, the benefits dominate the costs. In the next section we will see how mean transaction completion time is estimated.

10.4 Mean Transaction Completion Time

The mean transaction completion time is a function of the mean delay time or service time for the transaction over all components, plus queuing delays for contention, plus restart delays (Figure 10.2).

Queuing delays can be estimated for an open Jackson network configuration using the simple formula for the total time in the system, W:

$$\begin{aligned} W &= T_S/(1-\rho) \\ &= T_S/(1-\lambda T_S) \end{aligned} \tag{10.10}$$

where the service time $T_s = MD_j$, ρ is the utilization of the configuration, and λ is the mean arrival rate of queries. In other words, W represents the ideal mean completion time when no restarts are required. In Example 1, if we assumed the arrival rate of queries to be 2/sec (or .002/ms), then

$W = 329\ \text{ms} / (1 - .002*329) = 329/.342 = 962\ \text{ms} = .962\ \text{sec}$, and

$p(\text{success}) = [e^{-962/300000}(.984)]^3 = .9436$ for the given database.

When we consider both queuing and restart delays, mean completion time is estimated by computing the probability of different possible completion times. For example, if W were the given total time in the system, the mean completion time, MCT, can be easily derived, assuming probability p of a successful transaction, and for every failure, an average time to failure and recovery W/2 + MTTR, where W/2 is the mean time to failure of the transaction, given random failures of a collection of components over which that transaction must successfully execute.

$$\begin{aligned}
MCT &= p^*W + q^*p^*(W + W/2 + MTTR) + q^{2*}p^*(W + 2^*W/2 + 2^*MTTR) \\
&\quad + q^{3*}p^*(W + 3^*W/2 + 3^*MTTR) + \ldots \\
&= p^*W + q^*p^*W + q^{2*}p^*W + q^{3*}p^*W + \ldots + q^*p^*(W/2 + MTTR) \\
&\quad + 2q^{2*}p^*(W/2 + MTTR) + 3q^{3*}p^*(W/2 + MTTR) + \ldots \\
&= p^*W^*(1 + q + q^2 + q^3 + \ldots) + q^*p^*(W/2 + MTTR) \\
&\quad ^*(1 + 2q + 3q^2 + 4q^3 + \ldots) \\
&= W + (q/p)^*(W/2 + MTTR) \qquad (10.11)
\end{aligned}$$

by noting that

$$(1 + q + q2 + q3 + \ldots) = 1/(1-q) = 1/p \qquad (10.12)$$

and

$$(1 + 2q + 3q^2 + 4q^3 + \ldots) = 1/(1-q)^2 = 1/p^2. \qquad (10.13)$$

In our example, given W = .962 sec, p = .9436, MTTR=5 sec, and MTTF = 300 sec, we derive:

$$q = 1-p = .0564$$

$$MCT= .962 + (.0564/.9436)^*(.962/2 + 5.0 \text{ sec}) = .962 + .328 = 1.290 \text{ sec.}$$

Thus, we see that the actual mean completion time need not always be dramatically longer than the ideal completion time without any restarts.

10.5 Summary

We have derived expressions for availability and reliability in a repairable distributed database system for simple transactions involving both queries and updates. Reliability is derived in terms of the probability of success of an entire transaction and the mean transaction completion time due to both traffic congestion and restarts due to failure. We have also shown that simple decisions about data allocation, as an extension of the all beneficial sites algorithm, can be made from careful analysis of query and update costs.

Literature summary

[CePe84] Ceri, S. and Pelagatti, G. *Distributed Databases: Principles and Systems,* McGraw-Hill, New York, 1984.

[Duga90] Dugan, J.B. "On Measurement and Modeling of Computer Systems Dependability: A Dialog Among Experts," *IEEE Transactions on Reliability* 39,4 (Oct. 1990), pp. 506–510.

[Fell68] Feller, W. *An Introduction to Probability Theory and Its Applications* (3rd Ed.), John Wiley & Sons, New York, 1968.

[Gray90] Gray, Jim. "A Census of Tandem System Availability Between 1985 and 1990," *IEEE Transactions on Reliability* 39,4 (Oct. 1990), pp. 409–418.

[GrRe93] Gray, J. and Reuter, A. *Transaction Processing: Concepts and Techniques,* Morgan Kaufmann, San Mateo, CA, 1993.

[JoMa88] Johnson, A.M. Jr. and Malek, M. "Survey of Software Tools for Evaluating Reliability, Availability, and Serviceability," *ACM Computing Surveys* 20,4 (Dec. 1988), pp. 227–269.

[MaFe90] Maxion, R.A. and Feather, F.E. "A Case Study of Ethernet Anomalies in a Distributed Computing Environment," *IEEE Transactions on Reliability* 39,4 (Oct. 1990), pp. 433–443.

[OzVa90] Ozsu, M.T. and Valduriez, P. *Principles of Distributed Database Systems,* Prentice-Hall, Englewood Cliffs, NJ, 1990, pp. 327–328.

[SaMe86] Sanders, W.H. and Meyer, J.F. "METASAN: A Performability Evaluation Tool Based on Stochastic Activity Networks," *Proc. 1986 Fall Joint Computer Conference,* Nov. 2–6, 1986, AFIPS, New York, pp. 807–816.

[SaTr87] Sahner, R.A. and Trivedi, K.S. "Reliability Modeling Using SHARPE," *IEEE Transactions on Reliability* 36,2 (June 1987), pp. 186–193.

[SiSw82] Siewiorek, D.P. and Swarz, R.S. *The Theory and Practice of Reliable System Design,* Digital Press, Bedford, MA, 1982.

EXERCISES

Problem 10-1

For the network configuration given below, *derive an analytic expression* for the probability that fragment F1 is available for query Q1, given that there are three paths from query Q1 to fragment F1: A, BE, and BCD. Test your solution for $P_L = P_S = .98$.

> P_L = probability that a link is available (same value for all links)
> P_S = probability that a site is available (same value for all sites)

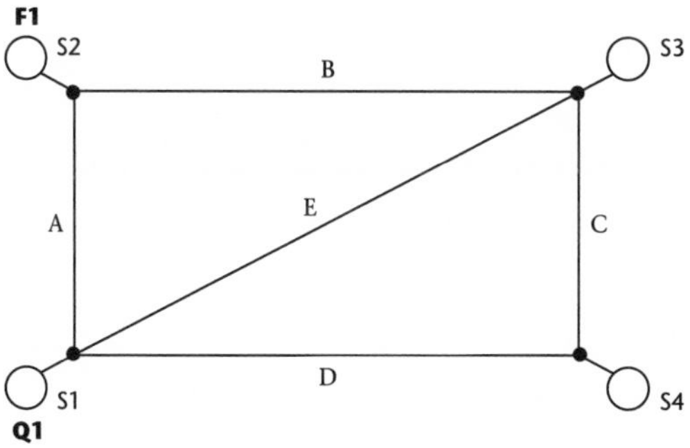

Problem 10-2

Using the configuration shown below, *estimate the mean completion time* for a simple remote query from site S3 to a fragment F3 at site S1, assuming that the fragment is a single block and is accessed randomly. The traffic for this query is 100/minute. Assume that availability of all resources can be derived from MTTF=2 hours, MTTR=5 min, and that QIT = 0 and QRDT = 0.

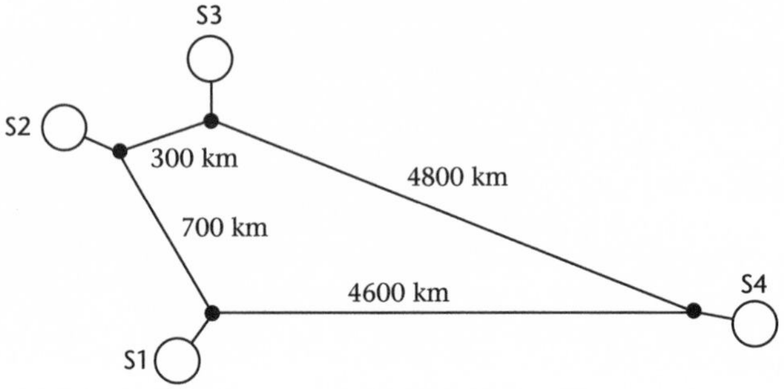

F3 has 50,000 records, blocking factor=25

Block size = 10,000 bytes; packet size = 1,000 bytes

Time for a random block access = Trba = 40 ms

Network propagation delay (200 km/ms)

Network transmission rate (1.544 Mbps)

APPENDIX A

REVIEW OF SQL

Structured Query Language, or SQL, is the ISO-ANSI standard data definition language and data manipulation language for relational database management systems. Individual relational database systems use slightly different dialects of SQL syntax and naming rules, and these differences can be seen by consulting the SQL user guides for those systems. In this text, where we explore each step of the logical and physical design portion of the database life cycle, many examples of database table creation and manipulation make use of SQL syntax.

SQL is, first of all, relational; its queries operate only on tables in a relational database, and produce only tables as the result. Similarly, SQL updates modify relational tables. Second, SQL is nonprocedural; each statement in the language specifies an atomic act to be carried out involving a set of rows. As a language, it is based more on relational calculus, which specifies what the result of the query looks like, than on the procedure-oriented relational algebra, which specifies the sequence of steps needed to obtain a database result. Third, SQL is unified; database administrators (DBAs), programmers, and system administrators all learn and use a single language and set of constructs, and use the same language on-line, in either batch files or individual programs.

The basic use of SQL can be learned quickly and easily by reading this appendix. More advanced features, such as statistical analysis and presentation of data, require more study and are beyond the reach of the typical nonprogrammer. However, SQL views can be set up by the DBA to help the nonprogrammer set up repetitive queries, and other languages such as forms are being commercially sold for nonprogrammers. For the advanced database programmer, embedded SQL (in C programs, for instance) is widely available for the most complex database applications that need the power of procedural languages.

This appendix introduces the reader to the basic constructs for SQL-92 (sometimes called SQL2) database definition, queries, and updates through a sequence of examples with some explanatory text. We start with a definition of SQL-92 terminology for data types and operators. This is followed by an explanation of the SQL-92 data definition language (DDL) constructs using the "create table" commands and including a definition of the various types of integrity constraints such as foreign keys and referential integrity. Finally we take a detailed look at the SQL-92 data manipulation language (DML) features through a series of both simple and complex practical examples of database queries and updates.

A.1 SQL Names and Operators

This section gives the basic rules for SQL-92 data types and operators according to the ISO-ANSI standard [MeSi93].

- SQL-92 names have no particular restrictions, but vendor-specific versions of SQL do have some restrictions. For example in Oracle, names of tables and columns (attributes), for instance, can be up to 30 characters long, must begin with a letter, and can include the symbols (a–z, 0–9,_,$,#). Names should not duplicate reserved words or names for other objects (attributes, tables, views, indexes) in the database.
- Data types for attributes: character, character varying, numeric, decimal, integer, smallint, float, double precision, real, bit, bit varying, date, time, timestamp, interval.
- Logical operators: and, or, not, ().
- Comparison operators: =, <>, <, <=, >, >=, (), in, any, some, all, between, not between, is null, is not null, like (see Examples 12 through 16 in Section A.3.1).
- Set operators (see Examples 4 and 5 in Section A.3.1):

  union—combines queries to display any row in each subquery

  intersect—combines queries to display distinct rows common to all subqueries

  except—combines queries to return all distinct rows returned by the first query but not the second (this is "minus" or "difference" in some versions of SQL)
- Set functions: count, sum, min, max, avg (see examples 6 through 11 in Section A.3.1).
- Advanced value expressions: CASE, CAST, row value constructors. The CASE is similar to the CASE expressions in programming languages in which a select command needs to produce different results when there are different values of the search condition. The CAST

expression allows you to convert data of one type to a different type, subject to some restrictions. Row value constructors allow one to set up multiple column value comparisons with a much simpler expression than is normally required in SQL (see [MeSi93] for detailed examples).

A.2 Data Definition Language (DDL)

The basic definitions for SQL objects (tables and views) are:

- *create table*—defines a table and all its attributes
- *alter table*—adds new columns, drops columns, or modifies existing columns in a table
- *drop table*—deletes an existing table
- *create view, drop view*—defines/deletes a database view (see "SQL Views," Section A.3.4)

Some versions of SQL also have create index/drop index, which defines/deletes an index on a particular attribute or composite of several attributes in a particular table.

The following table creation examples are based on a simple database of three tables: **customer**, **item**, and **order**. (Note that we put table names in boldface throughout the book for readability.)

```
create table customer
    (cust_num numeric,
    cust_name char(20),
    cust_addr varchar(256),
    credit_num numeric,
    check (credit_num >= 1000),
    primary key (cust_num));
```

Note that the attribute cust_num could be defined as "numeric not null unique" instead of explicitly defined as the primary key, since they have the same meaning. However, it would be redundant to have both forms in the same table definition. The check rule is an important integrity constraint that tells SQL to automatically test each insertion of credit_num value for something greater than or equal to 1000. If not, an error message should be displayed.

```
create table item
        (item_num numeric,
        item_name char(20),
        item_price numeric,
        item_wt numeric,
        primary key (item_num));

create table order
        (ord_num  char(15),
        cust_num  numeric not null,
        item_num numeric not null,
        quantity numeric,
        total_cost numeric,
        primary key (ord_num),
        foreign key (cust_num) references customer
                on delete no action on update cascade,
        foreign key (item_num) references item
                on delete no action on update cascade);
```

SQL-92, while allowing for the above format for primary key and foreign key, recommends a more detailed format, shown below for table **order**:

```
constraint pk_constr primary key (ord_num),
constraint fk_constr1 foreign key (cust_num) references customer
                (cust_num)
        on delete no action on update cascade,
constraint fk_constr2 foreign key (item_num) references item
                (item_num)
        on delete no action on update cascade);
```

where pk_constr is a primary key constraint name, and fk_constr1 and fk_constr2 are foreign key constraint names. The word "constraint" is a keyword, and the object in parenthesis after the table name is the name of the primary key in that table referenced by the foreign key.

The following constraints are common for attributes defined in the SQL create table commands:

- *Not null.* A constraint that specifies that an attribute must have a nonnull value.
- *Unique.* A constraint that specifies that the attribute is a candidate key—that is, that it has a unique value for every row in the table. Every attribute that is a candidate key must also have the constraint

not null. The constraint unique is also used as a clause to designate composite candidate keys that are not the primary key. This is particularly useful when transforming ternary relationships to SQL.

- *Primary key*. The primary key is a set of one or more attributes, which, when taken collectively, allows us to identify uniquely an entity or table. The set of attributes should not be reducible (see Section 5.1.2). The designation "primary key" for an attribute implies that the attribute must be "not null" and "unique," but the SQL key words NOT NULL and UNIQUE are redundant for any attribute that is part of a primary key, and need not be specified in the create table command.
- *Foreign key*. The referential integrity constraint specifies that a foreign key in a referencing table column must match an existing primary key in the referenced table. The references clause specifies the name of the referenced table. An attribute may be both a primary key and a foreign key, particularly in relationship tables formed from many-to-many binary relationships or from n-ary relationships.

Foreign key constraints are defined for row deletion on the referenced table and for the update of the primary key of the referenced table. The referential trigger actions for delete and update are similar:

- *on delete cascade*—the delete operation on the referenced table "cascades" to all matching foreign keys.
- *on delete set null*—foreign keys are set to null when they match the primary key of a deleted row in the referenced table. Each foreign key must be able to accept null values for this operation to apply.
- *on delete set default*—foreign keys are set to a default value when they match the primary key of the deleted row(s) in the reference table. Legal default values include a literal value, "user," "system user," or "no action."
- *on update cascade*—the update operation on the primary key(s) in the referenced table "cascades" to all matching foreign keys.
- *on update set null*—foreign keys are set to null when they match the old primary key value of an updated row in the referenced table. Each foreign key must be able to accept null values for this operation to apply.
- *on update set default*—foreign keys are set to a default value when they match the primary key of an updated row in the reference table. Legal default values include a literal value, "user," "system user," or "no action."

The "cascade" option is generally applicable when either the mandatory existence constraint or the ID dependency constraint is specified in the ER diagram for the referenced table, and either "set null" or "set default" is applicable when optional existence is specified in the ER diagram for the referenced table (see Chapters 2 and 4).

Some systems, such as DB2 have an additional option on delete or update, called "restricted." Delete restricted means that the referenced table rows are deleted only if there are no matching foreign key values in the referencing table. Similarly, "update restricted" means that the referenced table rows (primary keys) are updated only if there are no matching foreign key values in the referencing table.

Various column and table constraints can be specified as "deferable" (the default is "not deferable"), which means that the DBMS will defer checking this constraint until you commit the transaction. Often this is required for mutual constraint checking.

The following examples illustrate the alter table and drop table commands. The first alter table command modifies the cust_name data type from char(20) in the original definition to varchar(256). The second and third alter table commands add and drop a column, respectively. The add column option specifies the data type of the new column.

```
alter table customer
        modify (cust_name varchar(256));
alter table customer
        add column cust_credit_limit numeric;
alter table customer
        drop column credit_num;
drop table customer;
```

A.3 Data Manipulation Language (DML)

Data manipulation language commands are used for queries, updates, and the definition of views. These concepts are presented through a series of annotated examples, from simple to moderately complex.

A.3.1 SQL Select Command

The SQL select command is the basis for all database queries. We look at a series of examples to illustrate the syntax and semantics for the select command for the most frequent types of queries in everyday business applications. We use the indentation form of select command to emphasize readability and consistency.

1. Display the entire **customer** table. The asterisk (*) denotes that all records from this table are to be read and displayed.

```
select *
      from customer;
```

2. Display customer number and credit number for all customers in Toronto with credit number greater than 5. Order by ascending sequence of customer numbers (the order by options are asc, desc). Note that the first selection condition is specified in the "where" clause and succeeding selection conditions are specified by "and" clauses. Character type data and other nonnumeric data are placed inside single quotes, but numeric data is given without quotes.

```
select cust_num, credit_num
      from customer
      where cust_addr = 'Toronto'
      and credit_num > 5
      order by cust_num asc;
```

3. Display all customer and ordered item information (all columns), but omitting customers with credit number of 40. In this query the "from" clause shows the definition of abbreviations c and o for tables **customer** and **order**, respectively. The abbreviations can be used anywhere in the query to denote their respective table names. This example also illustrates a join between table **customer** and table **order** using the common attribute name cust_num, as shown in the "where" clause. The join finds matching cust_num values from the two tables and displays all the data from the matching rows, except where the credit number is 40.

```
select c.*, o.*
      from customer as c, order as o
      where c.cust_num = o.cust_num
      and c.credit_num <> 40;
```

4. Which items are ordered by customer 1 or customer 2? This query can be answered in two ways, one with a set operator (union) and the other with a logical operator (or).

```
select item_num, cust_num
      from order
      where cust_num = 1
union
select item_num, cust_num
      from order
      where cust_num =2;
```

```
select item_num, cust_num
    from order
    where (cust_num = 1 or cust_num = 2);
```

5. Which items are ordered by both customers 1 and 3? All the rows in table **order** that have customer 1 are selected and compared to the rows in **order** that have customer 3. Rows from each set are compared with all rows from the other set, and those that have matching item numbers have the item numbers displayed.

```
select item_num
    from order
    where cust_num =1
intersect
select item_num
    from order
    where cust_num = 3;
```

6. Display the total number of customers. This query uses the SQL function "count" to count the number of rows in table **customer**.

```
select count(*)
    from customer;
```

7. Display the total number of customers actually shipping items. This is a variation of the count function that specifies that only the distinct number of customers are to be counted. The "distinct" modifier is required because duplicate values of customer numbers are likely to be found, because a customer can order many items and will appear in many rows of table **order**.

```
select count (distinct cust_num)
    from order;
```

8. Display the maximum quantity of an order of item number 31. The SQL "maximum" function is used to search the table **order**, select rows where the item number is 31, and display the maximum value of quantity from the rows selected.

```
select max (quantity)
    from order
    where item_num = 31;
```

9. For each type of item ordered, display the item number and total order quantity. Note that item_num in the select line must be in a "group by" clause. In SQL any attribute to be displayed in the result of the select command must be included in a "group by" clause when the result of an SQL function is also to be displayed. The

"group by" clause results in a display of the aggregate sum of quantity values for each value of item_num. Item_num could appear in many different rows in table order, so the aggregate sums will be taken over all rows with the same value of item_num.

```
select item_num, sum(quantity)
    from order
    group by item_num;
```

10. Display item numbers for all items ordered more than ten times. This query requires the use of the "group by" and "having" clauses to display data that is based on a count of rows from table **order** having the same value for attribute item_num.

```
select item_num
    from order
    group by item_num
    having count(*) > 10;
```

11. Display item numbers and customer numbers and their largest quantity ordered, and group by item number as primary and customer number as secondary columns.

```
select item_num, cust_num, max(quantity)
    from order
    group by item_num,cust_num;
```

12. Display customer names for customers who order item 32. This query requires a join (equijoin) of tables **customer** and **order** in order to match customer names with item number 32. The equijoin is the most common type of join, and the only one we discuss here, but the reader may note that SQL-92 defines several other types [MeSi93].

```
select c.cust_name
    from customer as c, order as o
    where c.cust_num = o.cust_num
    and o.item_num = 32;
```

This query can be equivalently performed with a *subquery* (sometimes called *nested subquery*) with the following format. The select command inside the parentheses is a nested subquery and is executed first, resulting in a set of values for customer number (cust_num) selected from the **order** table. Each of those values is compared with cust_num values from the **customer** table, and matching values result in the display of customer name from the matching row in the **customer** table. This is effectively a join between tables **customer** and **order** with the selection condition of item number 32.

```
select c.cust_name
        from customer as c
        where c.cust_num in
        (select cust_num
        from order as o
        where o.item_num = 32);
```

13. Display customer names who order at least one item priced over $500.00. This query requires a three-level nested subquery format. Note that the phrases "in," "= some," and "= any" in the "where" clauses are often used as equivalent comparison operators; see [MeSi93].

```
select c.cust_name
        from customer as c
        where c.cust_num in
        (select o.cust_num
                from order as o
                where o.item_num = any
                (select i.item_num
                        from item as i
                        where i.item_price > '$500.00'));
```

14. Which customers have not ordered any item over $20? Note that one can equivalently use "not in" instead of "not any." The query first selects the customer numbers from all rows from the join of tables **order** and **item** where the item price is over $20. Then it selects rows from table **customer** where the customer number does not match any of the customers selected in the subquery, and displays the customer names.

```
select c.cust_name
        from customer as c
        where c.cust_num not any
        (select o.cust_num
                from order as o, item as i
                where o.item_num = i.item_num
                and i.item_price >'$20.00');
```

15. Which customers have only ordered items weighing more than 1000? This is an example of the universal quantifier "all." First the subquery selects all rows from table **item** where the item weight is over 1000. Then it selects rows from table **order** where all rows with a given item number match at least one row in the set selected in the subquery. Any rows in **order** satisfying this condition are joined with the customer table and the **customer** name is displayed as the final result.

```
select c.cust_name
    from customer as c, order as o
    where c.cust_num = o.cust_num
    and o.item_num = all
    (select i.item_num
        from item as i
        where i.item_wt > 1000);
```

16. Find all items that have the word "video" in their name. This requires the use of the "like" predicate which locates the character string 'video' anywhere in the string. Note that a % before and/or after a character string satisfies this query. An underscore specifies a particular position in a character string, but the value is unknown. An example of this would be '_xyz' which specifies a four character string with unknown first value and '%abcde_fg' specifies a variable length string in which the last eight characters are 'abcde', followed by an unknown character, and ending with 'fg'.

```
select item_name
    from item
    where item_name like '%video%';
```

17. How much has Schmidt made while working for this company? This illustrates a more complex query involving computation of an aggregate total from individual row data. Let us assume a new table, **salary_history**, with attributes last_name, monthly_salary, start_date, and end_date. (The special functions in this query are from Oracle SQL*Plus.)

```
select sum(monthly_salary*months_between(end_date,start_date))
    from salary_history
    where last_name = 'Schmidt';
```

A variation of this query checks to see if the last enddate is null. *Note:* the null value test function nvl(expr1, expr2) = expr1 if it is not null, or expr2 if expr1 is null.

```
select sum (monthly_salary*
        (months_between (nvl (end_date,sysdate), start_date)))
    from salary_history
    where last_name = 'Schmidt';
```

A.3.2 SQL Update Commands

The following SQL update commands relate to our continuing example and illustrate typical usage of insertion, deletion, and update of selected rows in tables.

```
insert into customer
    values (35,'Smith','Detroit,MI',10);
delete from customer
    where credit_num < 2;
update order
    set quantity = 450
    where quantity = 500
    and cust_num =3
    and item_num = 31;
```

A.3.3 Referential Integrity

The following update to the **item** table resets the value of item_num for a particular item, but because item_num is a foreign key in the **order** table, SQL must maintain referential integrity by triggering the execution sequence named by the foreign key constraint "on update cascade" in the definition of the **order** table (Section A2). This means that, in addition to updating a row in the **item** table, SQL will search the **order** table for values of item_num equal to 53300 and reset each value to 53327.

```
update item
    set item_num = 53327
    where item_num = 53300;
```

If this update had been a "delete" instead, such as the following:

```
delete from item
    where item_num = 53300;
```

Then the referential integrity trigger would have caused the additional execution of the foreign key constraint "on delete set default" in order (as defined in Section A.2), which finds every row in order with item_num = 53300 and takes the action set up in the default. A typical action for this type of database might be to set item_num to either null or a predefined literal value to denote that the particular item has been deleted; this would then be a signal to the system that the customer needs to be contacted to change the order. Of course, the system would have to be set up in advance to check for these values periodically.

A.3.4 SQL Views

A view in SQL is a named, derived (virtual) table that derives its data from base tables, the actual tables defined by the "create table" command. While view definitions can be stored in the database, the views (derived tables) themselves are not stored, but derived at execution time when the view is invoked as a query using the SQL select command. The person who queries the view treats the view as if it were an actual (stored) table, unaware of the difference between the view and the base table.

Views are useful in several ways. First, they allow complex queries to be set up in advance in a view, and the novice SQL user is only required to make a simple query on the view. This simple query invokes the more complex query defined by the view. Thus, nonprogrammers are allowed to utilize the full power of SQL without having to create complex queries. Second, views provide greater security for a database because the DBA can assign different views of the data to different users and control what any individual user sees in the database. Third, views provide a greater sense of data independence—that is, even though the base tables may be altered by adding, deleting, or modifying columns, the view query may not need to be changed. While view definition may need to be changed, that is the job of the DBA, not the person querying the view.

Views may be defined hierarchically, that is, a view definition may contain another view name as well as base table names. This allows for some views to become quite complex.

In the following example, we create a view called "orders" that shows which items have been ordered by each customer and how many. The first line of the view definition specifies the view name and (in parentheses) lists the attributes of that view. The view attributes must correlate exactly with the attributes defined in the select statement in the second line of the view definition:

```
create view orders (customer_name, item_name, quantity) as
    select c.cust_name, i.item_name, o.quantity
        from customer as c, item as i, order as o
        where c.cust_num = o.cust_num
        and o.item_num = i.item_num;
```

The "create view" command creates the view definition, which defines two joins among three base tables **customer**, **item**, and **order**; and SQL stores the definition to be executed later when invoked by a query. The query shown below selects all the data from the view "orders." This query causes SQL to execute the select command given in the view definition above, producing a tabular result with the column headings for customer_name, item_name, and quantity.

```
select *
    from orders;
```

Views are usually not allowed to be updated, because the updates would have to be made to the base tables that make up the definition of the view. When a view is created from a single table, the view update is often unambiguous, but when a view is created from the joins of multiple tables, the base table updates are very often ambiguous and may have undesirable side effects. Each relational system has its own rules about when views can and cannot be updated.

As an example of an ambiguous update situation, consider the two tables, **table1** and **table2**, with columns named one, two, three, and four:

table1	one	two	three	**table2**	three	four
	a	b	e		e	k
	a	d	f		e	m
	a	d	e		f	n

```
create view view1 (one, two, three, four) as
    select t1.one, t1.two, t1.three, t2.four
        from table1 as r1, table2 as r2
        where t1.three = t2.three;
```

The resulting view produced by a query "select * from view1" would be displayed as

view1	one	two	three	four	
	a	d	f	n	/* row 1 */
	a	b	e	k	/* row 2 */
	a	b	e	m	/* row 3 */
	a	d	e	k	/* row 4 */
	a	d	e	m	/* row 5 */

If we try to delete row 2 from view1, there are serious problems in trying to delete the corresponding data from the base tables, **table1** and **table2**. One approach is to delete row 1 in **table1**, but this has the unintended side effect of deleting row 3 in view1 as well as row 2. Similarly, deleting row 1 in **table2** has the side effect of deleting row 4 in view1 as well as row 2. Deleting row 1 in both **table1** and **table2** makes matters even worse, deleting rows 3 and 4 in view1.

If we try to update row 2 in view1, attribute three from "e" to "f," we have more problems. If we update row 1 of **table1** to be (a,b,f) and update row 1 of **table2** to be (f,k), the join of these two updated rows in the view query will produce several superfluous rows as a result, and view1 will be incorrect. As a result, deleting or updating of rows from view1 is not recommended!

Literature Summary

[ISAN89] ISO-ANSI Database Language SQL2 and SQL3, ANSI X3H2-89-110, ISO DBL CAN-3 (working draft), J. Melton (editor), February 1989.

[ISAN92] ANSI X3.135-1992 Database Language SQL and ISO/IEC 9075:1992 Database Language SQL.

[MeSi93] Melton, J. and Simon, A.R. *Understanding the New SQL: A Complete Guide*, Morgan Kaufmann Publishers, San Francisco, 1993.

EXERCISES

Problem A-1

Given the following schema for a presidential database, write SQL queries (in correct syntax) for each of the three queries listed below:

```
create table president
    (identifier integer not null unique,
    last_name char(16),
    first_name char(16),
    middle_init char(2),
    political_party char(16),
    state_from char(16));
create table administration
    (pres_identifier integer,
    start_date date not null unique,
    end_date date,
    vp_last_name char(16),
    vp_first_name char(16),
    vp_middle_init char(2));
create table state
    (state_name char(16) not null unique,
    date_admitted date not null,
    area integer,000000
    population integer,
    capital_city char(16));
```

Queries

Q1. Which presidents were from the state of Ohio and also members of the Republican party?

Q2. Which states were admitted when President Andrew Johnson was in office?

Q3. Which vice-presidents (vp's) did *not* later become president? Assume that no one could be president and then vice-president, but could be vice-president and then president.

Problem A-2

For the relational table definitions given below, write the SQL queries and updates for the English queries and updates specified.

Queries

Q1. Who does Bill Joy manage?

Q2. Is there a manager who manages *both* Ed Birss and Leo Horvitz? If so, who is it?

Q3. Display employee names and room numbers who work in the "special funds" department.

Q4. Which employees work in *either* the "engineering" or "data processing" departments?

Q5. Display the names of project managers who are *also* department heads.

Q6. Display all projects, sorted (ascending) by project name. Specify who manages each project, which employees work on it, and show what department the project manager is in. Within a project, sort employees by employee name.

Q7. Which programmers are *not* assigned to the "new computers" project?

Q8. How much money has Mike Wilens made while working for this company?

Q9. Which employees make over $5000/month and have no project management responsibility?

Q10. Who are the first-, second-, and third-level managers above Beverly Kahn? Use the "manager" attribute in the employee table. Create three "views," one for the first-level manager, another for the second-level manager, and yet another for the third-level manager. Then specify three separate queries in terms of these three "views."

Updates

U1. Create a new table that has your last name and first initial as its name-prefix, and that lists employee names and three hobbies. Make up four rows for this table. (Example table name: **deppe_m_hobbies**.) In this way each member of the class can add to the database without damaging the existing database. See if you can print out a nonredundant list of hobbies for those employees working in the "special funds" department.

U2. Delete one of the rows in your table.

U3. Modify one of the remaining rows to change one of the hobbies.

```
create table dept (dept_no char(6),
    dept_name char(20),
    dept_head char(10),
    primary key (dept_no));
create table employee (emp_no char(10),
    emp_name char(20),
    room_no char(8),
    dept_no char(6),
    manager char(10),
    primary key (emp_no),
    foreign key (dept_no) references dept
        on delete set null on update cascade,
    foreign key (manager) references employee
        on delete cascade on update cascade);
create table salary (salary_level integer,
    mon_salary float,
    primary key (salary_level));
create table job (job_code char(5),
    job_title char(15),
    primary key (job_code));
create table salary_hist (emp_no char(10),
    salary_level integer,
    job_code char(5),
    start_date char(8),
    end_date char(8),
    primary key (emp_no, salary_level),
    foreign key (emp_no) references employee
        on delete cascade on update cascade,
    foreign key (salary_level) references salary
        on delete cascade on update cascade);
```

```
create table project (proj_code char(6),
    proj_name char(15),
    start_date char(8),
    end_date char(8),
    proj_mgr char(10),
    primary key (proj_code),
    foreign key (proj_mgr) references employee
        on delete set default on update cascade);
create table workson (emp_no char(10),
    proj_code char(6),
    primary key (emp_no, proj_code),
    foreign key (emp_no) references employee
        on delete cascade on update cascade,
    foreign key (proj_code) references project
        on delete cascade on update cascade);
```

APPENDIX B

DATABASE PERFORMANCE TUNING

This appendix looks at the various parameters associated with relational database tuning in terms of what the database user can control and what the database administrator usually manages. For each parameter, we define how the concept works and what choices are possible, including trade-offs that should be considered. Some of the specific parameters and their values are taken from Oracle [OR89a, b], but the concepts can be applied to many commercial relational systems.

B.1 User-Defined Parameters

Relational database users typically have control over the table @FL = definitions, including primary and foreign keys, normalization, and usage refinement (see Chapters 4–6). However, they also have a significant amount of control over the indexing and clustering of tables.

1. Index. A method for speeding up the access to database tables compared to a full table scan. In general, it is better to build an index when fewer than 10–15% of the rows will be accessed. A full table scan is typically faster for greater than 10–15% of the rows scanned because of multiblock sequential access techniques (single reads of 64 KB or more).
   a. Number of indexes per table. More than one index per table allows a greater variety of efficient accesses for different types of queries. This flexibility and efficiency is created at the expense of greater space overhead and index update overhead.
   b. Unique index. An index created for primary keys only, with pointers to individual (unique) rows. This is very often implemented as a hashing table, but also can be implemented as a B^+-tree (sometimes referred to as a B* tree).

c. Nonunique index (secondary index). An index based on nonkey attributes, requiring a pointer array to possibly many rows that satisfy the attribute value(s) given in the search argument. This type of index is very efficient and flexible for complex Boolean queries involving several nonkey attribute values.

d. Concatenated index. An index created on more than one column, that is, based on a concatenated key of more than one column. This index is typically much larger than a single column index because of the many possible values for the combined keys. It tends to give faster database access for queries based on the concatenated key, but is less flexible than a simple index, requires more space, and has greater index update overhead. It is used for certain dominating queries in terms of frequency of execution.

e. Compressed index. Any index that is stored in compressed mode, thus having more index entries per B^+-tree node than a noncompressed index. Oracle does both front and rear compression, which is based on storing only the key value characters that are different from the value of the previous entry and an integer representing the number of overlapping characters between the current key value and the previous one. Compressed indexes require much less space (typically a 3 or 4 to 1 reduction) and thus less I/O, but at the expense of somewhat higher CPU cost to compress and decompress the entries.

f. Percent free. A numeric value that specifies how much free space will be allocated to B^+-tree leaf nodes during index creation. Typically, values of 10–15% are used to allow for expansion for new rows after the initial allocation of index values.

2. Clustering. The main idea of clustering is to physically store together data that is often queried together. Clustering has no effect on the type of SQL statements used to access the data, only on the efficiency of those statements. Tables selected for clustering are those that are frequently joined to satisfy queries. These tables typically have one or more columns in common, and the redundant data is eliminated in the cluster.

   a. Cluster key. Designates which columns are overlapping between two tables in a cluster, and thus indicates which data will be stored nonredundantly.

   b. Logical block size. The logical unit of clustered data that encompasses data from both tables in the cluster. This is typically smaller than the physical block size of the database and is used for conserving space and minimizing the I/O calls during cluster scans.

B.2 Database Administrator and System Defined Parameters

1. Blocks. The physical block is the basic unit of I/O for many systems and thus is an important parameter for database storage.
   a. Block size. Typical block size for most environments (UNIX, IBM, etc.) is either 2048 or 4096 bytes. However, multiblock scans of 64 KB per I/O have been used to increase the sequential processing efficiency of certain systems.
   b. Row length. Bytes per row, including overhead such as row sequence number and column id number, and compressed data such as null values.
   c. Percent free. A numeric value that specifies how much free space will be allocated to data blocks to allow for expansion due to insertions and updates. (Updates cause expansion when null values are replaced by nonnull values.)
   d. Blocking factor (bf). The number of rows (records) per block. This number takes into account the row length; all overhead for headers, and percent free space in the block.

bf = integervalue[(1 – freespace_fraction) * (blocksize – headersize)/rowsize]

   For example, if percent free is 20%, block size is 2048 bytes, header size is 76 bytes, and row size is 150 bytes, then the blocking factor is integer[(1 – .2) * (2048 – 76)/150] = 10.
   e. Blocks per table. The number of rows in the table divided by the the blocking factor, taken to the next higher integer if a fractional value.
2. Buffers. Space allocated in main memory to hold data accessed from I/O devices.
   a. Buffer size. Size of individual buffers, typically preset by the I/O block size, standardized for a given system; for example, UNIX uses 2048 byte blocks, whereas MVS uses 4096 byte blocks.
   b. Buffer pool size. The number of buffers allocated in main memory for a database application; for example, Oracle defaults to 50 buffers in the buffer pool. The greater the number of buffers cached in main memory the greater the likelihood that a record you need is in main memory and the lesser that you will need an I/O to get it. This probability is highly dependent on the locality of the database queries and the way the data is clustered.

Literature Summary

[OR89a] Oracle Database Administrator's Guide, Part No. 3601-V5.1, 1989.

[OR89b] Oracle RDBMS Performance Tuning Guide, Part No. 5317-V6.0, 1989.

REFERENCES

[Abri74] Abrial, J. "Data Semantics," Data Base Management, Proc. IFIP TC2 Conf., Cargese, Corsica, North-Holland, Amsterdam, 1974.

[ACM90] *ACM Computing Surveys* (Special Issue on Heterogeneous Databases) 22,3 (Sept. 1990), pp. 173-293.

[Aper88] Apers, P.M.G. "Data Allocation in Distributed Database Systems," *ACM Trans. Database Systems* 13,3 (Sept. 1988), pp. 263-304.

[Ariav86] Ariav, G.A. "Temporally Oriented Data Model," *ACM Trans. Database Systems* 11,4 (Dec. 1986), pp. 499-527.

[Bach69] Bachman, C.W. "Data Structure Diagrams," Database 1,2 (1969), pp. 4-10.

[Bach72] Bachman, C.W. "The Evolution of Storage Structures," *Comm. ACM* 15,7 (July 1972), pp. 628-634.

[Bach77] Bachman, C.W. "The Role Concept in Data Models," *Proc. 3rd Intl. Conf. on Very Large Data Bases,* Tokyo, Oct. 6-8, 1977, IEEE, New York, pp. 464-476.

[Bane87] Banerjee, J., Chou, H.T., Garza, J.F., Kim, W., Woelk, B., and Ballou, N. "Data Model Issues for Object-Oriented Applications," *ACM Trans. on Office Information Systems* 5,1 (Jan. 1987), pp. 3-26.

[BaLe84] Batini, C. and Lenzerini, M. "A Methodology for Data Schema Integration in the Entity Relationship Model," *IEEE Trans. on Software Engr.* SE-10,6 (Nov. 1984), pp. 650-664.

[BCN92] Batini, C., Ceri, S., and Navathe, S. *Conceptual Database Design: An Entity-Relationship Approach,* Benjamin/Cummings, Redwood City, CA, 1992.

[BLN86] Batini, C., Lenzerini, M., and Navathe, S.B. "A Comparative Analysis of Methodologies for Database Schema Integration," *ACM Computing Surveys* 18,4 (Dec. 1986), pp. 323-364.

[BaBu84] Batory, D.S. and Buchmann, A.P. "Molecular Objects, Abstract Data Types, and Data Models: A Framework," *Proc. 10th Intl. Conf. on Very Large Data Bases,* Singapore, Aug. 1984, pp. 172-184.

[BaMc72] Bayer, R. and McCreight, E. "Organization and Maintenance of Large Ordered Indexes," *Acta. Inf.* 1,3 (1972), pp. 173-189.

[BBG78] Beeri, C., Bernstein, P., and Goodman, N. "A Sophisticates Introduction to Database Normalization Theory," *Proc. 4th Intl. Conf. on Very Large Data Bases,* Berlin, Sept. 13-15, 1978, IEEE, New York, pp. 113-124.

[BFH77] Beeri, C., Fagin, R., and Howard, J.H. "A Complete Axiomization for Functional and Multivalued Dependencies in Database Relations," *Proc. 1977 ACM SIGMOD Int'l. Conf. on Management of Data,* Toronto, 1977, pp. 47-61.

[Bern76] Bernstein, P. "Synthesizing 3NF Relations from Functional Dependencies," *ACM Trans. Database Systems* 1,4 (1976), pp. 272-298.

[BeGo81] Bernstein, P.A. and Goodman, N. "Concurrency Control in Distributed Database Systems," *ACM Computing Surveys* 13,2 (June 1981), pp. 185-222.

[BlEs77] Blasgen, M.W. and Eswaran, K.P. "Storage and Access in Relational Data Bases," *IBM Syst. J.* 16,4 (1977), pp. 363-377.

[Booc86] Booch, G. "Object-Oriented Development," *IEEE Trans. on Software Engineering* SE-12,2 (Feb. 1986), pp. 211-221.

[Booc91] Booch, G. *Object Oriented Design with Applications,* Benjamin/ Cummings, Redwood City, CA, 1991.

[BPP76] Bracchi, G., Paolini, P., and Pelagatti, G. "Binary Logical Associations in Data Modelling," *Modelling in Data Base Management Systems* (C.M. Nijssen, Ed.), North-Holland, Amsterdam, 1976.

[BHHS85] Braind, H., Habrias, H., Hue, J., and Simon, Y. "Expert System for Translating an E-R Diagram into Databases," *Proc. 4th Intl. Conf. on Entity-Relationship Approach,* Chicago, IEEE Computer Society Press, Silver Spring, MD, 1985, pp. 199-206.

[BMS84] Brodie, M.L., Mylopoulos, J., and Schmidt, J. (editors). *On Conceptual Modeling: Perspectives from Artificial Intelligence, Databases, and Programming Languages,* Springer-Verlag, New York, 1984. — 0932 633 188 . ISBN

[Bruc92] Bruce, T.A. *Designing Quality Databases with IDEF1X Information Models,* Dorset House, New York, 1992. £50 - 2/3 week.

[Bube77] Bubenko, J. "The Temporal Dimension in Information Modelling," *Architecture and Models in Data Base Management Systems,* G. Nijssen (editor), North-Holland, Amsterdam, 1977.

[Card85] Cardenas, A.F. *Data Base Management Systems* (2nd Ed.), Allyn and Bacon, Boston, 1985.

[Case72] Casey, R.G. "Allocation of Copies of a File in an Information Network," *Spring Joint Computer Conf.,* 1972, AFIPS Press, Vol. 40, 1972.

[CePe84] Ceri, S. and Pelagatti, G. *Distributed Databases: Principles and Systems,* McGraw-Hill, New York, 1984.

[CNW83] Ceri, S., Navathe, S.B., and Wiederhold, G. "Distribution Design of Logical Database Schemes," *IEEE Trans. on Soft. Engr.* SE-9,4(1983), pp. 487-504.

[CNP82] Ceri, S., Negri, M., and Pelagatti, G. "Horizontal Data Partitioning in Database Design," *Proc. ACM-SIGMOD Int'l. Conf. on Management of Data,* Orlando, FL, June 2-4, 1982, pp. 128-136.

[CPW87] Ceri, S., Pernici, B., and Wiederhold, G. "Distributed Database Design Methodologies," *Proc. IEEE,* May 1987, pp. 533-546.

[Chen76] Chen, P.P. "The Entity-Relationship Model—Toward a Unified View of Data," *ACM Trans. Database Systems* 1,1 (March 1976), pp. 9-36.

[Chen87] Chen and Associates, Inc. *ER Designer* (User Manual), 1987.

[Chu69] Chu, W.W. "Optimal File Allocation in a Multiple Computer System," *IEEE Trans. on Computers* C-18,10 (Oct. 1969), pp. 885-889.

[Chu84] Chu, W.W. *Distributed Data Bases, Handbook of Software Engineering,* C.R. Vick and C.V. Ramamoorthy (editors), Van Nostrand Reinhold, New York, 1984.

[ClWa83] Clifford, J. and Warren, D. "Formal Semantics for Time in Databases," *ACM Trans. Database Systems* 8,2 (1983), pp. 214-254.

[CoYo90] Coad, P. and Yourdon, E. *Object-Oriented Analysis*, Prentice-Hall, Englewood Cliffs, NJ, 1990.

[CFT84] Cobb, R.E., Fry, J.P., and Teorey, T.J. "The Database Designers Workbench," Information Sciences 32,1 (Feb. 1984), pp. 33-45.

[Codd70] Codd, E. "A Relational Model for Large Shared Data Banks," *Comm. ACM* 13,6 (June 1970), pp. 377-387.

[Codd74] Codd, E. "Recent Investigations into Relational Data Base Systems," *Proc. IFIP Congress,* North-Holland, Amsterdam, 1974.

[Codd90] Codd, E. *The Relational Model for Database Management: Version 2,* Addison Wesley, Reading, MA, 1990.

[CoGe80] Coffman, E.G. et al. "Optimization of the Number of Copies in Distributed Databases," *Proc. of the 7th IFIP Symposium on Computer Performance Modelling, Measurement and Evaluation,* Springer-Verlag, New York, May 1980, pp. 257- 263.

[CACM92] *Comm. ACM* (Special Issue: Analysis and Modeling in Software Development) 35,9 (Sept. 1992), pp. 35-171.

[Date84] Date, C.J. *A Guide to DB2*, Addison-Wesley, Reading, MA, 1984.

[Date87] Date, C.J. "The Twelve Rules for a Distributed Data Base," *Computerworld,* June 8, 1987.

[Date89] Date, C.J. *A Guide to the SQL Standard* (2nd Ed.), Addison-Wesley, Reading, MA, 1989.

[Date90] Date, C.J. *An Introduction to Database Systems, Vol. 1* (5th Ed.), Addison-Wesley, Reading, MA, 1990.

[DBMS93] *DBMS* (Special Issue: Database Buyer's Guide) 6,7 (Sept. 1993).

[DeMa78] De Marco, T. *Structured Analysis and System Specification,* Yourdon Press, New York, 1978.

[DGL86] Dittrich, K.R., Gotthard, W., and Lockemann, P.C. "Complex Entities for Engineering Applications," *Proc. 5th ER Conf.,* North-Holland, 1986.

[DKM86] Dittrich, K.R., Kotz, A.M., and Mulle, J.A. "An Event/Trigger Mechanism to Enforce Complex Consistency Constraints in Design Databases," *SIGMOD Record* 15,3 (Sept. 1986), pp. 22-36.

[Duga90] Dugan, J.B. "On Measurement and Modeling of Computer Systems Dependability: A Dialog Among Experts," *IEEE Transactions on Reliability* 39,4 (Oct. 1990), pp. 506-510.

[DuHa89] Dutka, A.F. and Hanson, H.H. *Fundamentals of Data Normalization,* Addison- Wesley, Reading, MA, 1989.

[ElNa94] Elmasri, R. and Navathe, S.B. *Fundamentals of Database Systems* (2nd Ed.), Addison-Wesley/Benjamin/Cummings, Redwood City, CA, 1994.

[ElWi79] Elmasri, R. and Wiederhold, G. "Data Model Integration Using the Structural Model," *Proc. ACM SIGMOD Conf.,* Boston, ACM, New York, 1979, pp. 319-326.

[EHW85] Elmasri, R., Hevner, A., and Weeldreyer, J. "The Category Concept: An Extension to the Entity-Relationship Model," *Data and Knowledge Engineering* 1,1 (1985), pp. 75-116.

[Ever86] Everest, G.C. *Database Management: Objectives, System Functions, and Administration,* McGraw-Hill, New York, 1986.

[Fagi77] Fagin, R. "Multivalued Dependencies and a New Normal Form for Relational Databases," *ACM Trans. Database Systems* 2,3 (1977), pp. 262-278.

[FeMi86] Feldman, P. and Miller, D. "Entity Model Clustering: Structuring a Data Model by Abstraction," *Computer Journal* 29,4 (Aug. 1986), pp. 348-360.

[Fell68] Feller, W. *An Introduction to Probability Theory and Its Applications* (3rd Ed.), John Wiley & Sons, New York, 1968.

[Ferg85] Ferg, S. "Modeling the Time Dimension in an Entity-Relationship Diagram," *Proc. 4th Intl. Conf. on the Entity-Relationship Approach,* Chicago, IEEE Computer Society Press, Silver Spring, MD, 1985, pp. 280-286.

[FiHo80] Fisher, M.L. and Hochbaum, D., "Database Location in Computer Networks," *J ACM* 27,4 (Oct. 1980), pp. 718-735.

[FHS80] Fisher, P., Hollist, P., and Slonim, J. "A Design Methodology for Distributed Databases," *Proc. IEEE Conf. Distributed Computing,* Sept.1980, IEEE, pp. 199-202.

[FHJF85] Fong, E., Henderson, M., Jefferson, D., and Sullivan, J. *Guide on Logical Database Design,* NBS Spec. Pub. 500-122, U.S. Dept. of Commerce, 1985.

[FlvH89] Fleming, C.C. and von Halle, B. *Handbook of Relational Database Design,* Addison-Wesley, Reading, MA, 1989.

[Gadr87] Gadre, S.H. "Building an Enterprise and Information Model," *Database Programming and Design* 1,1 (Dec. 1987), pp. 48-58.

[GaSa79] Gane, C.P. and Sarson, T. *Structured System Analysis: Tools and Techniques,* Prentice-Hall, Englewood Cliffs, NJ, 1979.

[Gray81] Gray, J. "The Transaction Concept: Virtues and Limitations," *Proc. 7th Intl. Conf. on Very Large Data Bases,* Sept. 1981, IEEE, New York, pp. 144-154.

[Gray90] Gray, Jim. "A Census of Tandem System Availability Between 1985 and 1990," *IEEE Transactions on Reliability* 39,4 (Oct. 1990), pp. 409-418.

[GrAn87] Gray, J.N. and Anderson, M. "Distributed Computer Systems: Four Cases," *Proc. IEEE* 75,5 (May 1987), pp.719-729.

[GrRe93] Gray, J. and Reuter, A. *Transaction Processing: Concepts and Techniques,* Morgan Kaufmann, San Mateo, CA, 1993.

[Gros86] Grosshans, D. *File Systems Design and Implementation,* Prentice-Hall, Englewood Cliffs, NJ, 1986.

[HaMc82] Hammer, M. and McLeod, D. "Database Description with SDM: A Semantic Database Model," *ACM Trans. Database Systems* 6,3 (Sept. 1982), pp. 351-386.

[Harb88] Harbron, T.R. *File Systems Structures and Algorithms,* Prentice-Hall, Englewood Cliffs, NJ, 1988.

[Hawr84] Hawryszkiewycz, I. *Database Analysis and Design*, SRA, Chicago, 1984.

[Hawr90] Hawryszkiewycz, I. *Relational Database Design,* Prentice-Hall, New York, 1990.

[Heba77] Hebalkar, P.G. "Logical Design Considerations for Distributed Database Systems," *IEEE COMPSAC,* Nov. 1977, pp. 562-580.

[HeYa87] Hevner, A.R. and Yao, S.B. "Querying Distributed Databases on Local Area Networks," *Proc. IEEE* 75,5 (May 1987), pp. 563-572.

[Howe83] Howe, D. *Data Analysis and Data Base Design,* Arnold, London, 1983.

[HsKa89] Hsiao,D.K. and Kamel,M.N. "Heterogeneous Databases: Proliferations, Issues, and Solutions," *IEEE Trans. on Knowledge and Data Engineering* 1,1 (March 1989), pp. 45-62.

[HuKi87] Hull, R. and King, R. "Semantic Database Modeling: Survey, Applications, and Research Issues," *ACM Computing Surveys* 19,3 (Sept. 1987), pp. 201-260.

[IEEE92] *IEEE Computer* (Special Issue: Inheritance and Classification in Object-Oriented Computing) 25,10 (Oct. 1992), pp. 6-90.

[Inmo87] Inmon, W.H. "Optimizing Performance with Denormalization," *Database Programming and Design* 1,1 (Dec. 1987), pp. 34-39.

[IrKh81] Irani, K.B. and Khabbaz, N.G. "A Combined Communication Network Design and File Allocation for Distributed Databases," *2nd Intl Conf. on Distributed Systems,* Paris, IEEE Computer Society Press, April 1981.

[ISAN89] *ISO-ANSI Database Language SQL2 and SQL3,* ANSI X3H2-89-110, ISO DBL CAN-3 (working draft), J. Melton (editor), February 1989.

[ISO82] ISO/TC97/SC5/WG3-N695 Report. "Concepts and Terminology for the Conceptual Schema and the Information Base," J. van Griethuysen (editor), ANSI, New York, 1982.

[Jaco87] Jacobsen, I. "Object Oriented Development in an Industrial Environment," OOPSLA'87 as *ACM SIGPLAN* 22,12 (Dec. 1987), pp. 183-191.

[JaNg84] Jajodia, S. and Ng, P. "Translation of Entity-Relationship Diagrams into Relational Structures," *J. Systems and Software* 4,2-3 (1984) pp. 123-133.

[JWBT91] Janakiraman, J., Warack, C., Bhal, G., and Teorey, T.J. "Progressive Fragment Allocation," *Proc. 10th Int'l Conf. on the Entity Relationship Approach,* ER Institute, San Mateo, CA, October 23-25, 1991, pp. 543-560.

[JaKo84] Jarke, M. and Koch, J. "Query Optimization in Database Systems," *ACM Computing Surveys* 16,2 (June 1984), pp. 111-152.

[JoMa88] Johnson, A.M. Jr. and Malek, M. "Survey of Software Tools for Evaluating Reliability, Availability, and Serviceability," *ACM Computing Surveys* 20,4 (Dec. 1988), pp. 227-269.

[Kent81] Kent, W. "Consequences of Assuming a Universal Relation," *ACM Trans. Database Systems* 6,4 (1981), pp. 539-556.

[Kent83] Kent, W. "A Simple Guide to Five Normal Forms in Relational Database Theory," *Comm. ACM* 26,2 (Feb. 1983), pp. 120-125.

[Kent84] Kent, W. "Fact-Based Data Analysis and Design," *J. Systems and Software* 4 (1984), pp. 99-121.

[KiLo89] Kim, W. and Lochovsky, F. *Object-Oriented Concepts, Databases, and Applications,* Addison-Wesley, Reading, MA, 1989.

[KoSi91] Korth, H.F. and Silberschatz, A. *Database System Concepts* (2nd Ed.), McGraw-Hill, New York, 1991.

[LeSa83] Lenzerini, M. and Santucci, G. "Cardinality Constraints in the Entity-Relationship Model," *The Entity-Relationship Approach to Software Engineering,* G.C. Davis et al. (editors), Elsevier, North-Holland, New York, 1983, pp. 529-549.

[Lien81] Lien, Y. "Hierarchical Schemata for Relational Databases," *ACM Trans. Database Systems* 6,1 (1981), pp. 48-69.

[Lien82] Lien, Y. "On the Equivalence of Data Models," *J. ACM* 29,2 (1982), pp. 333-362.

[Ling85] Ling, T. "A Normal Form for Entity-Relationship Diagrams," *Proc. 4th International Conf. on the ER Approach,* Chicago, IEEE Computer Society Press, Silver Spring, MD, 1985, pp. 24-35.

[Loom83] Loomis, M.E.S. *Data Management and File Processing,* Prentice-Hall, Englewood Cliffs, NJ, 1983.

[Maci89] Maciaszek, L. *Database Design and Implementation," Prentice-Hall International, 1989.*

[MaRi76] Mahmood, S. and Riordan, J. "Optimal Allocation of Resources in Distributed Information Networks," *ACM Trans. Database Systems* 1,1 (March 1976), pp. 66-78.

[Maie83] Maier, D. *Theory of Relational Databases,* Computer Science Press, Rockville, MD, 1983.

[MSOP86] Maier, D., Stein, J., Otis, A., and Purdy, A. "Development of an Object-Oriented DBMS," *OOPSLA 1986 Proc.,* Sept. 1986, pp. 472-482.

[MMR86] Makowski, J.A., Markowitz, V.M., and Rotics, N. "Entity-Relationship Consistency for Relational Schemas," in *Proc. Intl Conf. on Database Theory,* G. Ausiello and P. Atzeni (Eds.), Springer-Verlag, Berlin, New York, Sept. 1986, pp. 306-322.

[MaTe88] Mantei, M.M. and Teorey, T.J. "Cost/Benefit Analysis for Incorporating Human Factors into the Software Lifecycle," *Comm. ACM* 31,4 (April 1988), pp. 428-439.

[Mark87] Mark, L. "Defining Views in the Binary Relationship Model," *Inform. Systems* 12,3 (1987), pp. 281-294.

[MaSh89] Markowitz, V.M. and Shoshani, A. "Name Assignment Techniques for Relational Schemas Representing Extended Entity-Relationship Schemas," *Proc. 8th Intl Conf. on the Entity-Relationship Approach,* Toronto, October 18-20, 1989, pp. 21-39.

[MaSh89] Markowitz, V.M. and Shoshani, A. "On the Correctness of Representing Extended Entity-Relationship Structures in the Relational Model," *Proc. ACM SIGMOD Conf. on Management of Data,* Portland, 1989, pp. 430-439.

[Mart82] Martin, J. *Strategic Data-Planning Methodologies,* Prentice-Hall, Englewood Cliffs, NJ, 1982.

[Mart83] Martin, J. *Managing the Data-Base Environment,* Prentice-Hall, Englewood Cliffs, NJ, 1983.

[MaFe90] Maxion, R.A. and Feather, F.E. "A Case Study of Ethernet Anomalies in a Distributed Computing Environment," *IEEE Transactions on Reliability* 39,4 (Oct. 1990), pp. 433-443.

[McGe74] McGee, W. "A Contribution to the Study of Data Equivalence, Data Base Management," J.W. Klimbie and K.L. Koffeman (editors), North-Holland, 1974, pp. 123-148.

[McKi79] McLeod, D. and King, R. "Applying a Semantic Database Model," *Proc. 1st Intl. Conf. on the Entity-Relationship Approach to Systems Analysis and Design*, North-Holland, Amsterdam, 1979, pp. 193-210.

[MeSi93] Melton, J. and Simon, A.R. *Understanding The New SQL: A Complete Guide*, Morgan Kaufmann, San Francisco, 1993.

[Meye88] Meyer, B. *Object-Oriented Software Construction*, Prentice-Hall Int'l, Hertfordshire, England, 1988.

[Mitt91] Mittra, S. S. *Principles of Relational Database Systems*, Prentice-Hall, Englewood Cliffs, NJ, 1991.

[MoLe77] Morgan, H.L. and Levin, K.D. "Optimal Program and Data Allocation in Computer Networks," *Comm. ACM* 32,5 (May 1977), pp. 345-353.

[MTM89] Moyne, J.R., Teorey, T.J., and McAfee, L.C. "Time Sequence Ordering Extensions to the Entity Relationship Model and their Application to the Automated Manufacturing Process," *Data and Knowledge Engr.* 6,5 (Sept. 1991), pp. 421-433.

[NaCh83] Navathe, S. and Cheng, A. "A Methodology for Database Schema Mapping from Extended Entity Relationship Models into the Hierarchical Model," *The Entity-Relationship Approach to Software Engineering*, G.C. Davis et al. (editors), Elsevier, North-Holland, Amsterdam, 1983.

[NaGa82] Navathe, S. and Gadgil, S. "A Methodology for View Integration in Logical Database Design," *Proc. 8th Intl. Conf. on Very Large Data Bases*, Mexico City, 1982, pp. 142-152.

[NEL86] Navathe, S., Elmasri, R., and Larson, J. "Integrating User Views in Database Design," *IEEE Computer* 19,1 (1986), pp. 50-62.

[NSE84] Navathe, S., Sashidhar, T., and Elmasri, R. "Relationship Merging in Schema Integration," *Proc. 10th Intl. Conf. on Very Large Data Bases*, Singapore, 1984, pp. 78-90.

[NiHa89] Nijssen, G.M. and Halpin, T.A. *Conceptual Schema and Relational Database Design: A Fact Oriented Approach*, Prentice-Hall, New York, 1989.

[NvS79] Nijssen, G., van Assche, F., and Snijders, J. "End User Tools for Information Systems Requirement Definition," *Formal Models and Practical Tools for Information System Design*, H. Schneider (editor), North-Holland, Amsterdam, 1979.

[OR89a] Oracle Database Administrator's Guide, Part No. 3601-V5.1, 1989.

[OR89b] Oracle RDBMS Performance Tuning Guide, Part No. 5317-V6.0, 1989.

[Oren85] Oren, O. "Integrity Constraints in the Conceptual Schema Language SYSDOC," *Proc. 4th Intl. Conf. on the Entity-Relationship Approach,* Chicago, IEEE Computer Society Press, Silver Spring, MD, 1985, pp. 288-294.

[Ossh84] Ossher, H.L. "A New Program Structuring Mechanism Based on Layered Graphs," *Proc. 11th Annual ACM SIGACT-SIGPLAN POPL,* Salt Lake City, Utah, Jan. 15-18, 1984, pp. 11-22.

[OzVa90] Ozsu, M.T. and Valduriez, P. *Principles of Distributed Database Systems,* Prentice-Hall, Englewood Cliffs, NJ, 1990.

[PaSp86] Parent, C. and Spaccapietra, S. "Enhancing the Operational Semantics of the Entity-Relationship Model," in *Database Semantics (DS-1),* T.B. Steel, Jr., and R. Meersman (editors), Elsevier, North-Holland, 1986, pp. 159-173.

[Parn72] Parnas, D.L. "On the Criteria to be Used in Decomposing Systems into Modules," *Comm. ACM* 15, 12 (1972), pp. 1053-1058.

[PeMa88] Peckham, J. and Maryanski, F. "Semantic Data Models," *ACM Computing Surveys* 20,3 (Sept. 1988), pp. 153-190.

[PoKe86] Potter, W.D. and Kerschberg, L. "A Unified Approach to Modeling Knowledge and Data," *IFIP WG 2.6 Working Conf. on Knowledge and Data,* University of South Carolina, Elsevier, North-Holland, Amsterdam, Sept. 1986.

[Rein85] Reiner, D., Brodie, M., Brown, G., Friedell, M., Kramlich, D., Lehman, J., and Rosenthal, A. "The Database Design and Evaluation Workbench (DDEW) Project at CCA," *Database Engineering* 7,4 (1985), pp. 10-15.

[Rein86] Reiner, D., Brown, G., Friedell, M., Lehman, J., McKee, R., Rheingans, P., and Rosenthal, A. "A Database Designers Workbench," *Proc. 5th ER Conference,* Dijon, France, North-Holland, Amsterdam, 1986, pp. 347-360.

[Rodg89] Rodgers, U. "Denormalization: Why, What, and How?" *Database Programming and Design* 2,12 (Dec. 1989), pp. 46-53.

[RoSt87] Rowe, L. and Stonebraker, M. "The Postgres Data Model," *Proc. 13th Intl. Conf. on Very Large Data Bases,* Brighton, England, Sept. 1-4, 1987.

[Rumb91] Rumbaugh, J., Blaha, M., Premerlani, W., Eddy, F., and Lorensen, W. *Object-Oriented Modeling and Design,* Prentice-Hall, Englewood Cliffs, NJ, 1991.

[Sacco87] Sacco, G.M. "The Fact Model: A Semantic Data Model for Complex Databases," *ESPRIT 86: Results and Achievements,* Elsevier, North-Holland, Amsterdam, 1987, pp. 587-594.

[SaTr87] Sahner, R.A. and Trivedi, K.S. "Reliability Modeling Using SHARPE," *IEEE Transactions on Reliability* 36,2 (June 1987), pp. 186-193.

[Saka83] Sakai, H. "Entity-Relationship Approach to Logical Database Design," *Entity-Relationship Approach to Software Engineering,* C.G. Davis, S. Jajodia, P. A. Ng, and R.T. Yeh (editors), Elsevier, North-Holland, New York, 1983, pp. 155-187.

[SaMe86] Sanders, W.H. and Meyer, J.F. METASAN: A Performability Evaluation Tool Based on Stochastic Activity Networks, *Proc. 1986 Fall Joint Computer Conference,* Nov. 2-6, 1986, AFIPS, New York, pp. 807-816.

[SSW80] Scheuermann, P., Scheffner, G., and Weber, H. "Abstraction Capabilities and Invariant Properties Modelling within the Entity-Relationship Approach," *Entity-Relationship Approach to Systems Analysis and Design,* P. Chen (editor), Elsevier, North-Holland, Amsterdam, 1980, pp. 121-140.

[ScSo80] Schkolnick, M. and Sorenson, P. "Denormalization: A Performance Oriented Database Design Technique," *Proc. AICA 1980 Congress,* Bologna, Italy, AICA, Brussels, 1980, pp. 363-377.

[Seli79] Selinger, P. G., Astrahan, M.M., Chamberlin, D.D., Lorie, R.A., Price, T.C. "Access Path Selection on a Relational Database Management System," *Proc. 1979 ACM SIGMOD Internatl. Conf. on Management of Data,* ACM, New York, pp. 23-34.

[Senk73] Senko et al. "Data Structures and Accessing in Data-base Systems," *IBM Syst, J.* 12,1 (1973), pp. 30-93.

[Shee89] Sheer, A.-W. *Enterprise-Wide Data Modelling,* Springer-Verlag, Berlin, 1989.

[ShMe88] Shlaer, S. and Mellor, S. *Object-Oriented Systems Analysis: Modeling the World in Data,* Yourdon Press, Englewood Cliffs, NJ, 1988.

[SiSw82] Siewiorek, D.P. and Swarz, R.S. *The Theory and Practice of Reliable System Design,* Digital Press, Bedford, MA, 1982.

[Smit85] Smith, H. "Database Design: Composing Fully Normalized Tables from a Rigorous Dependency Diagram," *Comm. ACM* 28,8 (1985), pp. 826-838.

[SmSm77] Smith, J. and Smith, D. "Database Abstractions: Aggregation and Generalization," *ACM Trans. Database Systems* 2,2 (June 1977), pp. 105-133.

[Spro76] Sprowls, R.C. *Management Data Bases,* Wiley/Hamilton, Santa Barbara, CA, 1976.

[StMa88] Stein, J. and Maier, D. "Concepts in Object-Oriented Data Management," *Database Programming and Design* 1,4 (April 1988), pp. 58-67.

[SMC74] Stevens, W., Myers, G., and Constantine, L. "Structured Design," *IBM Syst. J.* 13,2 (1974), pp. 115-139.

[StRo86] Stonebraker, M. and Rowe, L.A. "The Design of Postgres," *Proc. ACM-SIGMOD Intl. Conf. on Management of Data,* May 1986, pp. 340-355.

[Su83] Su, S.Y.W. "SAM*: A Semantic Association Model for Corporate and Scientific Statistical Databases," *Inform. Sciences* 29, 2-3 (May-June 1983), pp. 151-199.

[Swee85] Sweet, F. "Process-Driven Data Design," *Datamation* 31,16 (1985), pp. 84-85.

[TeHe77] Teichroew, D. and Hershey, E.A. "PSL/PSA: A Computer Aided Technique for Structured Documentation and Analysis of Information Processing Systems," *IEEE Trans. Software Engr.* SE-3,1 (1977), pp. 41-48.

[TeFr82] Teorey, T. and Fry, J. *Design of Database Structures*, Prentice-Hall, Englewood Cliffs, NJ, 1982.

[Teor89] Teorey, T.J. "Distributed Database Design: A Practical Approach and Example," *SIGMOD Record* 18,4 (Dec. 1989), pp. 23-39.

[TeYa91] Teorey, T.J. and Yang, D. "Usage Refinement for ER-to-Relation Design Transformations," *Information Sciences* 55, 1-3 (June 1991), pp. 49-67.

[TYF86] Teorey, T.J., Yang, D., and Fry, J.P. "A Logical Design Methodology for Relational Databases Using the Extended Entity-Relationship Model," *ACM Computing Surveys* 18,2 (June 1986), pp. 197-222.

[TCOU89] Teorey, T.J., Chaar, J., Olukotun, K., and Umar, A. "Distributed Database Design: Some Basic Concepts and Strategies," *Database Programming and Design* 2,4 (April 1989), pp. 34-42.

[TWBK89] Teorey, T.J., Wei, G., Bolton, D.L., and Koenig, J.A. "ER Model Clustering as an Aid for User Communication and Documentation in Database Design," *Comm. ACM* 32,8 (Aug. 1989), pp. 975-987.

[TsLo82] Tsichritzis, D. and Lochovsky, F. *Data Models,* Prentice-Hall, Englewood Cliffs, NJ, 1982.

[Ullm88] Ullman, J. *Principles of Database and Knowledge-Base Systems, Vols. 1 and 2,* Computer Science Press, Rockville, MD, 1988.

[VeVa82] Verheijen, G. and Van Bekkum, J. "NIAM: An Information Analysis Method,"*Information Systems Design Methodologies,* Olle, Sol, and Verryn-Stuart (editors), North-Holland, Amsterdam, 1982, pp. 537-590.

[WPM89] Wasserman, A.I., Pircher, P.A., and Muller, R.J. "An Object-Oriented Structured Design Method for Code Generation," *Software Eng. Notices* 14,1 (Jan. 1989), pp. 32-55.

[Wied83] Wiederhold, G. *Database Design* (2nd Ed.), McGraw-Hill, New York, 1983.

[Wied86] Wiederhold, G. "Views, Objects, and Databases," *IEEE Computer* (Dec. 1986), pp. 37-44.

[Wied87] Wiederhold, G. *File Organization for Database Design,* McGraw-Hill, New York, 1987.

[Wilm84] Wilmot, R. "Foreign Keys Decrease Adaptability of Database Designs," *Comm. ACM* 27,12 (Dec. 1984), pp. 1237-1243.

[Yao85] Yao, S.B. (editor). *Principles of Database Design,* Prentice-Hall, Englewood Cliffs, NJ, 1985.

[YoCo79] Yourdon, E. and Constantine, L.L. *Structured Design,* Prentice-Hall, Englewood Cliffs, NJ, 1979.

[YuCh84] Yu, C. and Chang, C. "Distributed Query Processing," *ACM Computing Surveys* 16,4 (Dec. 1984), pp. 399-433.

[ZaMe81] Zaniolo, C. and Melkanoff, M. "On the Design of Relational Database Schemas," *ACM Trans. Database Systems* 6,1 (1981), pp. 1-47.

[ZdMa90] Zdonik, S. and Maier, D. *Readings in Object-Oriented Database Systems,* Morgan Kaufmann, San Mateo, CA, 1990.

Additional References (1994 reprint)

[Codd79] Codd, E.F. "Extending the Database Relational Model to Capture More Meaning," *ACM TODS* 4,4 (Dec. 1979), pp. 397-434.

[Kent78] Kent, W. *Data and Reality,* Elsevier, Amsterdam, 1978.

[MMR86] Makowsky, J.A., Markowitz, V.M., and Rotics, N. "Entity-Relationship Consistency for Relational Schemas," *Proc. Int'l. Conf. on Database Theory,* G. Ausiello and P. Atzeni (editors), Springer-Verlag, New York, 1986, pp. 306-322.

[MaSh89] Markowitz, V.M. and Shoshani, A. "Name Assignment Techniques for Relational Schemas Representing Extended Entity-Relationship Schemas," *Proc. 8th Int'l. Conf. on the Entity-Relationship Approach,* Toronto, October 18-20, 1989, pp. 21-39.

[MaSh89a] Markowitz, V.M. and Shoshani, A. "On the Correctness of Representing Extended Entity-Relationship Structures in the Relational Model," *Proc. ACM SIGMOD Conf. on Management of Data,* Portland, 1989, pp. 430-439.

SOLUTIONS TO SELECTED EXERCISES

Problem 2-3 (page 41)

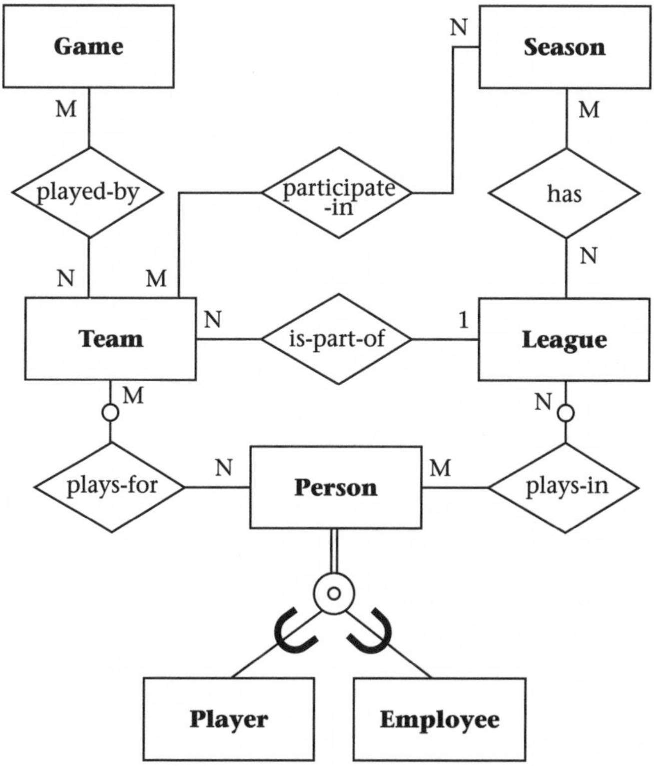

Problem 3-2 (page 73)

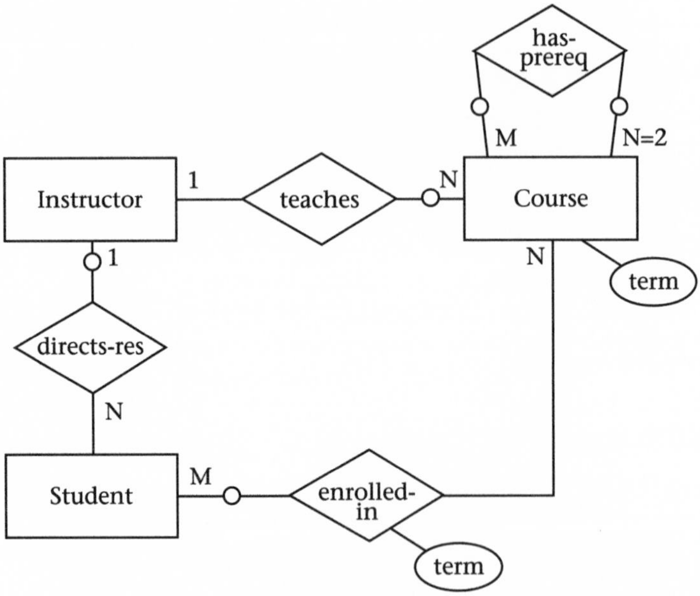

Problem 4-2 (page 89)

create table **instructor** (instr_id char(10),
    instr_name char(20),
    instr_office_no char(10),
    primary key (instr_id));

create table **student** (student_id char(10),
    student_name char(20),
    student_address char(30),
    res_instr_id char(10),
    primary key (student_id),
    foreign key (res_instr_id) references **instructor**
        on delete set null on update cascade);

create table **course** (course_id char(9),
    course_name char(20),
    term char(10),
    instr_id char(10) not null,
    primary key (course_id),
    foreign key (instr_id) references **instructor**
        on delete set default on update cascade);

```
create table enrolled_in (student_id char(10),
        course_id char(10),
        term char(10),
        primary key (student_id, course_id),
        foreign key (student_id) references student
                on delete cascade on update cascade,
        foreign key (course_id) references course
                on delete cascade on update cascade);
create table has_prereq (course_id char(10),
        prereq_course_id char(10),
        primary key (course_id, prereq_course_id),
        foreign key (course_id) references course
                on delete cascade on update cascade,
        foreign key (prereq_course_id) references course
                on delete cascade on update cascade);
```

Problem 5-2 (page 123)

1. No, R is not in 3NF because of the transitive functional dependencies.
2. Yes, R is in 3NF because A is a prime attribute (part of the candidate key AB).
3. Yes, R is in BCNF because BC is a candidate key, determining the only other attribute.
4. Yes, BC is a candidate key.
5. No, nonfully functional dependency exists.
6. Yes, if A–>C, then AB–>C.
7. No, because the transitive dependency A–>C–>B exists.

Problem 5-3 (page 124)

1. Functional dependencies
   course_id –> instructor_id
   student_id –> instructor_id (optional)
   student_id, course_id –> term (optional)
2. Level of normalization when implemented as a single table with no repeating columns: 1NF
3. Convert to BCNF: use separate relations for instructor, student, course, enrollment, and prerequisite (see solution to Problem 4-2).

Problem 5-6 (page 126)

Minimum set of 3NF relations. R1–R4 are BCNF; R5 is 3NF.

R1: AB with key A and functional dependency A –> B

R2: BCD with keys B and D and functional dependencies B –> CD and D –> B

R3: AEF with composite key AE and functional dependency AE –> F

R4: EJ with key E and functional dependency E –> J

R5: EGH with composite key EG and functional dependencies EG –> H and H –> G

Problem 5-8 (page 127)

Minimum set of 3NF (and BCNF) relations:

R1: ABC with key A (A –> BC)

R2: BDEFG with keys B, E (B –> DEFG, E –> B)

Problem 6-3 (page 159)

1. Sequential search of the student records:

   Disk access times: seek(disk) = 40 ms, rot = 20 ms, tr = 200 KB/sec

   Sequential block access time: Tsba = rot/2 + bks/tr = 20/2 + 1000/200 KB/sec = 15 ms

   Random block access time: Trba = Tsba + seek(disk) = 15 ms + 40 ms = 55 ms

   Sequential access is to be computed for a single pass through 20,000 records:

   blocking factor: bf = floor(1000 Bytes per block / 64 Bytes per student record) = 15

   lra = 20,000 logical record accesses

   sba = ceiling(lra/bf) = ceiling(20,000/15) = 1,334 sequential block accesses

   iotime = tsba*sba = 15 ms * 1,334 sba = 20.0 seconds

2. Secondary index access to student records:

   We assume that the foreign key research_instr_id in student records has a secondary index.

   We also assume that the attribute name index is small and fits into a single block in main memory.

Attribute value index size: 2500 instructors*9 Bytes = 22,500 Bytes => 23 blocks (thus a successful search requires an average of 12 blocks).

Accession list size = 10 (given each instructor has an average of 10 research students).

Pointer size = 5 Bytes (assumed).

iotime = time1 (access the index of attribute types)
+ time2 (access the index of attribute values)
+ time3 (access the accession list for a given instructor id)
+ time4 (access the 10 target records)
= 0 (attribute type index in main memory)
+ 12 rba*Trba (attribute value index search)
+ 1 rba*Trba (accession list has 10 entries of 5B each, fitting into a single block)
+ 10 rba*Trba (target data block accesses)
= 23*55 ms
= 1265 ms

Problem 8-1 (page 189)

Best fit nonredundant allocation:

Table R1 is allocated to site S2 (total local frequency of 100: 100 for Update 1)

Table R2 is allocated to site S3 (total local frequency of 60: 10 for Query 2 and 50 for Update 2)

Table R3 is allocated to site S1 (total local frequency of 20: 10 for Query 1 and 10 for Query 2)

All beneficial sites allocation (where to replicate after the initial allocation):

Table R1 is to be replicated at S1 (benefit of 101.2 seconds exceeds cost of 27 seconds).

No other replications are recommended: cost exceeds or equals benefit in all other cases.

Benefit computation for the replication of table R1 at site S1:

Query 1 accesses table R1 at site S1 with frequency of 10. Remote minus local query eliminates the local disk I/O.

Time per transaction = [request propagation delay + transmission of request packet + result propagation delay + result of the query (100 packets at 100 ms/packet)]*frequency

= [10 + 100 + 10 + 100*100]*10
= 101,200 ms (101.2 seconds)

Cost computation for the replication of table R1 at site S1:

Update 1 accesses table R1 at site S1 with frequency of 100.

Time per transaction = [request propagation delay + transmission of request packet + local update disk I/O (random read plus rewrite) + result propagation delay + result of the update (1 packet at 100ms)]*frequency

= [10 +100 + (40 + 40) + 10 + 100]*100
= 30,000 ms (30 seconds)

Problem A-1 (page 247)

Query 1.

select first_name, middle_init, last_name
from **president**
where political_party = 'Republican'
and state_from = 'Ohio';

Query 2.

select s.state_name
from **state** as s, **president** as p, **administration** as a
where p.first_name = 'Andrew'
and p.last_name = 'Johnson'
and p.identifier = a.pres_identifier
and a.start_date <= s.date_admitted
and a.end_date >= s.date_admitted;

Query 3.

select a.vp_first_name, a.vp_middle_init, a.vp_last_name
from **administration** as a
minus
select a.vp_first_name, a.vp_middle_init, a.last_name
from **administration** as a, **president** as p
where p.first_name = a.vp_first_name
and p.middle_init = a.vp_middle_init
and p.last_name = a.vp_last_name;

INDEX

ABOUT THE AUTHOR

Toby J. Teorey received the B.S. (1964) and M.S. (1965) degrees in Electrical Engineering from the University of Arizona and a Ph.D. (1972) in Computer Sciences from the University of Wisconsin.

He served as an EDP officer in the U.S. Air Force from 1965 to 1969 and was a White House Social Aide for President Lyndon Johnson from 1966 to 1968. At the University of Wisconsin (1969 to 1972), he became coordinator of the Operations Research Group in the Madison Academic Computing Center. He is currently Professor and Associate Chair of Electrical Engineering & Computer Science for CSE at the University of Michigan, Ann Arbor. He served as the program chair for the 1991 Entity-Relationship Conference and the general chair of the 1981 ACM SIGMOD Conference. This is his second book on database design.

Professor Teorey's current research interests are object data modeling, distributed databases, and network management and performance tools. Since 1986, he has led an effort resulting in the development of NetMod, a Windows-based analytical tool for predicting the performance of large-scale, interconnected local area networks. He is a member of the ACM and of the IEEE Computer Society.

He has consulted widely in the area of database design, including work with General Motors, Apple Computer, IBM, Northern Telecom, The World Bank, and NSA, as well as other corporations and agencies of the U.S. government.